From Snapshots to Social Media - The Changing Picture of Domestic Photography

Computer Supported Cooperative Work

For other titles published in this series, go to
http://www.springer.com/series/2861

Risto Sarvas · David M. Frohlich

From Snapshots to Social Media - The Changing Picture of Domestic Photography

 Springer

Dr. Risto Sarvas
Helsinki Institute for Information
Technology HIIT
Aalto University
Finland
risto.sarvas@hiit.fi

Professor David M. Frohlich
Digital World Research Centre
University of Surrey
UK
D.Frohlich@surrey.ac.uk

ISBN 978-1-4471-2633-1   ISBN 978-0-85729-247-6 (eBook)
DOI 10.1007/978-0-85729-247-6
Springer London Dordrecht Heidelberg New York

British Library Cataloguing in Publication Data
A catalogue record for this book is available from the British Library

Printed on acid-free paper

Springer is part of Springer Science+Business Media (www.springer.com)

To Tuula.
      – Risto

To Joel, Lily, and Hugh.
              – David

Acknowledgements

The possibility of focusing on a single research topic for roughly 2 years is a luxury that is found only in special circumstances. It requires the right people and place, time, and – of course – funding. We have been very fortunate in having all four to enable us to write a book together on such a rich topic as photography.

Most of the research for this book was done in 2009 during Risto's year as a visiting fellow at the Digital World Research Centre (DWRC), hosted by David at the UK's University of Surrey. The atmosphere at the DWRC inspired new ideas yet was peaceful enough for thinking. This book is the result of collaboration, brainstorming, and regular discussions between Risto and David in Guildford, on trains, and sometimes next to a pint of genuine English real ale. The write-up of the ideas and findings was divided between us such that Chap. 6 was written by David; Risto wrote Chaps. 1, 3, 4, and 5; and Chaps. 2, 7, and 8 were prepared collaboratively. The book was completed after Risto returned to the Helsinki Institute for Information Technology HIIT, in Finland. It turned out that HIIT was a perfect place to present and polish ideas, because the researchers there are multidisciplinary in approach, open to new ideas, and ready to offer constructive criticism of works in progress.

Regardless of the place, locations are about their people. We are grateful to the people we know and have grown acquainted with who have been friendly, helpful, and open to discussions of photography and information technology. Therefore, we take the opportunity here to thank those who have contributed to shaping a set of unorganised thoughts into (we hope) a coherent book.

Asko Lehmuskallio has been absolutely priceless in helping us to study photography, in discussions of photography, and in pointing us toward interesting and relevant research. He has also been our number-one reviewer and sparring partner for ideas.

We are also indebted to Richard Harper, who always found time to meet and talk about the book project and to offer his suggestions – comments that were precise and highly valuable. We thank Richard especially for giving us permission not to worry too much about making watertight arguments and for encouraging us instead to focus on writing what we wanted to say.

Putting together a book requires the help of experts. In particular, a book on photography needs to have photographs in it. We thank Olli Pitkänen for photographing many of the cameras and film cartridges in this book, and also for his comments and discussion during the writing of the book. Kristina Langhein did great work with editing of the photographs captured by Olli and Risto. Special thanks go to Abigail Durrant, who not only talked with us about changes in the 'domestic sphere' and photography but also shared with us her unpublished material and writings on domestic photography. Our special thanks also go to Katie Smith, who helped mould an engineer's mind to think more anthropologically. Especially 'hoppy' thanks also to Frode Skarstein for his help with referencing software.

In addition, many people have read through and commented on our drafts and discussed our ideas with us. We especially thank Peter Buse, Markus Huttunen, Sampsa Hyysalo, Mikael Johnson, Vesa Kantola, Vilma Lehtinen, Ralph London, Jukka Sarvas, Peter Sucy, and Sami Vihavainen for taking the time to read parts of the manuscript and to give us suggestions, feedback, and critiques. We also thank the following people for interesting, fun, and thought-provoking conversations and e-mail exchanges that helped to shape the book and guide us in our work: Ossi Asikainen, Ali al-Azzawi, Ellen Isaacs, Dave Kenyon, Ilpo Koskinen, Siân Lindley, Antti Oulasvirta, Daniella Petrelli, Gillian Rose, Daniel Rubinstein, Diane Schiano, Katrina Sluis, and Sarah Woods. We also thank Leena Sarvas, who helped Risto with the English language, and many thanks go as well to Anna Shefl, who proofread the whole book. We also kindly thank the authors and publishers who gave their permission for us to use their images in this book.

Risto is extremely grateful to his family for their support, especially during the year in England. Very special thanks go to Tuula Savola, who took time off from her work to move to the UK and supported Risto in keeping the book project within office hours. Many thanks go also to the grandparents – Lea, Raija, Asko, and Jukka, who were always willing to fly from Finland to England and spend time with Risto's family. David would also like to thank Julie, Joel, Lily, and Hugh for their patience and support with writing work that eventually crept into the weekends.

Risto's work for this book has been funded by the Aalto University School of Science and Technology and by the Academy of Finland. He thanks both organisations for their support.

Risto Sarvas
David M. Frohlich

Contents

Chapter 1
Introduction

There is hardly a person in the developed world who does not have photographs from his or her past. Even those who do not keep large collections of prints or photo albums know how to take photos, how to pose for a photograph, when it is acceptable to take photos, and when it is almost compulsory to have a photo taken. It is quite common to take photographs while travelling, to carry photographs in one's wallet, to give photographs as a gift, and to hang photographs on the wall at home or have them on one's desk in the workplace. It would be strange not to do these things.

Photography is embedded in our lives. It is present from our birth to our death, and beyond: parents today can obtain the first pictures of their future child from ultrasound images several months before the birth, and those who have passed away often remain present with the family through photographs on bookshelves or in albums. Whether one is a professional photographer or an amateur who takes pictures by happenstance, most probably the first photos he or she ever saw were family photos and the first camera was a family camera. Taking photographs, looking at them, and talking about them are activities so common in our lives that they almost escape our notice.

Domestic photography is now going through a change. More precisely, it has been changing for the past two decades. Not only have the cameras replaced film with digital capture, but also the uses ordinary people have for photographs have shifted into new forms. Today, many of the activities previously involving film photography and paper prints use computers of different sorts: PCs, laptops, mobile phones, tablets, and large servers. Activities such as sharing, editing, publishing, storing, copying, posting, commenting upon, praising, printing, and displaying are still in our photo vocabulary, but the tools and media for these have changed. We really appear to be living in times of major changes and continuous innovation – are we?

We are indeed witnessing a great change in domestic photography: the constellation of technologies, businesses, conventions, practices, artefacts, etc. that constitute photography has changed. However, the change has not come about overnight. It has been happening since the beginning of the 1990s, when the first digital consumer camera became available. Nor is this change unprecedented in domestic

R. Sarvas and D.M. Frohlich, *From Snapshots to Social Media - The Changing Picture of Domestic Photography*, Computer Supported Cooperative Work,
DOI 10.1007/978-0-85729-247-6_1, © Springer-Verlag London Limited 2011

photography: a similar fundamental change was the invention of photography in the 1830s, and the second major change was the advent of consumer photography in 1888. Lastly, not everything has changed. For example, the cameras of today use the same technical principle as did cameras in the 1830s; family portraits have been popular throughout the history of photography, and still are; and most of the major brands we see in photography were familiar 50 years ago. We are witnessing a major change, but what is actually changing and when will the change be over?

In this book we identify three consecutive paths in the history of domestic photography: the Portrait Path (ca. 1830s–1888), the Kodak Path (ca. 1888–1990s), and the Digital Path (starting in the 1990s). Each of these paths is characterised by an innovation that disrupted the existing *status quo* of technologies, businesses, and practices related to the creation of images within the domestic sphere. Each disruption was followed by an era of ferment in which technological change, business actors, and changing practices interacted to form a new *status quo* – a new path. In Chap. 2, we go through the key terms and concepts *domestic photography* and *snapshot photography*, and we describe our analytical tool of *technological paths*.

In the following chapters (Chaps. 3–6), we identify the actors, influences, and stakeholders shaping these paths – in other words, the people, businesses, technologies, practices, economic changes, and other societal actors that shaped domestic photography into what it is today. We end the journey (with Chap. 7) by discussing what and who will shape domestic photography in the future and how. Then, in the book's conclusion (Chap. 8), we also recommend methodological directions for future research in this area. These include taking greater account of the technical, social, and cultural contexts into which new technology is introduced.

Before going into the history of domestic photography, we finish this introduction by discussing why this book was written and for whom. We hope that researchers into visual culture and in science and technology studies find this book an interesting and useful study of the history and future of domestic photography and its associated technologies. However, the main audience for this book is researchers, engineers, and designers of digital imaging technologies, social media, and Web services or other products relying on mediated social interaction.

Why should the designers of 'tomorrow's technology' pay attention to the past? What can a historical overview of domestic photography tell us about people's imaging habits today or offer for designing the technology of tomorrow? For a designer, or any builder of technology, looking at history enables 'thinking outside the box'. No matter how novel an invention is, it carries a legacy. Any technology has to connect with a world that includes old technologies, existing business models and economic structures, and laws and regulations written a year or a century ago, as well as with people, who have certain values, attitudes, practices, and uses for technologies. If a designer knows the history of a technology, such as in domestic photography, he or she has a better chance of being creative and innovative.

Second, the history of technology is a history of changes. By looking at the previous major changes in domestic photography, we see how the process of technological change occurs. As we will discuss, technological change is not linear but marked by discontinuities that have potential to disrupt whole industries.

By understanding the evolution of technology, and the difference between incremental and disruptive innovations, a designer can identify whether an idea or invention is radical or conservative. Without knowledge of the past, it is impossible to estimate the novelty, innovativeness, and potential impact of a new technology. It is not enough to study the past few months or years, no matter how rapid the technological change seems to be. As our book will show, contemporary uses for domestic photography were strongly influenced by actors and actions of a century ago.

Bill Buxton too has drawn attention to the lack of historical perspective and knowledge in the design of products and services. One of his examples is IBM and BellSouth's Simon, released in 1993. This was a touchscreen mobile phone that could be used as a pager, a calendar, a scheduler, an address book, a calculator, a sketchpad, and a platform on which to read e-mail. In other words, it was a touchscreen smartphone a decade before smartphones came to the market. Buxton's point is that hardly anyone reporting on, reviewing, blogging about, or admiring the Apple iPhone (released in 2007), especially its touchscreen user interface, was aware of Simon. Buxton also points out that hardly anyone is familiar with any of the touchscreen interfaces for wristwatches, which were available even earlier. Buxton hammers his point home by contrasting reviews of new technological gadgets to reviews of a theatrical play (or any other new art). In summary, no professional theatre critic could ignore the historical and societal context of a new release, yet in technology reviews, the historical, cultural, and political contexts are often absent.

A consequence of this absence is that issues such as privacy, power, social structures, and economic factors are almost missing from design-oriented science and engineering research. In the context of photography, a clear gap exists between research on interactive system design and visual media studies (including traditional photography studies). Our objective is to bridge this gap between interaction design and visual culture studies by presenting a socio-technical history of domestic photography in which we pay attention to the variety of actors shaping domestic photography: the technologies, the business models and commercial organisations, regulation, people and their practices, and broader phenomena in society. Our analytical lens in studying the history of domestic photography is the concept of a *technological path*, which has its background in science and technology studies (STS) and in technology management literature.

We rely for our historical data on literature on photography, visual culture, and imaging technology. However, we also use marketing reports and figures, as well as newspaper and magazine articles, in our discussions of technology-adoption in the past two decades.

In studying the technological paths in domestic photography (and those paths that did not become dominant), we do our best to find a middle ground between interaction design research, which has a technology-centric background, and visual culture studies, which have a strong background in cultural studies. By adopting an analytical approach from science and technology studies, we hope to contribute in both ways: to interaction design by emphasising the historical study of technologies as socio-technical constellations of heterogeneous actors and, second, to visual culture studies by emphasising the agency of these socio-technical constellations in shaping and maintaining specific visual cultures.

Chapter 2
Domestic Photography and Technological Paths

2.1 What Is Domestic Photography?

In this book, we use the term *domestic photography* to describe the photographic activities of ordinary people taking and using images for non-professional purposes. Also, in our use of the term we focus on the kind of use in which photography is not a hobby as such but embedded in other activities. The word 'domestic' implies that the activities take place mainly in homes, and the home is the headquarters for this activity.[1] Many photographs are taken in the home of people who live or visit there. People go abroad and take photographs, then return home to view, show, share, and store the captured pictures. The cameras, photo albums, prints, printers, computers, mobile phones, television sets, and other photographic technologies can be taken out of the home space, but they do 'live' at home as much as the owners of these technologies. Their resting place is at home.

The ordinary activities performed with cameras and photographs are also related to the people living in the home. Traditionally this has been the family unit. The connection between photography and the family has been so strong in the past that *family photography* has become almost synonymous with domestic photography. It has often been the members of the family who are photographed and who do most of the photographing. It is through family relations and the home that photography is introduced to babies and small children. The home is the place and the family is the social context inherent in the photographic practices we are all so familiar with. Also, the concept of family photography hints at the family-centric values that are often present in domestic photography: depicting the stereotypical father–mother–two-children nuclear family as a single coherent happy unit with no domestic problems or friction between familial relationships. Nevertheless, in our use of the term, domestic photography does not assume a family – even a person living alone without a partner or children can participate in domestic photography.

A third term, again used synonymously with the concepts of domestic and family photography, is *snapshot photography*. Although this is a common term today, its

---

[1] Holland 2009, p. 130.

R. Sarvas and D.M. Frohlich, *From Snapshots to Social Media - The Changing Picture of Domestic Photography*, Computer Supported Cooperative Work, DOI 10.1007/978-0-85729-247-6_2, © Springer-Verlag London Limited 2011

origins lie in the way in which people took photographs with early cameras. The term 'snapshot' is a British hunting term from the 1860s referring to shooting from the hip without careful aim.[2] The very first consumer cameras, from the late 1880s, did not have a viewfinder; therefore, the photographers 'shot' these cameras without much aiming. The word 'snap' resonates with a simplicity of consumer cameras with which the operator of the camera needs only to point the camera and squeeze a single button: the image is captured in an instant with the sound of a shutter snapping.

A snapshot photographer (*i.e.*, a snapshooter) is a person who takes photographs with consumer cameras, and snapshots are the photographs created in the process. Not all family photographs are snapshots, though. Often some of the photographs on display in a home are studio photographs taken by a professional photographer to celebrate an event such as a wedding or a birthday. Family photographs can also include newspaper clippings about friends, family, or other relatives. In other words, snapshot photography is the part of family and domestic photography wherein the members of the family or their acquaintances (*i.e.*, amateurs or non-professionals) capture the photographs themselves.

In the following three sections of this chapter, we are going to look at domestic photography from three perspectives: the practice, the technology, and the business. We believe these three factors are central for an understanding of domestic photography and the way it gets transformed through innovation and domestication. In the rest of the book, we review the interaction of these factors over time to identify how domestic photography came to be the way it is today, and how it is changing.

2.1.1   The Practice: Constructing Positive Images

Domestic photography has traditionally been about constructing images as one has wished to see them – often wishing to see them at their best.[3] Home photographers (*i.e.*, snapshooters) hardly ever take photographs of friends or family members arguing, painful experiences, or unhappy people, and if relations and situations change after a photograph has been taken, the unwanted photographs are removed from frames or albums. As Don Slater points out, domestic photography is *constructed* by how we present ourselves to the camera; what we decide to photograph and how we frame it; and, after the capture, the selection of photographs to share, archive, or throw away.[4] In turn, photographs help us to construct our individual, family, and cultural identities as they appear to others.[5] Through domestic photography we create an ideal image, wherein happiness flourishes in everyday life, in holidays, and in travel with friends and family. If there are unhappy memories, they are sentimental and nostalgic in nature.

---

[2]Coe and Gates 1977, p. 6.
[3]Chalfen 1987; Holland 2009; Musello 1979; Zuromskis 2009.
[4]Slater 1995, p. 134.
[5]Chalfen 1987; Durrant et al. 2009; Musello 1979.

The tools and technology for constructing domestic photography are the cameras and photographs, along with media for displaying the photographs: frames, albums, slides, photo paper, photo prints, photo books, mouse pads, Christmas cards, computers, phone and television displays, etc. The tools also include concrete tools for editing, selecting, organising, and transferring the photographs: scissors, software, boxes, pens for writing, envelopes, and so on. However, capturing photographs with the camera is a key activity in this process, and the content of those photographs the main material for construction.

Events and experiences are captured and documented, among them vacations, holidays, festivals, parties, and travels. Especially change, growth, and the passing of time are captured in photographs of familial rites like weddings, baptisms, graduations, and birthdays.[6] Also, children are photographed to capture the changes in them, often in an attempt to preserve a memory of them at a certain age and time. Richard Chalfen draws attention to how these documented changes are predictable and socially 'allowable',[7] such as via a child's first day at school, a cousin's graduation, or one's father's retirement. People do not photograph the progress of diseases, the changes propagated by a divorce, failed projects, or other changes that are perceived as not appropriate. And it is perhaps because domestic photography steers away from these negative and inappropriate memories and experiences that snapshots can trigger painful memories, sadness, loneliness, and trauma. A family portrait that is all smiles can trigger in someone memories of childhood trauma, such as domestic violence, alcoholism, or serious illness. The positive snapshot becomes an icon for an artificially constructed and unrealistic past.

However, not all domestic photography is done for reminiscing and recollecting the past. Photographs are also captured to communicate the present for the present. Photographs are captured and sent to distant relatives and friends to show 'how our life is here, right now'. Photographs are also taken and displayed to presents one's current self for wider audiences. A photograph on an office desk or a set of photographs in a wallet, a wallpaper photo on one's mobile phone, and profile pictures on social networking sites are all building blocks in constructing an ideal image of us. The audiences for these photographs range from intimate friends to total strangers who happen to catch a glimpse of these images.

The assumption that photographs are objective proof plays an important role in the documentation of domestic life. Proof of the way people looked, the places they visited, and the events that took place. Once these documents are put together and presented, for example, in a family album, the collection of photographs becomes a narrative of historical events, which is treated as truthful and objective. What we tend to overlook is the active selection process in the making of a family album, which can make the truthfulness of the narrative questionable: the family album may not be false as such, but it is a subjective perspective of what has taken place in a family's history.

As mentioned above, through framing, capturing, deleting, editing, selecting, organising, positioning, and sharing, we select only a fraction of the potential body

---

[6]Chalfen 1987; Musello 1979.
[7]Chalfen 1987.

of photographs to tell the past for potential viewers. We are all familiar with the rules and conventions of that selection process. We all know how to create and to identify appropriate snapshots, and the rules and conventions are learnt as part of our culture.[8] We learn the snapshot culture in the ways in which our parents, friends, and acquaintances use cameras and photographs; the ways in which these technologies are advertised; the ways in which news, magazines, operating manuals, and guidebooks present photography; and the ways in which the people and activities we idealise are depicted. Chalfen writes that the snapshot culture is introduced to us in childhood and in the process of learning we are introduced to social patterns and models of social organisation deemed acceptable and proper.[9]

In the process of learning to snapshoot, we are taught to capture photographs that are often criticised as visually banal, aesthetically challenged, or simply boring. Catherine Zuromskis describes how snapshots are framed centrally, people pose frontally, affection is demonstrated by obvious gestures, and more often than not people put on a smile.[10] A visually beautiful and exceptional snapshot is most probably accidental. However, as we discussed above, the purpose of snapshots is not to please aesthetically but to construct a positive representation of domestic life and to trigger positive emotions in people.

Typical of snapshots is that the emotions they stir are personal and private. A snapshot often remains banal and insignificant without a personal connection to the people or the context captured in the photograph. Roland Barthes[11] calls this personal relationship with a photograph the *punctum*: the piercing, prickling effect a photograph can have in bringing back personal and private memories and emotions. The counterpart of the *punctum* is the *studium*: the effect a photograph has for an average viewer, the more public and communal reading of a photograph. It is from the standpoint of the *studium* that snapshots are uninteresting and meaningless. From the personal *punctum*, the very same snapshot can be the most important image in a person's life.

In contrast to pre-planned studio photographs, snapshot photographs are often informal and spontaneous.[12] Perhaps the most obvious change in photographs that occurred once people started to take them themselves was the playfulness and informality captured. Previous photographs, created by professionals, lacked the close and affectionate relationship that can exist between a photographer and his or her subject. It is this relationship that gives the camera a function of bringing togetherness that does not even necessarily require the captured photographs: pushing the button of the camera signifies that the moment and the people present are elemental in constructing a positive image of the photographer's life.[13] 'May I take a photograph of you?' is a statement

---

[8]*Ibid*; Zuromskis 2009, p. 57.
[9]Chalfen 1987.
[10]Zuromskis 2009, p. 53.
[11]Barthes 2000.
[12]Coe and Gates 1977, p. 9; Holland 2009, p. 132; Zuromskis 2009, p. 53.
[13]Chalfen 1987; Musello 1979.

about the relationship between the photographer and the subject independent of whether the photographs will ever be displayed or looked at. Whether the purpose of a photograph is to communicate love, friendship, camaraderie, or mere acknowledgement, domestic photography's important function is to strengthen social relationships.

In a nutshell, domestic photographic has an inherent duality. From the point of view of the general public, snapshots and family photographs can be insignificant, banal, and visually uninteresting. They are trivial, inaccessible, and predictable, and perhaps the only interesting thing about them is that they do tell us about what domestic life looked like in the past. From the private point of view, and the point of view of immediate family and friends, the snapshots are probably the most important pictures in the world. They trigger rich memories and emotions (good and bad); they create togetherness, social bonding, and belonging; they capture and store personal histories for current and future generations; and they are building blocks for constructing a socially acceptable image of us. Another way of summarising this is to say that the core *values* of domestic photography are to support memory, communication, and identity.[14]

2.1.2 The Technology: Capturing and Creating an Image

The basics of a camera are simple: reflected light travels through a small hole and hits a surface, creating an image of what it initially reflected from. Ancient philosophers knew the principle, and the first dark room with a hole in the wall was built in the mediaeval Arab world. The Latin name for such a dark chamber is *camera obscura*, and the 'chamber' part of that term, *camera*, is the contemporary name of the device for capturing photographs. Before the invention of what we today call a camera, the *camerae obscurae* of the nineteenth century were small boxes with a hole in the front (or a lens) and a mirror in the back that would display the image to the viewer.

Mounting a lens and a diaphragm on the hole in front of the box made it possible to change the size of the hole (aperture), focus the image, and use different lenses to bend the light rays so that objects that are far away seem closer (a telephoto lens) and nearby objects can fit into a single image (a wide-angle lens). This is still the principle of any camera: by the use of a lens and changing aperture, to make a clear and focused image on the back of the camera.

The image at the back of the camera is recorded on a medium, which enables the picture to be viewed separate from the camera. It is the invention of the means to record the image produced by the *camera obscura* that is considered the invention of the photographic camera. The name that is most often mentioned in history books is Joseph Nicéphore Niépce, who, in 1822, was the first to successfully record a positive image on a medium ('positive' meaning that light was recorded as light and dark as dark, not *vice versa*, which is a negative image). In his case, the medium was a pewter plate covered with a mixture of bitumen (asphalt) and lavender oil.[15]

---

[14]Chalfen 1987; Musello 1979.

[15]Peres 2007, p. 130.

For the years to come, photography technology would be a combination of optics, chemistry of light-sensitive materials (mainly light-sensitive silver salts), and mechanics for getting the physics and the chemistry to work together to create an image.

After almost two centuries of producing photographs chemically, the process has become one of computation and information technology. As the captured image is digitised it becomes a set of numbers – computational data. Some practical effects of this fundamental change are already quite familiar: photographs can be stored in minimal physical space, there are hardly any costs for capturing thousands of images, the images can be copied indefinitely without loss of quality, they can be transferred over information networks over enormous distances in a very short time, they can be edited and manipulated in ways previously unimaginable, and they can be displayed immediately after capture on a variety of screen types. It is the digitalisation of images that has enabled the new domestic photography practices that use the internet, and it is digitalisation and digital technology that has enabled the creation of the new type of consumer camera: the camera phone.

However, perhaps the most basic change in domestic photography technology is that the photographs captured are no longer physical objects. Digital photographs always require some kind of device to view them, and the device has to have some kind of computational power to convert the numerical representation into an analogue signal visible to humans – often the image is converted into light emitted from an LCD screen. In contemporary society, this is not a problem: computers and displays are widespread, and the ways in which digital images are encoded into bits are standardised. Also, because of digitalisation, photography has become an integral part of information and communications technology: digital cameras and photographs are components of an ecosystem of computers, networks, hardware, and software. Photography as a practice, technology, and business is integrated into everything that current and future information and communications technology encompasses.

2.1.3   The Business: Camera, Film, and Service

Niépce achieved the recording of the image on the back of a *camera obscura* as early as 1822. Why was there a need to change his invention? And as it was changed, where did the requirements for new technology and design originate? The key driver of technological progress is the ways in which the technology is foreseen to profit its owner – to find a market for the new invention and turn it into a commercial innovation. In other words, domestic photography has responded to business needs as well as user needs down through the years. It has been a consumer business since its birth in the early nineteenth century.

The business of capturing and creating images was already familiar in Niépce's France. A painted portrait was an expensive luxury item, but miniature paintings, silhouettes, and physiognotraces were within the financial reach of the rising middle classes. Whether the motives of Niépce and other inventors working with image-capturing in 1826 were of a commercial nature or not, they must have been aware of the existing market for producing images to be sold for a price. Geoffrey Batchen points out that there was already from the late eighteenth century a "widespread social imperative" pointing toward finding a way to record the image in a *camera obscura*.[16]

The consumer photography business in the nineteenth century was one of the two: the sales of publicly appealing photographs and the sales of photographic services in portrait studios. The former included sales of photographs, taken by professionals, of celebrities, exotic places and people, historical events (actual and enacted), beautiful landscapes, and even erotic imaginary. These images were produced in bulk and sold by the thousands. The latter business involved the familiar studio practice of taking customers' photograph and then selling the image or images to them. In the early decades of photography, studio photographs were more of a luxury item and only single copies existed.

In the 1880s, George Eastman invented the technologies and a business model to make the camera a consumer product, and the development and printing of domestic photographs a commodity business. The sales slogan for the first Kodak cameras summarises Eastman's business model for snapshot photography: "You push the button, we do the rest". For the next 120 years, the basic model for the snapshot photography business would be the sales of simple and inexpensive cameras (the capture process automated into a single push of a button), and the commercial service of turning the captured images into paper prints (the complex development process externalised into a simple service). To link these two parts together, the camera and the prints, a standard disposable roll of film was the medium for recording the pictures, and the sale of film was the business.

This model was challenged somewhat after the Second World War with the introduction of the first instant cameras by Polaroid Corporation. Polaroid cameras automated the development process in addition to the capture process. Nevertheless, the business model eliminated only one component from the Kodak model: the development service. What remained were the sale of the cameras and the special Polaroid film.

In hindsight, the Polaroid instant camera was a predecessor of the digital camera. Like the instant camera, the digital camera does not require an external development service in order for the photographer to see the captured image. However, digital photography eliminates also the need for a disposable capture medium – the film. Digital photographs are often stored on a separate medium, the memory card, but the same memory card can be used over and over again. Of the three main sources of revenue in the Kodak era (sales of cameras, sales of film, and the development service), only the sales of cameras remains a major business today.

As digital photography has become the dominant form of domestic photography, it is easier to see how the Kodak business model restricted and enabled a specific set

---

[16]Batchen 1997.

of practices. In the digital era, capturing a photograph is not separated from seeing the captured image: no longer is it necessary to 'wait until the roll is full' before taking it to a developing service and waiting for them to develop the prints; this was what Polaroid had already achieved. Digital photos have the potential to be of any physical size and shape, but it remains the legacy of the Kodak era that the prints are often the standard rectangular 10 × 15 cm. Gone are the paper envelopes containing developed prints, as are many of the 'one-hour' photo shops and mail-order services that produced them. But perhaps the most visible change is the possibility of editing photographs. In the Kodak model, the only influence the snapshot photographer had on the developed photographs was selecting from among a few standard sizes and whether the photos were to be developed on glossy or matte paper. In comparison, the possibilities now afforded by image editing software are enormous.

Perhaps the most iconic device of the post-Kodak digital era is the camera phone. It fulfils none of the three business models of Kodak: it is not sold as a camera, it has a built-in storage medium, and it requires no development process to produce the photographs. At the same time, it integrates the advances in information, communication, and media technology: it is a handheld programmable computer with an inherent network connection and a built-in camera for taking still and moving pictures. How will such networked camera–computers shape domestic photography? Will there be a dominant business model for snapshot photography in the post-Kodak era, and how will it shape the practices?

It seems that the turn of the millennium will show a similar milestone in domestic photography to the invention of the camera in the first half of the nineteenth century, and the birth of snapshot photography at the dawn of the twentieth century. Old and existing practices have been reshaped as new practices have emerged, and these practices are still being reshaped by people adopting new products and services made publicly available by commercial organisations.

How did domestic photography end up being what it is today, and how have the business, technology, and practices interacted to shape it? As we asked at the beginning of this book, what has changed in domestic photography and what has remained the same? To begin our journey into the history of domestic photography, we next describe and discuss our analytical tool for understanding it.

2.2 Technological Paths in Domestic Photography

Most previous histories of domestic photography have been written from only one of the three perspectives outlined above. Many concentrate on the technical inventions that made it possible.[17] Some focus on photographic content and practices.[18] Yet others outline the business drivers and models, and provide histories

---

[17]See, *e.g.*, Auer 1975; Benson 2008; Gustavson 2009; Lewis 1991; Wade 1979.

[18]See, *e.g.*, Bourdieu 1990; Chalfen 1987; Chambers 2003; Coe and Gates 1977; Czech 1996; Drucker et al. 2004; Goldberg 1991; Holland 2009; King 1984; Musello 1979; Van Dijck 2008.

of organisations that made certain forms of photography popular.[19] However, as we pointed out in Chap. 1, domestic photography can be seen as a socio-technical system involving various interactions between technology, people, and the social organisations in which they live and work. Furthermore its technology and business models have been in flux for over 170 years.[20] This has taken place in particular societal contexts and been subject to creative accommodation and misuse.

These two insights underpin work in Computer Supported Cooperative Work (CSCW) and Science and Technology Studies (STS) and suggest the need for a more integrated history of the area. This should combine insights from technology, practice, and business perspectives. To undertake this work, we draw on the STS literature regarding technology and business evolution and social construction of technology. We focus on the agency of technology in shaping practice and the agency of business in shaping technology. This is because our main audience is the builders of future imaging technologies and we want to alert them to the fact that the artefacts they create are not morally or politically neutral; they embody values, preferred uses, politics, presumptions, and business models.

We emphasise the role of technology also because often the technology is dominant in sustaining certain structures. However, we do not propose technological determinism, while we do draw attention to how artefacts favour certain uses over others, and often these more 'compatible' uses support specific business models. This is not surprising, given that practically all photographic technology has been made public by commercial organisations. Therefore, we also pay special attention to the business and commercial incentives of producers and users of technologies.

2.2.1   The Cyclical Evolution of Technology

Our view on the history of domestic and snapshot photography is based on the model of technological evolution paced by discontinuities and dominant designs. We refer to the model published by Philip Anderson and Michael Tushman,[21] but other literature from technology management research, such as the work of Clayton M. Christensen and James Utterback,[22] presents similar models. In our approach, we also refer to science and technology studies, and within STS we mainly reference work from social construction of technology studies (SCOT). These studies recognise the non-linear and cyclical nature of technology development and progress, and they bring into the foreground the heterogeneous actors shaping the process.

By cyclical we mean that the consecutive phases of technology development follow each other in a cyclical manner. An established and stabilised technology

---

[19] See, *e.g.*, Collins 1990; Jenkins 1975; Munir 2005; Olshaker 1978; Wensberg 1987.

[20] Lehmuskallio discusses how the 'technological logics' driving photography and image capture in general range back centuries (Lehmuskallio 2010 (unpublished work)).

[21] Anderson and Tushman 1990.

[22] Christensen 1997; Utterback 1994.

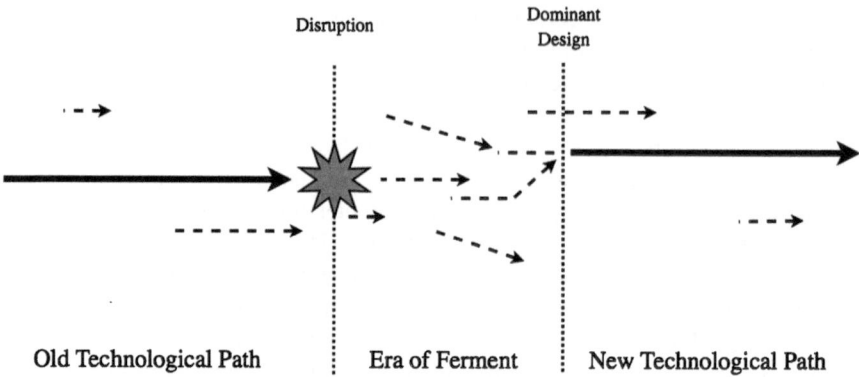

Fig. 2.1 The model of technological evolution used in this book. The *solid arrows* are dominant technological paths and the *dashed arrows* are alternative non-dominant paths (The figure is adapted from Fig. 1 from Anderson and Tushman 1990, p. 606. © Risto Sarvas, 2010)

can be seen to follow a certain *technological path*. At some point, this path is *disrupted* by a radical invention (or some other major change), which launches an *era of ferment* ending with a new stable and established technology path characterised by a *dominant design* (see Fig. 2.1). By non-linear we mean that in a 'Kuhnian'[23] fashion, technological evolution is not cumulative or incremental, but major changes happen in 'paradigm shifts' that shake the very foundations of technological knowledge, business models, and industry, and that pressure people to reconfigure their practices and invent new ones.

According to the model, a radical invention, at an unforeseen moment, disrupts the existing and established industry. Radical about the invention is that the new technology is not based on the existing business models and competencies in the industry, but is dramatically different from the norm of existing innovation in an industry.[24] Kamal A. Munir and Nelson Phillips go as far as to suggest that a radical innovation questions the whole concept of 'industry', since the idea of an industry assumes a central product and this becomes undermined.[25] Anderson and Tushman call this kind of radical innovation a *technological discontinuity*. Hughes discusses inventions in relation to a technological system, and a *radical invention* in his model is something that does not become a component in the incumbent and existing system.[26]

Inventions that are not radical or disruptive are *incremental*[27] or *conservative*.[28] Although they can be inventive, they support the existing, established business and industry structures, popular practices, and technological systems.

---

[23] Kuhn 1962.

[24] Anderson and Tushman 1990.

[25] Munir and Phillips 2002.

[26] Hughes 1989, p. 57.

[27] Anderson and Tushman 1990.

[28] Hughes 1989.

In the Anderson and Tushman model, a technological discontinuity launches an *era of ferment* in which the old technology competes against the new technology (and different variations of the new technology compete against each other).[29] Typical of the fermentation era is that there is no clear combination of actors that is stable and dominant. The potential benefits of becoming the new dominant design make the era of ferment exceptionally competitive, as previous structures, models, power relations, and organisations are potentially all due for change.

According to W. Brian Arthur, in an era of ferment the competition between technologies that have increasing returns to adoption can be strongly influenced by small events and factors: in a competition between new technologies, one of them might get a head start on adoption and benefit from the snowball effect of increasing returns.[30] Photography technology for domestic use is a good example of a technology with increasing returns to adoption: the more people use a specific technology (*e.g.*, glass plates, 35 mm film, or JPG images), the more standard or compatible with others it becomes; hence, it grows more attractive.

The outcome of an era of ferment is non-obvious and complex. Bijker and Law explain that in technological change the heterogeneous actors (*e.g.*, businesses, regulators, users, organisational structures, and existing technologies) each have their own strategies for winning in the conflict and beating any opposition.[31] The strategies and actions are shaped by the actions of other actors (and their strategies); this makes the strategies and their consequences emergent phenomena, and, more importantly, it makes technological change contingent and messy.[32] Hughes draws attention to the processes that take place between an invention and its commercialisation: after the initial invention has been made, further invention and development continue as the new technology is turned into an innovation within complex systems such as manufacturing, marketing, logistics, and service.[33] As Anderson and Tushman point out, the initial invention that started the era of ferment will not itself become the final stabilised dominant design forming the technological path, because of the active shaping processes.[34]

The era of ferment is not only a business competition between the stakeholders of different technologies. The users of the old and new technologies also face change and have a critical role in influencing the outcome. Elizabeth Shove et al. discuss how the proponents of new technologies – namely, digital photography – have to capture, enlist, and engage practitioners.[35] People have existing practices based on the incumbent or old technology, and taking new technology into use requires reconfiguring these practices. It is these new and reconfigured practices

---

[29] Anderson and Tushman 1990.

[30] Arthur 1994.

[31] Bijker and Law 1992.

[32] *Ibid.*

[33] Hughes 1989, p. 64

[34] Anderson and Tushman 1990, p. 616.

[35] Shove et al. 2007.

that shape what the new technology will be. Shove et al. take as an example how photography itself is defined, constituted, reproduced, and reconfigured through participation – in other words, the 'doing' of practices.[36]

The stakeholders of a new technology try to influence the process of adapting old practices to better suit the new technology. Munir and Jones draw attention to the active process of 'problematisation' by the stakeholders: to frame actors' understanding so that they perceive themselves as having problems for which the promoted technology is the solution.[37] In other words, rather than consumers having pre-existing needs, consumer needs are constructed in a process by various actors (*e.g.*, consumers themselves, technology promoters, and public media), and these needs are elemental in motivating people to adopt new technologies and adapt existing practices to fit them.

The era of ferment ends when the relations between the actors are stabilised: the technologies, businesses, regulators, retailer organisations, people and their practices, advertisers etc. reach an implicit consensus on what the technology design is. The technology becomes a 'black box' the internal workings of which are not disputed or questioned but taken for granted.[38] Anderson and Tushman call the stabilised technology a *dominant design* emerging from the era of ferment as the norm and industry standard.[39] However, Bijker and Law emphasise that it is not only the technology or the industry that stabilises but all relations between the actors.[40] In other words, in addition to a dominant technical design (*i.e.*, technology), the business model and actors producing and profiting from the technology are stabilised, as are people's practices for using the technology, and also societal factors such as regulation and levels of income.

2.2.2   Technological Paths

The Kodak model in snapshot photography is an example of how a technology (rolls of film and a simple camera), a business model (selling film and a photo-finishing service), and practice (capturing images of family members and familial events) stabilised in the Kodak Culture in the twentieth century and remained the dominant form of photography for almost a century. The Kodak example also demonstrates that a dominant design can be surprisingly resilient. The time period in which the technological path described by the Kodak model was dominant was anything but stable: two world wars, economic depressions, major emigrations and immigrations, and unprecedented technological development. Quite surprisingly, the technological path set by Kodak was not disrupted until the 1990s.

---

[36]*Ibid.*

[37]Munir and Jones 2004, p. 571, referencing Latour 1987.

[38]Latour 1987.

[39]Anderson and Tushman 1990.

[40]Bijker and Law 1992, p. 10.

Once a dominant design is established (*i.e.*, the stabilisation of relations between the actors), the era of ferment is over and technological development becomes *incremental* in improving the dominant design.[41] This marks the beginning of an era of incremental change,[42] which we refer to as a *technological path*. The technology, business models, and practices support each other, and changes occur gradually and do not diverge from the path. In other words, there is less opposition from other actors and stakeholders if a potential change follows the path rather than diverging from it. The actors and stakeholders benefiting from the dominant design and technological path have incentives in keeping the situation stabilised and dominant. Hughes discusses the incentive in organisations to avoid radical inventions that would make existing skills and structures obsolete.[43]

Anderson and Tushman make a distinction between *competence-enhancing* and *competence-destroying* discontinuities,[44] with the former meaning an invention that does not make the skills of an organisation completely obsolete. For example, the digitalisation of cameras was a competence-enhancing invention for camera manufacturers, who could still build on their knowledge of lenses, light-metering, exposure automation, automatic focusing, and so on. On the other hand, for businesses based on the sales or processing of photographic film, digital image capture was a competence-destroying technological discontinuity: it rendered the expertise required in film manufacture and processing obsolete.

The concept of a technological path is supported by Arthur's model concerning increasing returns, mentioned above: a technology that has achieved a dominant position has a clear advantage over the competition, even if the competition is in some respects 'superior'.[45] Following the technological path has advantages in compatibility and in existing knowledge and experience. An invention diverging from the path would have to overcome the critical mass of the existing path. Hughes discusses the 'momentum' of technological systems: organisations and people commit to a system (*i.e.*, a technological path) by means of various interests, fixed assets, and sunk costs.[46] In other words, once a combination of technologies, business models, organisations, legislation, and practices achieves a dominant position, it becomes difficult to overthrow the 'regime'. This is not necessarily because the *status quo* is somehow 'superior' to alternatives but because there are significant interests for established actors in maintaining the existing situation, and in the case of increasing returns, any alternative would have to compete against the head start of the incumbent 'regime'.[47] It is this 'regime' that we call a technological path.

---

[41] Anderson and Tushman 1990.

[42] *Ibid.*

[43] Hughes 1989.

[44] Anderson and Tushman 1990.

[45] Arthur 1994.

[46] Hughes 1989, pp. 76–77.

[47] *Ibid*; MacKenzie and Wajcman 1999.

More precisely, we define a technological path as a network of stabilised relations between heterogeneous actors, and the stability is based on alternative paths requiring a significant disruption in the relations of the actors (*e.g.*, a technological discontinuity, a societal change, a major business change, or a combination of these). The reason we call it a *technological* path even though technology is only one actor among others is that the technology as a material artefact is a concrete representation (or an icon) for the path. As we discuss below in more detail, we do not suggest that the inherent qualities of the technology are the sole determiners of the path. Nor do we suggest that the path chosen is necessarily better than alternative paths.

Like any theoretical model, the concept of a technological path is not without its problems and pitfalls. Bijker discusses how historical analyses of technology often focus on successful technologies rather than failed ones.[48] The focus on successes runs the risk of suggesting that "the success of an artefact offers some explanatory ground for the dynamics of its development".[49] For example, often histories of cameras do not mention that the Kodak camera made public in 1888 was, in fact, the *third* camera put forth for sale by the Eastman Dry Plate Company, and that the first two cameras were commercial failures. The commercial failure of the first two cameras was elemental in forcing George Eastman and his associates to look for new markets for their film-roll cameras and to rethink the process of developing images.[50] Describing the Kodak camera (*i.e.*, the third camera by Eastman and his associates) as the starting point of snapshot photography technology would then miss the actual dynamics of development and failure that shaped the organisation's thinking and business models.

To balance our historical overview of technological paths, we describe products and services that did not become dominant but nevertheless had an important impact on snapshot and domestic photography.

The second pitfall in using technological paths as a tool for understanding history is reading it as technological determinism. A technological path may suggest that it is somehow only the technology and its qualities that define the path and that the technology of a path is 'the best' among alternatives. As we have mentioned above, we do not believe in such a simple and technologically deterministic view. The superiority of a technology or a technological system is relative to time, place, and actors. Bijker and Law explicitly call for caution in using concepts such as technological paradigms and trajectories because they often afford a technologically deterministic view.[51]

So how do we justify the use of technological paths in our overview if we are not proponents of technological determinism? First, it is hard to deny that technological paths have existed and do exist. As we will describe in the following pages, there are clear eras in the history of photography when a technology–business

---

[48] Bijker 1995, p. 7.

[49] *Ibid*, p. 7.

[50] Jenkins 1975.

[51] Bijker and Law 1992, p. 8.

combination was dominant: metal plate photography and studio portrait practice, wet collodion plates and mass sales of stock photographs, the Kodak business model, and snapshot photography. During these periods, alternative paths did exist, but there were dominant technologies that formed a technological path.

It is in the interpretations of these technological paths that the siren song of technological determinism lies. For example, often the first Kodak camera from 1888 is described as a success by referring to its technical qualities: small size, ease of use, and 100 images without reloading. However, as mentioned above, the camera formed only one part of the commercial success of Kodak and the birth of the snapshot culture. Without the invention of a photo-finishing service, the idea of marketing to unskilled amateurs, and the societal and economic situation of the American middle class, the Kodak camera would not have been a success. The two unsuccessful cameras preceding the 'first' Kodak further support this view. Nevertheless, this Kodak camera was elemental in forming the Kodak Path, even though it was not solely the technology that formed that path.

On the other hand, undermining technological determinism by emphasising the agency of business models, commercial incentives, and business actors runs the risk of suggesting business determinism. We hope to avoid this pitfall by discussing how these business decisions and factors were shaped by society, people's practices, and also the technology. Generally, in our use of technological paths we attempt complete avoidance of *reductionism* – that is, the explanation of historical events by reducing all actors and their actions to one event, person, decision, technology, artefact, and so on.

2.2.3   Three Technological Paths in Domestic Photography

In summary, on the basis of cyclical and non-linear models of technological development, we look at the history of domestic photography from the point of view of technological paths and dominant designs. We use the term *technological path* to describe a time period of incremental development of technologies, stable domestic practices (*i.e.*, not the practices of the professionals), and gradual change of relations between the actors constituting the technology. The beginning and the end of a technological path are defined by a significant disruption in the relations between the actors, such as a technological innovation that forces the actors to react. Once the relations between the actors stabilise and a new dominant technology emerges, a new technological path is formed.

In our historical analysis, we look at the actors and activities from a relatively broad perspective based on literature on the history of photography, and as we move closer to the twenty-first century, we include academic literature from visual culture studies, interactive systems design, and also newspaper articles and marketing reports. Approaching domestic photography as a history of techno-socio-economic changes enables us to look at it from a 'macro' perspective and to identify outlines and contours that could be overlooked from a more 'micro' perspective. From this perspective, we see three paths, each of which began with a technological discontinuity (*i.e.*, a disruptive/radical innovation) and after an era of ferment stabilised into a technological path. These are summarised in Fig. 2.2.

The first path is the era in the nineteenth century starting with the parallel attempts at, and successes in, capturing a photograph in the 1830s and ending in the decade following the introduction of the Kodak camera in 1888. We call this the Portrait Path, and it is covered in Chap. 3. This technological path is characterised by the combination of photography technology (metal and glass plate capture and paper printing), the businesses of studio portraiture and stock photography, and the practices of having one's photographic portrait taken by a professional and of buying publicly sold photographs. It is this last characteristic that we use to define the path, because it is the domestic practice from the perspective of the non-professional consumer. Although technologies did vary within the Portrait Path, the domestic perspective of photography being associated with studio portraits and stock photography did not change until the late nineteenth century.

The second path is characterised by film as a capture medium, the selling of film rolls and photo-finishing services as dominant business models, and the practice and culture of snapshot photography (*i.e.*, unskilled amateurs taking pictures themselves, using their own cameras). This path started with the introduction of the Kodak camera in 1888 and the associated business model, both of which were elemental in the emergence of snapshot photography. As mentioned before, this path covers most of the twentieth century, ending in the 1990s, when digital image capture started to emerge as the disruptive technology. We call this second era the Kodak Path because the dominant form of domestic photography was snapshot photography and it was both invented and practically monopolised by Kodak. The Kodak Path is described in Chap. 4. Although camera and film technologies made huge advances during the time of the Kodak Path, and alternative technological paths competed for dominance, the basic model and process of taking snapshots persisted for over a century.

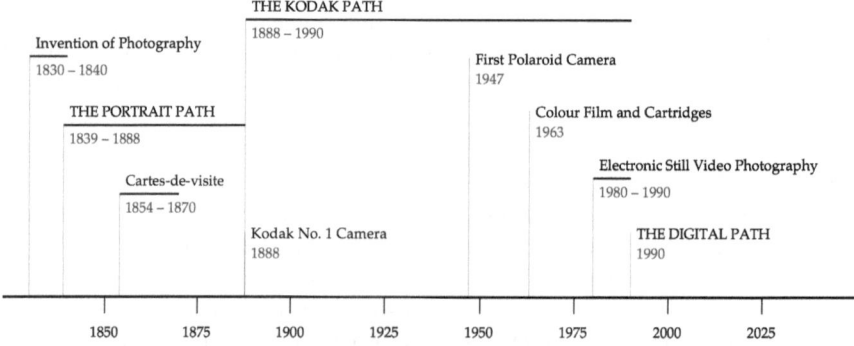

Fig. 2.2 A timeline of the three technological paths in the history of domestic photography and the six milestones we draw attention to in the chapters that follow (© Risto Sarvas, 2010)

Our third path is the Digital Path, which started in the 1990s and has, at the moment, no end in sight. On the contrary, we discuss at the end of the book how the Digital Path is still in an era of ferment. We go over the Digital Path in two separate chapters. Chapter 5 covers the stepwise transformation of domestic photography from a film-based infrastructure into a digital information and communications (ICT) infrastructure. Chapter 6 continues the treatment of the Digital Path by studying the digital photography literature in the disciplines of human–computer interaction, computer-supported co-operative work, and interaction design research to shed light on people's practices with the new technologies.

References

Anderson P, Tushman M (1990) Technological discontinuities and dominant designs: a cyclical model of technological change. Adm Sci Q 35(4):604–633

Arthur WB (1994) Increasing returns and path dependence in the economy. University of Michigan Press, Ann Arbor

Auer M (1975) The illustrated history of the camera from 1839 to the present. New York Graphic Society, Boston

Barthes R (2000) Camera Lucida: reflections on photography. Vintage Books, London

Batchen G (1997) Burning with desire: the conception of photography. MIT Press, Cambridge

Benson R (2008) The printed picture. Museum of Modern Art, New York

Bijker WE (1995) Of bicycles, bakelites, and bulbs: toward a theory of sociotechnical change. MIT Press, Cambridge

Bijker WE, Law J (1992) Shaping technology/building society: studies in sociotechnical change. MIT Press, Cambridge

Bourdieu P (1990) Photography: a middle-brow art. Polity Press, Cambridge

Chalfen R (1987) Snapshot versions of life. Bowling Green State University Popular Press, Bowling Green

Chambers D (2003) Family as place: family photograph albums and the domestication of public and private space. In: Schwartz JM, Ryan JM (eds) Picturing place: photography and the geographical imagination. I.B. Tauris, London

Christensen CM (1997) The innovator's dilemma: when new technologies cause great firms to fail. Harvard Business School Press, Boston

Coe B, Gates P (1977) The snapshot photograph: the rise of popular photography, 1888–1939. Ash & Grant, London

Collins D (1990) The story of Kodak. H.N. Abrams, New York

Czech KP (1996) Snapshot: America discovers the camera. Lerner, Minneapolis

Drucker S, Wong C, Roseway A, Glenner S, Mar S (2004) MediaBrowser: reclaiming the shoebox. In: Proceedings of the working conference on advanced visual interfaces (AVI '04), Gallipoli

Durrant A, Taylor A, Frohlich D, Sellen A, Uzzell D (2009) Photo displays and intergenerational relationships in the family home. In: Proceedings of The 23rd BCS conference on human computer interaction, Cambridge, 2009. British Computer Society

Goldberg V (1991) The power of photography: how photographs changed our lives, 1st. Abbeville, New York

Gustavson T (2009) Camera: a history of photography from daguerreotype to digital. Sterling Pub, New York

Holland P (2009) 'Sweet is to scan...': personal photographs and popular photography. In: Wells L (ed) Photography: a critical introduction. Routledge, London, pp 113–158

Hughes TP (1989) The evolution of large technological systems. In: Bijker WE, Hughes TP, Pinch TJ (eds) The social construction of technological systems. MIT Press, Cambridge, pp 51–82

Jenkins R (1975) Images and enterprise: technology and the American photographic industry, 1839–1925. Johns Hopkins University Press, Baltimore

King G (1984) Say 'cheese'!: the snapshot as art and social history. Collins, London

Kuhn TS (1962) The structure of scientific revolutions. University of Chicago Press, Chicago

Latour B (1987) Science in action. Harvard University Press, Cambridge

Lehmuskallio A (2010) Non-professional camera pictures in a 'Cam Era' – empirical studies in non-professional uses of user-created pictorial content. Unpublished work

Lewis G (1991) The history of the Japanese camera. The international museum of photography at George Eastman House, Rochester, New York

MacKenzie DA, Wajcman J (1999) Introductory essay: the social shaping of technology. In: MacKenzie DA, Wajcman J (eds) The social shaping of technology. Open University Press, Buckingham/Philadelphia, pp 3–27

Munir KA (2005) The birth of the 'Kodak Moment': institutional entrepreneurship and the adoption of new technologies. Organ Stud 26(11):1665–1687

Munir KA, Jones M (2004) Discontinuity and after: the social dynamics of technology evolution and dominance. Organ Stud 25(4):561–581

Munir KA, Phillips N (2002) The concept of industry and the case of radical technological change. J High Tech Manag Res 13:279–297

Musello C (1979) Family photography. In: Wagner J (ed) Images of information: still photography in the social sciences. Sage, Beverly Hills, pp 101–118

Olshaker M (1978) The instant image: Edwin Land and the Polaroid experience. Stein and Day, New York

Peres MR (2007) Focal encyclopedia of photography: digital imaging, theory and applications, history, and science, 4th edn. Focal, Amsterdam/London

Shove E, Watson M, Hand M, Ingram J (2007) The design of everyday life. Berg, New York

Slater D (1995) Domestic photography and digital culture. In: Lister M (ed) The photographic image in digital culture. Routledge, London, pp 129–146

Utterback JM (1994) Mastering the dynamics of innovation: how companies can seize opportunities in the face of technological change. Harvard Business School Press, Boston

Van Dijck J (2008) Digital photography: communication, identity, memory. Vis Commun 7(1):57–76

Wade J (1979) A short history of the camera. Fountain Press, Watford/New York

Wensberg PC (1987) Land's Polaroid: a company and the man who invented it. Houghton Mifflin, Boston

Zuromskis C (2009) On snapshot photography: rethinking photographic power in public and private spheres. In: Long JJ, Noble A, Welch E (eds) Photography: theoretical snapshots. Routledge, London, pp 49–62

Chapter 3
The Portrait Path (ca. 1830s–1890s)

3.1 The Invention of Photography in the 1830s

In the first decades of the nineteenth century the invention of photography involved low-hanging fruit. There was existing demand in the growing middle classes for affordable 'likenesses' (i.e., portrait pictures), a practice well established in that stratum of society. The *camera obscura*, technology known for centuries, could render a more detailed image than any painting or carving and without apparent effort. Also, the light-sensitive nature of silver salts (silver nitrate and silver chloride) was widely known among contemporary practitioners. All that was needed was a way to permanently record the *camera obscura*'s image in order to produce likenesses for an existing market.

Camera obscura is a general name for the dark rooms and boxes that have a pinhole (and often a lens) letting light through so that it projects an image on the opposite side of this 'chamber dark'. As a result of the laws of physics, the image is upside down and mirrored. The *camera lucida* ('chamber light') is an adaptation of the phenomenon captured in a *camera obscura*. The *camera lucida* is an optical device for superimposing the image from a pinhole on a plate or table so that an artist can use the image in drawing (see Fig. 3.1).

The rise of the middle classes in the late eighteenth and early nineteenth centuries created a demand for portraits. By having one's portrait made, an individual of the ascending middle classes could visually affirm his new social status.[1] This demand in the early nineteenth century resulted in popular and inexpensive means of creating one's likeness or portrait.[2]

Silhouettes (i.e., a cut-out or drawn profile of a person) had been around for decades, and there were even mechanical apparatuses to assist in the drawing process. Physiognotraces were more detailed likenesses than silhouettes but more laborious. They were made by tracing a person's profile on a copper plate and engraving the 'inside' of the profile. The miniature was literally a small-sized painting,

---

[1] Freund 1982, p. 9.
[2] Johnson et al. 2005; Rosenblum 2007, p. 39; Freund 1982.

R. Sarvas and D.M. Frohlich, *From Snapshots to Social Media - The Changing Picture of Domestic Photography*, Computer Supported Cooperative Work, DOI 10.1007/978-0-85729-247-6_3, © Springer-Verlag London Limited 2011

Fig. 3.1 An 1807 engraving of a *camera lucida* in use (Unknown artist. Wikimedia Commons. No known restrictions on publication)

the cost of which was less than that of a full-size portrait. Having a skilled artist paint a large portrait was beyond the finances of all but the wealthy. By contrast, having one's silhouette, a miniature, or a physiognotrace made was within the reach and interests of the middle classes.

Not only was there an existing practice of portraiture, and familiarity with the *camera obscura*; the photosensitivity of certain materials was known. The chemistry required in a photographic process had been available and widely known for some time. Already in 1725, Johann Heinrich Schulze had conducted experiments on silver salts demonstrating their light-sensitive qualities.[3] Geoffrey Batchen also draws attention to the published works of Elizabeth Fulhame (1794) and Thomas Wedgwood (1802), who experimented with and wrote about using silver salts to imprint images.[4]

Who, then, was the first to succeed in capturing the image of the *camera obscura*? Who invented photography?

Ever since the technology became popular knowledge in 1839, the title of inventor of photography has been a matter of fierce competition without a clear winner. Pierre Harmant listed 24 people who have been claimed to be the inventor of photography.[5] Geoffrey Batchen lists 20 "proto-photographers" – that is, people who between 1794 and 1837 "practiced, recorded, or subsequently claimed for themselves a precocious onset of the desire to photograph".[6]

However, one person was able to make photography popular knowledge. Frenchman Louis Jacques Mandé Daguerre was one of the people who were working on fixing the *camera obscura*'s image in the 1820s–1830s. His work was done partly in partnership

---

[3] Batchen 1997; Rosenblum 2007, p. 193.

[4] Batchen 1997.

[5] Harmant 1977.

[6] Batchen 1997.

with Joseph Nicéphore Niépce, who had succeeded in fixing an image on a pewter plate in 1827. However, Niépce died in 1833, 6 years before the co-operation was to bear fruit. In the late 1830s, Daguerre finally mastered a process for fixing the image: a copper sheet was coated with silver, then sensitised with iodine; after exposure, the plate was subjected to mercury vapour and finally fixed with sodium thiosulfate.[7]

What made Daguerre's invention a milestone in the history of photography and resulted in him often being credited as the inventor of photography was the way he made his process of photography public. Daguerre convinced the French government to purchase his invention from him and place it in the public domain.[8] On 19 August 1839, the process was made public in the joint meeting of the French Academies of Science and Fine Arts. At the same time, the invention purchased by the government was turned over to the public domain.[9]

The French government succeeded in promoting the new process and technology for creating photographs, called *daguerreotypes*. Paris was quickly overtaken by *daguerréotypomanie*[10] (see Fig. 3.2). An example of the popularity of the

Fig. 3.2 A cartoon by Theodore Maurisset from 1840 commenting on the *daguerréotypomanie* that took over Paris after the publication of Daguerre's photography process (Lithograph. Library of Congress Prints and Photographs Division, USA [Reproduction Number LC-DIG-ppmsca-02343]. No known restrictions on publication)

---

[7]Benson 2008, p. 100.

[8]Rosenblum 2007.

[9]*Ibid.*, p. 17. However, Rosenblum (2007, p. 18) points out that Daguerre's process was not royalty-free on the other side of the English Channel. Daguerre patented his invention in England, and British subjects had to purchase a franchise from Daguerre's agent.

[10]*Ibid.*, p. 21.

daguerreotype is that in the 18 months following the announcement, the manual describing Daguerre's process went through 30 editions and was translated into eight languages.[11]

Whether or not Daguerre was the first to invent photography, he was the first to make it popular knowledge, and the first to make a profit out of photography: Daguerre received an annual government pension of 6,000 francs for selling the invention to the government.[12]

After hearing the news of Daguerre's patent in January 1839, Englishman William Henry Fox Talbot quickly published the photographic process he had been working on for several years. In Fox Talbot's process, a paper coated with silver salts was exposed to light and an image would form on the paper: dark where more light hit the surface and light where less light was exposed – in other words, a *negative* image. Fox Talbot's photographs were called *calotypes* or *Talbotypes*. The resulting image was the opposite of Daguerre's process, which created a *positive* image on a metal plate. To produce a positive image, the calotype negative had to be printed on another light-sensitised paper, and exposing light through the negative produced a positive image. Importantly, unlike with the daguerreotype, one could produce numerous positive images from the same calotype negative – several copies could be made of a single photograph. This possibility would later be critical in the negative/positive process overtaking the daguerreotype process.

Neither of the processes published in 1839 was very practical even by nineteenth-century standards. Daguerreotypes had to be exposed to light for 10–15 min to get a photograph, the final picture was easily damaged, and the mercury fumes required in the process were unhealthy. The problem with the calotype was that the image was not as sharp and detailed as the competing daguerreotype (see Figs. 3.3 and 3.4), and, most discouragingly, it faded away. Nevertheless, a technological discontinuity had emerged in the business of creating likenesses, especially in portraiture but also in the business of selling images of landscapes etc. as lithograph and engraving prints. Compared to paintings, drawings, silhouettes, and physiognotraces, the

---

→

Figs. 3.3 and 3.4   On the *top* is a daguerreotype from 1844, and on the *bottom* is a calotype made in the same year. The clarity and detail of the daguerreotype were appreciated over the roughness and softness of the calotype (*Top figure*: Unknown photographer. Original title: Emlen Cresson, his mother Sarah Emlen Cresson, his wife Priscilla Prichett Cresson, and his mother-in-law Mrs. Edith Hatten Prichett in a group family portrait, 1844. Daguerreotype. Library of Congress Prints and Photographs Division, USA [Reproduction Number LC-USZC4-12733]. No known restrictions on publication. *Bottom figure*: Unknown photographer. Robert Adamson and David Octavius Hill. Original title: Thomas Duncan, 1807–1845, Artist, 1844. A calotype print. National Galleries of Scotland. No known restrictions on publication)

---

[11] Auer 1975, p. 35.

[12] Rosenblum 2007, p. 642. For lack of a better estimate, 2 litres of red wine cost, in August 1839, 0.36 francs in France; therefore, Daguerre's annuity would have purchased him around 33,000 litres of wine (data from Michaud 2010).

creation of a photograph was amazingly accurate and fast. Photography was received with public enthusiasm; the ability to create images as realistic as photographs was quite exceptional and previously unheard of.

3.1.1 Competing Technical Processes

The technical invention of the photography process launched an era of ferment in which both Daguerre's and Fox Talbot's inventions were improved and modified. Only 2 years after the announcements in 1839, there had been significant advances in lenses, the sensitivity of the photosensitive materials, and the surface of the plates.[13] In those 2 years following the announcement, the exposure time for a daguerreotype was reduced to 5–8 s (from 10 to 15 min) and lenses were made that were 16 times faster than Daguerre's original lens.[14] A key driver in the rapid development was the goal of making the process commercially feasible for portraiture.[15] The rapid progress was possible also because there were already professional opticians, lens-manufacturers, and *camera obscura* and *lucida* manufacturers who could easily adapt their competencies to improve the photographic processes.

At the time, the daguerreotype process was considered superior because of the sharp images it produced, and also it was royalty-free (at least in France), because the French government had purchased the rights from Daguerre and shared them in the public domain. Therefore, the daguerreotype became the *de facto* standard for portrait photography in the 1840s and remained the dominant design until the 1850s. In other words, the daguerreotype had a faster adoption rate, and, therefore, the technology had the benefits of increasing returns: more and more photographers adopted the process, creating a larger market for the materials and equipment, and the process became more widely known. Although the competing calotype process remained an alternative, the dominant design was the daguerreotype.

In the years immediately following the announcements of 1839, it was the negative/positive process that was commercially less feasible. The calotype's grainy and soft image was considered inferior to the sharp details of the daguerreotype. Also, the process was somewhat more complex. Unlike Daguerre's process, Fox Talbot's had two distinct parts: the *capture* of the image as a negative and exposing light through the negative to create a positive (i.e., printing). However, these two separate processes enabled the photograph to be reproduced several times.

The capture and printing parts of Fox Talbot's process were dramatically improved at the beginning of the 1850s. In 1851, the negative capture process reached a milestone in the wet collodion process credited to Frederick Scott Archer. A negative image was captured on a glass plate covered with a wet collodion (a chemical solution of pyroxylin in ether and alcohol that held the light-sensitive

---

[13] Jenkins 1975, p. 31.
[14] Rosenblum 2007; Wade 1979.
[15] Jenkins 1975, p. 30.

silver salts on the glass[16]). The image captured was more precise and exact than the calotype on paper. It did not, however, attain the level of detail of the daguerreotype, and the negative was a heavy and breakable glass plate. Nevertheless, both the immediate and potential advantages of reproduction eventually led to it overtaking the daguerreotype process, and for three decades it was the dominant technology in photography.[17]

A year before, in 1850, Louise Désiré Blanquart-Evrard announced improvements to the so-called albumen print process that had been invented by Claude Félix Abel Niépce de Saint-Victor, Nicéphore Niépce's nephew.[18] The characteristics of paper, which created a soft, grainy image and limited the tonal range, were overcome. In the albumen print process, the paper is coated with a layer of albumen (a protein in egg white), which effectively holds the image-forming chemicals on top of the fibres of the paper. The albumen print was able to do justice to the clarity and tonal range achieved in wet collodion glass negatives.[19]

The combination of the wet collodion negative and the albumen print positive marked the beginning of the end for the daguerreotype in the 1850s.[20] The picture qualities of the negative/positive process started to match those of the daguerreotype: exact, detailed, sharp images with a wide tonal range. Once the image quality was matched, the possibility of making copies of the original image proved to be the characteristic that threw off the dominance of the daguerreotype.

The wet collodion process remained the standard capture method from the 1850s until the 1870s, when the dry plate method (dried gelatine replacing the wet collodion) proved more practical, faster, and of standard high quality. The albumen print process remained the dominant design for photographic prints till the end of the century and the emergence of gelatine-prepared paper prints and ink-based photograph printing.

The collodion process was applied also to the singular (i.e., non-reproducible) metal plate photography. These adaptations of the collodion process can be seen as applications of a disruptive innovation from existing technologies. Nevertheless, these hybrid processes combining plates and collodion had clear advantages over the glass plate negative/positive process. A popular and inexpensive capture process was the tintype (also called the ferrotype), invented in 1853, which was an application of the collodion process captured on a black-lacquered metal plate.[21] The tintype was not reproducible, but its low cost and easy production made it popular with beach photographers, who sold their services to vacationers, and during the American Civil War, where tin-typists followed the army with their wagons and made a lucrative business of capturing the soldiers' portraits.[22]

---

[16]Benson 2008, p. 106.

[17]Auer 1975, p. 27; Jenkins 1975, p. 39.

[18]Auer 1975, p. 26.

[19]Benson 2008, p. 108.

[20]*Ibid.*, p. 108. However, the daguerreotype remained popular in the United States for longer than in Europe (Rosenblum 2007, p. 23).

[21]An underexposed negative image appears as a positive against a black background (Benson 2008, p. 118).

[22]Allison 1989, p. 48.

Another relatively popular capture format was the ambrotype, which was a further application of the collodion process invented in the first half of the 1850s. In the ambrotype process, a collodion-coated glass plate is underexposed, which creates a positive image when the plate is mounted on a black background.[23] Like the tintype, the ambrotype process was fast, and a finished ambrotype could be given to the customer in a matter of minutes.[24] The tintype and the ambrotype retained popularity in the portrait business in the 1850s, until the methods for mass production of *cartes-de-visite* proved more popular.

In the next section, we turn to parallel developments in the creation and use of images recorded in this first era of photography. This covers the business and practice of early photography and photographic content, which was itself subject to innovation, dominance, and change.

3.1.2 Selling Portraits and Landscapes

The new technology published in 1839 created the photography business, which would later develop into the printing and imaging industry. However, neither of the two processes published in 1839 was suitable as it was for commercial portrait-making: to capture a portrait, the subject had to sit for 15 min in blazing sunlight. Nevertheless, the potential for more efficient and accurate portrait production than allowed by existing non-photographic methods (i.e., painting, physiognotraces, and silhouettes) must have been obvious, because substantial effort was poured into making the daguerreotype process commercially viable.[25] As mentioned above, within 2 years of its announcement, the daguerreotype process was made faster with better lenses, use of chemicals, and other means, such that the exposure time was reduced to 5–8 s. This made commercial portrait photography much more feasible.[26]

The new photographers came from the professions that the new technology replaced: especially in France, it was the miniature and landscape painters who took up photography, as well as engravers and draughtsmen; but also watchmakers, opticians, tinkers, and other artisans saw a business opportunity in portrait photography.[27]

Some of the most successful portrait photographers left their names in history. Richard Beard opened the world's first photography studio (producing daguerreotypes) in London in 1841 (see Fig. 3.5).[28] In the United States, in 1843, Southworth & Hawes was established, a famous daguerreotype studio in Boston, and in 1844 Mathew Brady opened his studio in New York City. In the US national census of 1850, 938 citizens listed their profession as 'daguerreotypist'.[29]

---

[23] *Ibid.*, Benson 2008, p. 118.

[24] Allison 1989, p. 48.

[25] Rosenblum 2007, p. 40.

[26] *Ibid.*, p. 41.

[27] *Ibid.*, pp. 41–42.

[28] Auer 1975, p. 47.

[29] Czech 1996, p. 13.

Fig. 3.5 A daguerreotype of Richard Beard's studio in 1843. Beard's business was very successful, and he was said to be photography's first millionaire[30](Unknown photographer. Original title: Jabez Hogg and Mr. Johnson, 1843. Science & Society Picture Library. Republished with permission)

Relatively quickly, only a few years after the announcements of 1839, the profession and business of studio portrait photography was established, and to support that a small industry of camera and other device and chemical manufacturers was created.[31] The technology, exposure times, fashions, and images have changed, but the basic idea of studio portrait photography was the same then as it is now.

However, photography did not remain within the studio. The possibility to capture views previously unseen created a demand for those views. Places, people, objects, animals, events, fantasies, and other views that intrigued the mind could now be seen in a photograph. And a photograph captured every detail and was considered more truthful than a manually made picture – and it was less costly. Much due to their documentary nature, photographs became an important part of science, politics, news, medicine, crime investigations, marketing, and domestic life. In addition to the business of studio photography, selling interesting photographs to the general public was another way to profit from photography. The photographs at the home of a Western middle-class family of the time were one of two types: studio portraits and photographs bought from retailers.

---

[30]Holland 2009, p. 127.

[31]Jenkins 1975, p. 2.

The landscape photography business started with the selling of views of famous or extraordinary natural formations, such as Niagara Falls, to travellers.[32] In the 1830s, there already existed a market for engraved and lithographed scenes, and the first landscape photographers targeted the buyers of these scenes by having daguerreotypes translated by artists into engravings, lithographs, and aquatints.[33] Also, the urban scene was a popular subject of early daguerreotypes, as were panoramas and scenic views.[34]

However, the daguerreotype process was cumbersome, especially outside the comforts of a studio, and the metal plate was difficult to view, because of reflections. Most importantly, the daguerreotype process produced a single image that could not be easily duplicated. With the improvements made in the negative/positive process in the 1850s (i.e., glass negatives and albumen prints), it overtook the daguerreotype in capturing landscapes and scenery. Although hauling glass plates, a darkroom, and developing chemicals to exotic locations was anything but easy, it was less laborious than daguerreotypes, and the captured images could be reproduced.[35] The combination of glass plate negatives and the albumen print enabled the mechanised production of images of high quality, and publishers selling landscape images created a new consumer business from photography.[36]

One of the popular formats for photographic prints was the stereograph, or stereo cards, as they were called (see Fig. 3.6). The principle of the stereographic image was

Fig. 3.6 A stereo card of the Boston Coliseum at the World's Peace Jubilee in 1872 (Unknown photographer. Original title: World's Peace Jubilee, 1872 – Boston Coliseum, 1872. Photographic print on stereo card. Library of Congress Prints and Photographs Division, USA [Reproduction Number LC-DIG-ppmsca-17488]. No known restrictions on publication)

---

[32]Rosenblum 2007, p. 96.

[33]*Ibid.*, p. 97.

[34]*Ibid.*, p. 96.

[35]*Ibid.*, p. 98.

[36]*Ibid.*, p. 105.

known long before its popularity in the 1850s. Charles Wheatstone described it in 1838, but the mass production methods made possible by albumen prints and glass plates turned stereo cards into household items, an early mass consumer product.[37]

The stereograph required a special viewer that allowed each eye to see only the image meant for it and hence created an illusion of depth to the image. The stereo cards proved extremely popular and were the dominant format in sales of photographs to the public. Popular themes were travel and tourist views, city and rural life, wars and military campaigns, 'still life' settings and statuary, exhibitions, moralising and humorous tableaux, circus, pets and animals, trades and occupations, and so on.[38] One of the major retailers of stereo cards, the London Stereoscopic Company, had 100,000 different subjects in its catalogue of 'Groups and Scenes'.[39] F.J. Haynes, a photographer for the Northern Pacific Railroad, calculated that he sold 540,000 stereoscopic views of Western scenery.[40] The popularity of stereo cards declined in the late 1870s but was revived a decade later because of effective mass production methods and remained popular all the way into the late 1910s.[41]

The demand for photographs created a need for photographers to travel the world and capture its views, people, landscapes, and iconic landmarks for a mass audience.[42] A single photograph could sell as many as 38,000 copies,[43] and, as mentioned above, publishers had as many as 100,000 different views in stock.[44] Albumen prints as book illustrations became popular in the 1850s, and the first monthly magazines with photographs appeared.[45] Photographs were also sold as single images – for example, for tourists as souvenirs.[46]

Some publishers of photographs accumulated vast collections of landscapes and views. For example, by 1870, Francis Frith & Co. had become one of the largest photographic enterprises and had a collection of over one million views captured of the British Isles and continental Europe. A successful photo publisher, or a studio selling views and landscapes, had a network of freelance photographers who could capture images that appealed to the mass audience. Also, a studio such as the famous Carlo Ponti's in Venice had to have a good location for attracting tourists and business, and a well-organised mail-order distribution system.[47] Finally, a successful business had to be able to reproduce images efficiently with low costs to address the demand. For example, George Washington Wilson's publishing

---

[37] Jenkins 1975, p. 50.

[38] Allison 1989, p. 58.

[39] *Ibid.*, p. 58.

[40] Czech 1996, p. 37.

[41] Jenkins 1975, p. 60.

[42] Rosenblum 2007, p. 107.

[43] A view of Mammoth Hot Springs, in the US's Yellowstone National Park, captured by F.J. Haynes. Czech 1996, p. 37.

[44] Allison 1989; Holland 2009.

[45] Rosenblum 2007, pp. 109–110.

[46] Johnson et al. 2005, p. 165.

[47] *Ibid.*, p. 173.

works in Aberdeen, Scotland, could produce in the 1880s one million prints a year and had up to 1,300 printing frames on racks in its exposure yard.[48]

We can view the early decades of the photography business and technology as involving demand for private personal portraits and publicly sold landscapes and views (i.e., stock photographs). These two types of photographs were the domestic photographs in the middle-class home of the nineteenth century. For millions of ordinary people who could not afford to travel, the public photographs in books, prints, stereo cards, and albums brought home the world.[49] The portraits of the people themselves enabled a new way of presenting self, the family, and the status achieved in society, but portraits also were exchanged and shared as tokens of love, kinship, and friendship in an industrialising world of growing distances and mobility.

From a technical point of view, the metal plate daguerreotypes were better suited to the single image portrait business, and the negative/positive process of collodion plates and albumen prints being the 'best' technology for mass production of images. The head start enjoyed by the daguerreotype process was not enough for that process to remain competitive against the improved negative/positive process, which enabled, first and foremost, the reproduction of images. In other words, the daguerreotype was initially considered 'better' technology than the calotype, and this was because from the perspective of the portrait business it clearly was. The detailed and sharp images of metal plate photographs suited the capture of portraits better than the soft and grainy calotype did. The limitation of a single copy of a daguerreotype was not critical in the portrait business, where a single image satisfied the demand. Also, as the daguerreotype got a head start, it enjoyed the benefits of increasing returns; it was in the beginning synonymous with photography.

However, as the demand for images other than personal portraits grew, the negative/positive process proved ideal. A single calotype could be copied and sold thousands of times, and this suited mass production perfectly. The invention of the glass plate collodion process eventually became the dominant design, after a decade of modifying and varying the initial calotype process published by Fox Talbot. The same can be said of the albumen print, which evolved from the salt prints and waxed-paper prints developed in the 1840s. The negative/positive process was always 'better' than the daguerreotype for mass production, but not until the technical qualities of the image reached the level of the daguerreotype was the negative/positive process able to overthrow the dominant daguerreotype.

In summary, these examples show an interaction between different actors shaping photography: technologies, business models, people's practices, political decisions, innovative individuals, etc. A dominant technology supports particular practices and business models: daguerreotypes supported the portrait business and practice, but not landscape photography business and sales. One can speculate as to whether the single plate images would have remained the norm for portrait photographs longer if the commercial incentives of mass sales of images had not encouraged

---

[48] Allison 1989, p. 53.
[49] *Ibid.*, p. 54.

development of the negative/positive process to the point that it overtook daguerreotypes, ambrotypes, and tintypes in portrait photography.

On the other hand, the plate-based portraits did survive for a relatively long time: daguerreotypes were still popular in the United States in the 1860s, and the tintypes continued to be made even into the twentieth century.[50] Nevertheless, the collodion plate and albumen print technology became the dominant design and path that the technology's development followed from the 1850s. This led to another interaction with practice by enabling the mass production and circulation of portraits in the form of *cartes-de-visite*. *Carte* portrait photography became a new, big business in photography, which not only paved the way for snapshot photography and family albums but also anticipated some aspects of today's online social networking.

3.2   *Cartes-de-visite*: Mass-Market Portraits and Albums

The *carte-de-visite* was the portrait photography format for mass production. In its popular years between the 1860s and 1880s, estimated hundreds of millions of *cartes-de-visite* were sold.[51] In addition to stereographic pictures, the *carte* was the format for selling photographs of scenery, landscapes, urban views, and any other popular images. However, the biggest impact of *cartes* was in popularising studio portrait photography. The cost of a *carte-de-visite* portrait put personal photographs within the reach of a wider range of people than daguerreotypes or ambrotypes.

Carte-de-visite refers to a photograph of a certain size and material: a 63 mm × 100 mm (2.5″ × 4″) albumen print photograph pasted on a slightly larger piece of cardboard. A *carte* was the size of a visiting card, and initially the photographs were used as such.[52] However, the small size proved more important in bringing down the price and costs of portrait photography.

As discussed above, technical advancements in the negative/positive process had enabled the mass production of photographs and created the business of photo publishing and retailing. What had happened to landscape and scenery photographs in the 1850s was to happen to portrait photography in the 1860s. Wet plate negatives (i.e., collodion glass plates) and albumen printing were well-established technologies in the 1850s, and effective mass production of prints from the negatives was also the norm in photo production. A portrait of an ordinary person had a very limited market; therefore, the cost per photograph would remain high. However, a photograph of a landscape, scenery, a celebrity, etc. could be sold hundreds or thousands of times.

The French studio photographer André Adolphe Eugène Disderi came up with the last piece of the puzzle to bring down the costs of personal portrait photography. In his

---

[50] Rosenblum 2007, p. 196.

[51] Allison 1989; Wichard and Wichard 1999, p. 5.

[52] Batchen 2009, p. 81.

patent in 1854, he described a method of capturing several images on a single glass plate. His idea was that a camera could have several lenses so that it could capture several images at the same time, or the glass plate in the camera could be moved so that each capture would expose only a portion of the glass plate. Either way, a single plate could have several images (2, 4, 6, 8, or 10), most often eight, and the time and effort required to print a single plate now produced several images; the cost per image was reduced. Also, with little extra effort, the 2–10 images could all have different exposures, which meant that a customer could have 2–10 different portraits in one sitting. Further savings were achieved by not expending time and effort in retouching the image; most defects were unnoticeable in small-sized photographs anyway.[53]

The cost of a dozen *cartes* in the US was about $2–3 when the average cost of a single 1/6-plate-size daguerreotype was $2 (in 1851, the American Daguerreotype Association agreed to sell for no less that $1.50).[54] The price per picture for *cartes* was less than 1/8 that of the daguerreotype. The wages paid for the unskilled labour, not the photographer, creating these prints in the back rooms and on the roofs of studios was $3 a week. For the low-wage employee, a dozen *cartes* meant a week's salary. Although still expensive for the lower classes, getting one's portrait taken had come within the reach of more people of the middle classes.

The method in which the price of a portrait was reduced was an example of "true industrial-era efficiency".[55] As mentioned above, a well-organised photograph-printing business could produce millions of prints a year, or 200 *carte* sittings a day.[56] David Allison describes the industrial practice of a *carte* printing establishment of the early 1860s: "A highly organized mass-production business trading on its technical expertise, good customer relations, advertising, use of machines, [a] flexible work force earning low wages, quality and quantity control, and recycling procedures, supported by strong consumer demand."[57] By breaking photography into separate tasks, some of which could be assigned to unskilled labour (i.e., developing, printing, cutting, and mounting), the craft of photography was transformed into an industry.[58]

The mechanised reproduction was also reflected in the images themselves. Portrait photography had been, and still was, a way for the members of the middle classes to present themselves as successful members of that layer of society. One of the ways to make sure that the message was correctly received was to follow the almost strict visual code for *cartes-de-visite* at the time: "a man stands in front of a high-backed chair with his arm resting on a square column; a boy rests his arm on a balustrade that seems to disappear into the floor; a woman in her bonnet stands

[53] *Ibid.*, p. 81.

[54] Allison 1989; Jenkins 1975, p. 20; Johnson et al. 2005, p. 82.

[55] Goldberg 1991, p. 104.

[56] Batchen 2009, p. 81.

[57] Allison 1989, p. 55.

[58] Batchen 2009, p. 88.

next to a table with an open book on its top[...]".[59] The function of the shared and repeated visual code was for the subjects to visually declare their social class and belonging to that class.[60]

Publicly sold *cartes* of the aristocracy were elemental in defining that code. Batchen discusses, for example, the influence of the *carte* portraits taken of Emperor Napoleon III and how the clothing, posing, and framing of thousands of *cartes* imitated the emperor's portrait.[61] The photographers were the professionals who knew how to make a *carte* portrait look as it was supposed to: just like other *cartes*.

The profile pictures in online social networking services have the same function as *cartes* of demonstrating membership in a specific social stratum or a subculture. Also, the public images of celebrities have a strong influence on the visual code of online profile images. As we discuss in the conclusion of this chapter, the commercial value of celebrity *cartes-de-visite* was quickly understood and the seeds of celebrity culture and visual marketing were sown.

The tremendous popularity of the *carte-de-visite*, which was termed 'cartomania', brought about the birth of another key element of domestic photography: the family album. The metal and glass plates of daguerreotypes and ambrotypes had to be kept inside a case. The daguerreotype was vulnerable to scratches, and the ambrotype required a black background (cloth, varnish, or paper) to make the negative image seem positive.[62] Therefore, there was great demand for various types of photograph cases: metal, wooden, and so on.[63]

The paper albumen prints, of which *cartes* were one type, required no case but were kept in albums for protection, and importantly, as a convenient way of showing and storing the images.[64] Despite its name, the *carte-de-visite* was marketed not as a visiting card but as 'the album portrait'.[65] Not only did the sales of albums create a parallel business (a British firm claimed to have sold almost a million albums by 1867[66]), but the empty pages of albums encouraged the purchase of more *cartes*.[67] The standard size of *cartes* was also important for the album business: it provided a standard format for images (portraits, landscapes, etc.), and albums could be made to support that specific format by cutting sleeves for inserting the *cartes*.[68]

Albums varied in their size, the number of images they could hold, and the decorations and illustrations printed on the pages (see Fig. 3.7). A pen-and-ink-style illustration could frame the *carte* photograph, and "popular topics included spring

---

[59] *Ibid.*, p. 88.

[60] *Ibid.*

[61] *Ibid.*

[62] Allison 1989, p. 46.

[63] Auer 1975, p. 46.

[64] Wichard and Wichard 1999, p. 74.

[65] *Ibid.*, p. 74.

[66] *Ibid.*, p. 76.

[67] *Ibid.*, p. 74.

[68] *Ibid.*, p. 75.

Fig. 3.7 A *carte-de-visite* album from the 1880s (© Olli Pitkänen and Risto Sarvas, 2010. Published with permission)

flowers, seashells, scenic views interspersed with small spaces for vignetted portraits, trailing ivy, rope chains, autumn leaves, playing cards and suits, and ecclesiastical symbols".[69] According to Wichard and Wichard (1999), the albums were designed to reflect the external features of Bibles and prayer books: a heavy leather binding and metal clasps.[70] The resemblance gave the albums a feeling of respect, luxury, and prestige, and the similarity resonated with the function of the Bible as the family record: the front page of the family Bible normally was used for recording birth dates and important events in family history as they occurred.[71] Albums were sold for specific topics, such as the dead in the family, and in the late 1880s wedding albums were introduced.[72]

The family albums were a popular feature of the late-nineteenth-century home, and in Victorian Britain, no drawing room was considered complete without an album.[73] Collecting *cartes* in albums and decorating them was, at the time, considered a useless but suitable hobby for the women in the home.[74] The album contained photographs of

---

[69] *Ibid.*, pp. 74–75.

[70] *Ibid.*, p. 75.

[71] *Ibid.*, p. 75.

[72] *Ibid.*, p. 76.

[73] Allison 1989; Wichard and Wichard 1999, p. 79.

[74] Holland 2009, p. 128.

members of the family but also of friends, celebrities, royalty, statesmen, and well-known landscapes and scenes.[75] The photographs of public figures and institutions at the front of the album told its viewers of the larger community and world the family subscribed to, effectively linking the family members and their relatives with eminent individuals of politics, power, and pedigree, as well as celebrated symbols of nature and 'high culture'.[76]

Some portraits of public figures became very popular. The above-mentioned *carte-de-visite* photograph of Emperor Napoleon III of France, taken by Disderi in 1858, sold thousands of copies[77] and was perhaps one of the factors in launching the 'cartomania' of the 1860s. In July 1860, there were 14 *cartes* of Queen Victoria (an active *carte* collector herself), Prince Albert, and their children taken; these were published in the same year in the 'Royal Album'.[78] At least 60,000 sets of these royal portraits were sold in the UK and its colonies.[79] In the week after Prince Albert died in 1861, 70,000 photographs of him were ordered from the photograph retailer Marion & Co., which was, at the time, perhaps the world's largest retailer of *cartes-de-visite*.[80]

In addition to the aristocracy, the *carte* promoted a new breed of fame that Vicki Goldberg calls "aristocracy of achievement": artists, writers, clergymen, scientists, composers, and actors.[81] In bookstores and magazine shops, all of these public figures, or celebrities, were sold side by side, to be collected in albums at home or exchanged with friends.[82] Some celebrities used the *carte* business to their own advantage: the mass production and sale of photographs was an entirely new channel of promotion and publicity. Sojourner Truth, a former slave who gave public talks in the United States against slavery, sold *carte* portraits of herself (see Fig. 3.8) at the end of her talks as her main income.[83] To promote her career, actress Adah Isaacs Menken had her photograph frequently taken and sold in the places she toured (an example is shown in Fig. 3.9). Her seductive poses in the photographs, the scarcity of clothing in her theatre roles, and her publicly discussed affairs and scandals made her one of the first celebrities to gain widespread publicity through photographs.[84] In the 9 years she was on stage, thousands of *cartes* of her were made, and she is said to have been the most photographed woman in the world.[85]

---

[75] Chambers 2003; Wichard and Wichard 1999, p. 78.

[76] Chambers 2003, p. 99.

[77] Johnson et al. 2005, p. 328; Batchen 2009, p. 83.

[78] Allison 1989; Goldberg 1991, pp. 104, 128.

[79] Goldberg 1991, p. 104.

[80] Allison 1989; Goldberg 1991, p. 104.

[81] Goldberg 1991, p. 105.

[82] *Ibid.*, p. 105.

[83] *Ibid.*, p. 104.

[84] *Ibid.*, pp. 107–108.

[85] *Ibid.*, p. 108.

Fig. 3.8 The *carte* image of Sojourner Truth taken in 1864. She sold this *carte* at her public talks as her main income: "I Sell the Shadow to Support the Substance" (Unknown photographer. Original title: Sojourner Truth, 1864. Albumen print on a carte-de-visite mount. Library of Congress Prints and Photographs Division, USA [Reproduction Number LC-DIG-ppmsca-08978]. No known restrictions on publication)

Menken did not get paid to pose for photographers. However, soon celebrities recognised the value of their own image. For example, in his American tour in 1867–1868, the author Charles Dickens posed for photographs for public sale only for a fee.[86] The actress Sarah Bernhardt was paid $1,500 for a set of theatrical poses, and actress Lillie Langtry, some years later, demanded $5,000 for being photographed.[87] Goldberg summarises: "Once photography had helped establish the cult of personality, appearance became as salable as talent itself."[88]

The albums had a more social and interactive function as well. They were a source of entertainment and stimuli for conversation,[89] and the albums also encouraged

---

[86] *Ibid.*, p. 112.

[87] Czech 1996; Goldberg 1991, p. 112.

[88] Goldberg 1991, p. 108.

[89] Wichard and Wichard 1999, pp. 79–80.

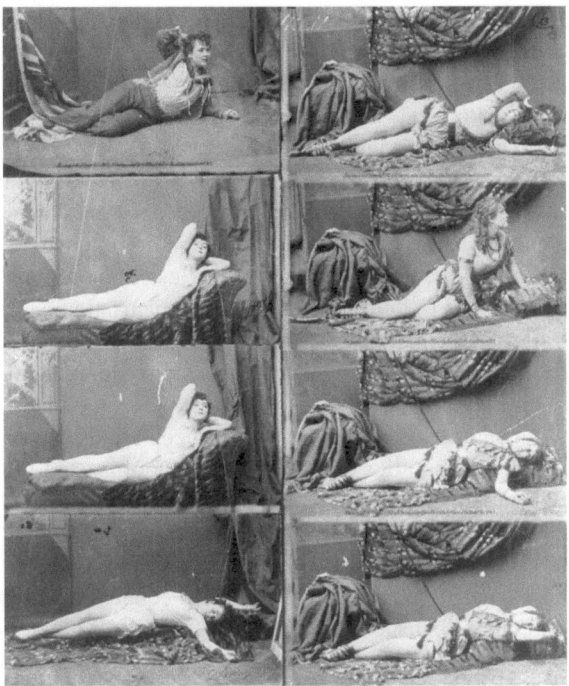

Fig. 3.9 Eight images captured on a single plate, producing eight *carte-de-visite*-size photographs. The images are of actress Adah Isaacs Menken, taken in 1868. Menken was perhaps the first celebrity who used public photographs to promote her career (Unknown photographer. Original title: Adah Isaacs Menken, 1835–1868, in 8 seductive reclining poses, 1866. Photographic print. Library of Congress Prints and Photographs Division, USA [Reproduction Number LC-USZ62-62681]. No known restrictions on publication)

the practice of exchanging photographs among friends and family. Often the album would have introductory text, such as this:

> Yes, this is my album,
> But learn ere you look,
> That all are expected
> To add to my book.
>
> You are welcome to quiz it,
> The penalty is
> That you add your own portrait
> For others to quiz.[90]

Therefore, the album contained the images not only of public figures, and members of the family, but of friends and relatives as well. Effectively, the family album became a catalogue of who belongs to the family, who their acquaintances are, and the wider public context that the family wants to associate itself with.

---

[90] Chambers 2003; Wichard and Wichard 1999.

The album, as a visual catalogue of private and public social circles, was a way of emphasising the coherence and unity of a family in a world of major societal changes. The rapid changes in communications and transportation technology in the mid-nineteenth century as well as political and social changes had broken down the pre-industrial communities and family structures. Economic opportunities had pulled family members and relatives to distant places made accessible by growing railway networks. Telegraph messages had replaced personal contact, and contemporaries complained about the loss of face-to-face communication.[91] The photo album became the nostalgic compensation for the loss of close family and the loss of a romantic, rural world to industrialisation and urbanisation.[92]

Drawing parallels to contemporary twenty-first-century society is not difficult. The online sharing of photographs in Web services or sending them via e-mail can be seen to serve the same function of holding together social relationships strained by distance and changes. Social networking services are a way of holding on to people, groups, and communities that present-day mobility and life changes have torn apart: school and university friends, office-mates and colleagues, sports teams, old neighbours, and other social ties from the past.

The *carte-de-visite* was 'the' format in the portrait photography business from the late 1850s to the early decades of the twentieth century.[93] The invention of the format is often credited to Disderi and his idea of small-format portraits that were more economical to produce than larger images; this idea was manifested in his camera invention. In addition, as we have discussed, the established methods of mass production and division of labour played a fundamental role in the popularity of the *carte*. Therefore, the technology behind the popularity of *cartes* was rather more a configuration of existing technologies in an economical manner than a disruptive innovation in the form of technological discontinuity. In the language of innovation models, Disderi's invention was *competence-enhancing*, because existing technologies could be used and skills applied.

The standard, dominant format and the accessibility of portrait photography to a large part of the population created the 'cartomania' discussed above. The technology and business model for selling *cartes* supported sales of more than one portrait picture per customer, and having 'extra' portraits suggested the exchange of them. As the price per photograph was lower, giving them to other people or exchanging them was less costly.

The *cartes* were also integral in enabling the growing middle classes to pose, in the most literal sense, as successful members of society – especially as the aristocracy (such as Emperor Napoleon III and Queen Victoria) met the middle class half way: the upper layers of society were keen to demonstrate their closeness to the bourgeoisie by posing in the format of choice of the middle classes: the *carte-de-visite*.

---

[91] Goldberg 1991, p. 105.

[92] Holland 2009, p. 125.

[93] Batchen 2009, p. 81.

Perhaps most significantly for domestic photography, the family album provided the covers between which the family could collect the pictures of themselves, their social circles, and the wider societal network they subscribed to. The public image of the domestic was presented in the same format and in the same book as the public images of members of the aristocracy, celebrities, statesmen, clergymen, and scientists, along with views, events, news, and moralising or humour-focused commentaries. As mentioned, much as do the twenty-first century's social networking service profile pages, which present the person; his or her social network; and the larger-scale public figures, events, news, etc. that he or she supports or values. Also, both *cartes* and the profile pictures on the Internet adhere to a specific visual code, the purpose of which is to declare one's belonging to a specific social group or class.

From a technological point of view, *cartes* and images on Web pages share a common feature: the format for personal and mass-use images is the same; i.e., the physical dimensions of the *carte* and the technical specifications of the digital image allow the two types – the self and the larger associations – to be presented side by side. However, the shared format between mass-produced and popularly sold public images and the private portraits of family and friends was eventually to disappear with the almost simultaneous introduction of the consumer camera and half-tone printing process.

3.3   Conclusions

The Portrait Path can be summarised as a transition from portraits to mass-produced portraits. Once it was public knowledge and available, photography found its uses in the portrait business for producing likenesses for people of themselves. By the end of the 1880s, these likenesses were produced with the same mass production methods as public stock photographs. Nevertheless, the photographs people could get of themselves still were portraits, while the other photographs in a household were publicly sold stock photographs. From the perspective of agency and actors, who and what shaped domestic photography on the Portrait Path?

It is quite possible that photography would have been invented even if both Daguerre and Fox Talbot had never taken even the slightest interest in recording the image of a *camera obscura*. However, these two individuals did ponder the mystery of recording images and, therefore, shaped history quite significantly. Daguerre made the conscious decision to convince the French government to buy his invention and make it publicly available (and receive a government pension in the process). His decision to benefit from his invention in such a way made the daguerreotype known and available to the public very efficiently. By contrast, Fox Talbot's decision to keep his invention from the public was elemental in giving the daguerreotype process a head start. Only when Fox Talbot heard of Daguerre's public invention did he make his work known. In other words, the personalities and decisions had a profound effect on how photography was introduced to the public domain.

Despite the head start, the daguerreotype process (and other metal plate processes) in the end lost their popularity, and the recording principle invented by Fox Talbot (i.e., the negative/positive process) became the dominant recording process in photography. The commercial potential of the negative/positive process had a major role in this competition between the two processes. The metal plate process was almost perfect for studio photography because it produced high-quality images and there was no demand for more than one portrait. It fit perfectly the existing business of producing likenesses. On the other hand, the original Fox Talbot calotypes were of not as high quality as the metal plate images, though the technology had commercial potential in reproduction of images, just as lithographs and other print techniques did. Therefore, the research and development effort put into the negative/positive process was commercially justifiable. The commercial potential was a key factor in eventually producing the combination of wet collodion glass plates and albumen prints that matched the quality of the metal plate photographs. Whether Fox Talbot designed his process for mass production of images in questionable, but once his invention was public some people saw that potential and invested in the technology. They required production processes that enabled mass production.

It was the *carte-de-visite* in which the mass production processes perfected for stock image reproduction were applied to personal portraits, and it was this application of mass production in portraiture that was the death blow to metal plate photography. The daguerreotype and ambrotype studios could not compete with the low production costs of *carte-de-visite* studios.

Was it Disderi's special camera that launched the 'cartomania' that spread throughout the newly industrialised societies, or was it the *carte* Disderi took of Emperor Napoleon III that inspired people? History does not provide a definitive answer, but many fingers point toward Disderi as playing an important role in shaping domestic photography. However, in hindsight, it seems probable that the mass production methods would have been adopted in the studio portrait business even without him.

The mass production methods suggested also a new business model for studio photography: sell by the dozen. Rather than selling a single portrait, it was more profitable to sell a dozen copies of the same portrait. This was something the metal plate processes would have never achieved. The plenitude of 'self-portraits' supported the giving and exchanging of images as never before. And because the personal portraits and the publicly sold stock photographs were produced in the same *carte-de-visite* format, it was possible to put these images side by side in an album – the family photo album. The giving of self-portraits was a popular use for photographs, and the combination of surplus personal portraits and convenient albums only fed into people's desire to use photographs for tokens of friendship and affection, self-presentation, and demonstration of memberships within their culture.

It was from this *status quo* that two inventions surfaced that disrupted both domestic photography and mass production of photographic images. For the next 100 years, domestic photography would be separated from the production methods and print formats of mass-produced images. The Portrait Path was going to end, and the Kodak Path was beginning.

References

Allison D (1989) Photography and the mass market. In: Ford C (ed) The Kodak Museum: the story of popular photography. Century, London, pp 42–59

Auer M (1975) The illustrated history of the camera from 1839 to the present. New York Graphic Society, Boston

Batchen G (1997) Burning with desire: the conception of photography. MIT Press, Cambridge

Batchen G (2009) Dreams of ordinary life: Cartes-de-visite and the Bourgeois imagination. In: Long JJ, Noble A, Welch E (eds) Photography: theoretical snapshots. Routledge, London, pp 80–97

Benson R (2008) The printed picture. Museum of Modern Art, New York

Chambers D (2003) Family as place: family photograph albums and the domestication of public and private space. In: Schwartz JM, Ryan JM (eds) Picturing place: photography and the geographical imagination. I.B. Tauris, London

Czech KP (1996) Snapshot: America discovers the camera. Lerner, Minneapolis

Freund G (1982) Photography & society. David R Godine, Boston

Goldberg V (1991) The power of photography: how photographs changed our lives, 1st. Abbeville, New York

Harmant P (1977) Anno Lucis 1839: 1st Part. Camera 5

Holland P (2009) 'Sweet is to scan...': personal photographs and popular photography. In: Wells L (ed) Photography: a critical introduction. Routledge, London, pp 113–158

Jenkins R (1975) Images and enterprise: technology and the American photographic industry, 1839–1925. Johns Hopkins University Press, Baltimore

Johnson WS, Rice M, Williams C (2005) The George Eastman House collection, a history of photography, from 1839 to present. Taschen, Hong Kong

Michaud F (2010) Monthly Prices in Angoulême, 1819–1880. International Institute of Social History.http://www.iisg.nl/hpw/angouleme.php. Accessed 7 Sep 2010

Rosenblum N (2007) A world history of photography, 4th edn. Abbeville, New York

Wade J (1979) A short history of the camera. Fountain Press, Watford/New York

Wichard R, Wichard C (1999) Victorian cartes-de-visite. Shire, Princes Risborough

Chapter 4
The Kodak Path (ca. 1888–1990s)

The birth of snapshot photography (*i.e.*, unskilled amateurs taking images with their own cameras) is the story of the commercial success of George Eastman and his company Kodak (originally the Eastman Dry Plate Company). Eastman was the perfect example of the new entrepreneurial spirit in the United States in the last decades of the nineteenth century. His business vision in combination with knowledge of technology was critical in the invention of the consumer camera coupled with developing and printing as a service. Kodak's products and 'photo-finishing' service, and the wide adoption of both by unskilled amateurs, transformed photography perhaps as much as did the announcements in 1839.

George Eastman, through his Kodak enterprise, was the first to lead photography from commerce targeted at professionals and serious amateurs toward a global business aimed at ordinary people. In this expansion to the consumer market, the practice of snapshot photography was born and the business of Kodak was interwoven tightly into what emerged as the snapshot culture of the twentieth century.[1] The main characteristic of this culture was that photography was made available to almost everyone: it required little skill, and as the prices of cameras, film, and photo-finishing gradually decreased, it did not require much money either. For the first time in the history of photography, large proportions of the population took the opportunity to capture photographs themselves.

While the snapshot revolution was occurring, another major change in photography took place. The halftone printing process became commercially feasible, and newspapers and magazines started printing photographs on a regular basis (the basic idea of the halftone process was familiar already to Fox Talbot but was not made commercially feasible until the 1880s[2]). Previously, all newsworthy (and gossip-worthy) photographs were bought from newsagents, bookstores, etc. separately as *cartes-de-visite*, stereographs, or other types of paper prints. In the 1890s, as halftone pictures became regular in newspapers, the business of selling separate

---

[1] Richard Chalfen calls the snapshot photography culture the 'Kodak Culture' (Chalfen 1987).
[2] Peres 2007, p. 6.

R. Sarvas and D.M. Frohlich, *From Snapshots to Social Media - The Changing Picture of Domestic Photography*, Computer Supported Cooperative Work, DOI 10.1007/978-0-85729-247-6_4, © Springer-Verlag London Limited 2011

pictures to consumers gradually faded away; the public hunger for photographic images could be satisfied by newspapers and magazines.

The almost simultaneous birth of snapshot photography and photojournalism separated these images into specific spheres within the domestic environment. Previously professional photographs of statesmen, celebrities, famous landscapes, and major public events were collected as photographs: stereographs in the family's own collection or as *cartes* in the family albums. In the twentieth century, the private snapshots were still collected as individual photographs mainly in albums. The public images of the twentieth century were mainly printed in newspapers and magazines alongside text and advertisements, and hardly collected at all.

The snapshot culture began gradually as the nineteenth century drew to a close, at a time when industrialisation had reached most of the Western world, spurring on modernisation of family life. Kodak's technology found fruitful ground with the middle class, especially the American upper middle class, who found themselves with spare time and cash, which they spent on leisure. The first Kodaks were marketed in the context of upper-middle-class leisure alongside bicycles, automobiles, outdoor picnics, tennis, etc.[3] Later, in the first two decades of the twentieth century, Kodak's advertising and marketing shifted the context of snapshooting more toward the privacy of the home: the snapshot camera became both a symbol of a modern home and the tool for representing that modern home in images.[4] The foundation stones of snapshot culture – the *home* as the location of snapshots; *leisure* as the time of snapshots; and *family* as the people in the snapshots – were all laid at the beginning of the century. And, as we discuss later in the book, these foundation stones still form the basis of current, twenty-first-century snapshot photography.

In this chapter, we focus on the beginnings of the snapshot culture and the technological path dominated by Kodak. We also discuss the practices and images that emerged as ordinary people started taking photographs. Then we discuss further the parallel change in photojournalism and its impact for domestic photography. Lastly, we go through potentially disruptive innovations in the Kodak Path that were established but did not fully succeed in casting off the dominant path: instant photography, colour film cartridges, and electronic still video photography.

4.1   Film Photography for a Mass Market

Following the invention of the dry plate method in 1871, photography was in the turmoil of yet another change. Richard Maddox published his method for covering glass plates with a gelatine of photosensitive material in 1871, but the new process and the plates only gradually superseded the existing norm of collodion wet plates. Because the new plates required much shorter exposure times,

---

[3] West 2000.
[4] Slater 1995; West 2000.

photographers had to cast away some of their existing practices and knowledge.[5] According to Reese Jenkins, professional photographers familiar with the collodion processes and its quirks and rules of thumb were not keen on learning a new process, even if it was faster.

However, the dry plates enabled another major change in photography. The dry plates could be prepared beforehand and stored significantly longer than the wet plates, which had to be used almost immediately after preparation. This made it possible to manufacture plates centrally at a factory and sell them pre-processed. Photography was made one step easier, as photographers did not have to bother with preparing plates.

Half a decade after the introduction of the dry plates, the same gelatine coating process was applied to printing paper, and the gelatinised paper (gelatine bromide paper) was introduced.[6] The switch from albumen prints to gelatine prints required also learning and new skills on the photographers' part. Nevertheless, not only could the gelatinised plates be manufactured centrally but the paper could be similarly prepared and sold, mainly to new amateur photographers not burdened with the legacy practices of the collodion era.

The increasing market of serious amateur photographers and the growing popularity of dry plates among professionals made the manufacture of dry plates and gelatinised paper a growing business. George Eastman had begun amateur photography in the late 1870s and soon began to produce gelatine dry plates himself.[7] In 1881, already with a foothold in the dry plate business, Eastman acquired the financing of businessman Henry A. Strong and established the Eastman Dry Plate Company in Rochester, New York. In the first half of the 1880s, Eastman's company was the third largest dry plate manufacturer in the United States.[8]

According to Jenkins,[9] the end of the collodion plate era spurred innovation in photography in general. The relatively stable reign (from roughly the 1850s to the end of the 1870s) of the collodion process and albumen prints was overthrown. The new spirit of innovation took on the challenge of replacing the cumbersome, heavy, and breakable glass plates altogether.[10] This was also the path that George Eastman started to pursue. Although his company had a significant market share in the dry plate business, he saw business potential in replacing glass plates completely. The dry plate business was in a state of price competition, which was not lucrative for the manufacturers. Also, the dry plate manufacturing technology was firmly established and there was little room for gaining a monopoly on patent rights within that field.[11]

On the other hand, the technology for using film as the capture medium was new and not commercially established – in particular, the technologies for mass production

---

[5] Jenkins 1975, p. 84.

[6] *Ibid.*, p. 80.

[7] *Ibid.*

[8] *Ibid.*, p 80.

[9] *Ibid.*

[10] *Ibid.*

[11] *Ibid.*

of film. Eastman's objective became to invent and patent a complete system of machinery, products, and processes for film photography; if successful, the whole business of film photography would be covered by his company.[12] Therefore, his main foci for invention were roll film, a roll-film holder for cameras, and film-making machinery.[13] Eastman wrote about film photography in March 1889: "If we can fully control it I would not trade it for the telephone. [...] because the patents are young and the field won't require 8 or ten years to develop it & introduce it."[14]

In 1883, Eastman and employee William H. Walker, a camera manufacturer, started their work on a film-roll-based system. They based their work on Leon Warnerke's roll-film camera with a roll holder system from 1877.[15] By 1885, Eastman and Walker had patented their own roll holder and paper film.[16] However, the commercialisation of these inventions was not successful. The negative paper film and the stripping film did not find a market among professionals and serious amateurs.[17] Eastman had to find a new market for his film technology.

In the second half of the 1880s, the Eastman company was the largest American producer of gelatine bromide paper.[18] Nevertheless, professional photographers did not enthusiastically adopt the gelatine paper, because of the new processes its use required, though the new amateurs embarking on photography were keen to use the faster paper for printing. Thirdly, the stripping film sold by Eastman's company required complex processing and was not necessarily what the new amateurs wanted in otherwise simplified photography. To promote the sales of its gelatine bromide paper and stripping film, Eastman's company provided a service for its customers. The Enlarging and Printing Department would print the customer's glass negatives to the bromide paper, it would make enlarged prints if needed, and it would also process the stripping film for the customer.[19]

After the failure to introduce film to the professional and amateur market, Eastman decided to address the mass market with his film photography. To keep photography as simple as possible, he utilised the existing Enlarging and Printing Department to provide potential customers with a service to develop and print the captured images. In Eastman's own words: "When we started out with our scheme of film photography, we expected that everybody that used glass plates would take up films, but we found that the number that did this was relatively small and that in order to make a large business we would have to reach the general public and create a new class of patrons."[20]

With existing film and film roller technology, and the developing and printing service, all the company needed was a camera. The Eastman Dry Plate & Film

---

[12]*Ibid.*

[13]*Ibid.*

[14]As quoted in Ibid., p. 131.

[15]*Ibid.*

[16]US patents #306,470; #306,594; and #317,049.

[17]Jenkins 1975.

[18]*Ibid.*

[19]*Ibid.*

[20]As quoted on p. 112 in *Ibid.*

Company had already designed and introduced two cameras to promote its film roller, so it had gained some experience in camera manufacturing. However, a camera for the unskilled general public would have to be simple to use and inexpensive. Also, Eastman wanted the camera to be easy to manufacture in large quantities. In late June 1888, the new cameras were in production, and then in July, at the annual photographers' convention, a panel of judges awarded the camera a medal as the photographic invention of the year. The camera, named Kodak, was ready to change photography forever.[21]

The Kodak camera (see Fig. 4.1) cost \$25 in 1888, and it included a roll of film for 100 images. Once the 100 images were taken, the whole camera was shipped to

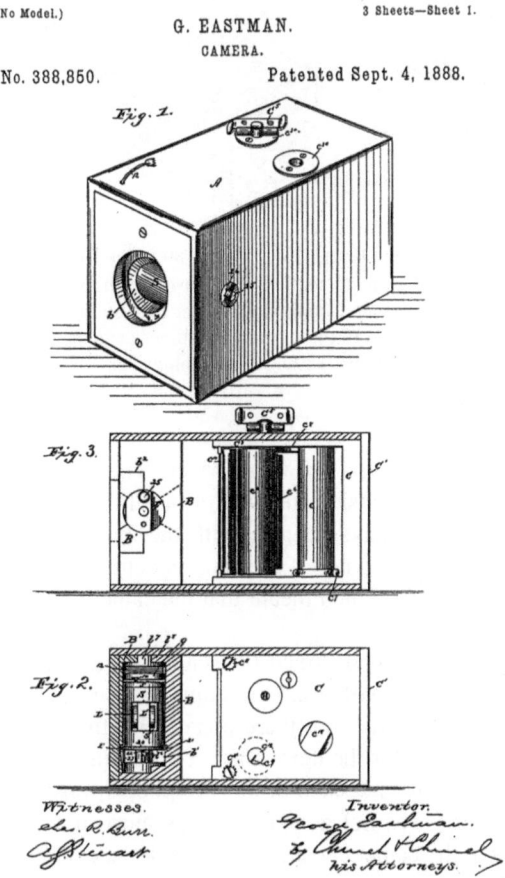

Fig. 4.1 The illustrations of Eastman's patent[22] for the first Kodak camera. The *top* drawing is the complete device, the *middle one* is a side view, and at the *bottom* is a view from above (George Eastman. Figures 1–3 from U.S. Patent #388,850, 1888. United States Patent and Trademark Office. No known restrictions on publication)

---

[21] *Ibid.*

[22] Eastman 1888.

Fig. 4.2 A photograph taken with a Kodak No. 1 circa 1890. The lack of a viewfinder made the cropping and straightening of the image challenging. However, the woman's relaxed expression suggests that the photographer was an acquaintance rather than an unknown professional, something that was not often the case before the days of consumer cameras (Unknown photographer. Original title: Woman at market stall, ca. 1890. Photographic print. National Media Museum. No known restrictions on publication)

Rochester for the developing and printing service. The service shipped back the camera with a new roll of film inside and with prints of the 100 images; this service cost $10 and took about 10 days.[23] Later, with the introduction of the daylight-loading film roll in 1891, the owner of the camera could load and unload the film roll in and out of the camera, which meant that the camera did not have to be sent for development.[24]

The Kodak weighed 624 g, had a fixed-focus lens with aperture f/9, and captured circular images (see Fig. 4.2) with a 2.5 in. radius (6.4 cm). To take a photograph, the user had to cock the shutter, point (there was no viewfinder), release the shutter, and advance the roll of film for the next image, by winding. A memorandum book was supplied to write down what each of the 100 photos was.[25]

Although this camera was not as expensive as most, it was not accessible to everyone (the $25 that the camera cost in 1888 would be equal in worth to $582 in 2009[26]). The weekly wage for many at the time was around $5, so the camera cost

[23]Coe and Gates 1977, p. 17.

[24]Jenkins 1975; Wade 1979, p. 64

[25]Coe and Gates 1977, p. 17.

[26]Calculated according to the consumer price index (CPI).

much more than a month's wages.[27] However, 13,000 sold in the first year, and it was a success.[28] In the following decade, the sales of Kodak roll-of-film cameras more than doubled: in 1892, Eastman's company's camera sales came to almost $200,000, and 8 years later, in 1900, sales were $540,000.[29] But as Eastman had planned, it was not the sale of cameras that brought the main business. In 1900, the sales of film ($730,000) were already more than camera sales.[30]

The Kodak Camera combined two characteristics: mobility and ease of use. It was smaller than contemporary plate cameras, and because there were no heavy glass plates, it was lighter to carry and easier to handle. The externalisation of the development and printing process to a service bypassed the difficulties and complexities of actually creating a picture on paper from the film.

The simplicity and mobility of the new type of camera suited the snapshooter perfectly, but it also made photography readily accessible for other uses as well. At the end of the century, photography expanded to areas in which mobility and ease of use were important. Doctors, botanists, meteorologists, and other scientific professionals took up use of the snapshot camera.[31] In the early 1890s, American explorer Robert E. Peary took a Kodak camera with him in his explorations of the Arctic and snapped over 2,000 pictures, and, as Kenneth P. Czech points out "just a generation earlier, not even a professional photographer could have made so many photographs in such harsh terrain".[32]

Soon, at the turn of the century, the mobility and simplicity inherent in the snapshot camera would become key characteristics required by the growing number of photojournalists. These professionals did their best to satisfy the demand for photographs from newspapers and magazines that were now able to print photographs in the cost-effective halftone process. The idea of a mobile camera that was fast to use (*i.e.*, simple) in dynamic circumstances was ideal for photojournalists. However, the requirements for image quality were higher for journalism than for snapshooting; therefore, the cameras designed for photojournalists were mobile and fast to use but of higher technical quality than the Kodaks for consumer use.

4.1.1 Planting the Seeds of the Kodak Culture

The idea of making cameras so easy to use that anyone could create photographs turned out to be quite disruptive. It changed photography from a specialist activity into a practice for everyone – almost everyone. The costs of photography were still

---

[27]Coe 1989, p. 62. West 2000, p. 23, estimates that $25 was the yearly income of a farm labourer.

[28]Coe and Gates 1977, p. 17.

[29]Jenkins 1975, p. 210.

[30]*Ibid.*, p. 278.

[31]Czech 1996, p. 54.

[32]*Ibid.*, p. 54.

not within the reach of everybody, even if the act of taking photographs and turning them into prints required no special skills. As mentioned earlier, the first Kodak camera was expensive: the price of the first Kodak, $25 in 1888, would have been equal in worth to $582 in 2009, and the developing and printing service, $10 in 1888, would have been equal in worth to $233 in 2009[33] (*i.e.*, $2,33 per photo). The first snapshooters came from the upper middle class, who had enough surplus time and money to spend; the lower middle class, skilled artisans, and unskilled labour of that time could not afford the Kodak.[34]

In the era of ferment of the disruptive consumer camera, the social changes of industrialisation had reached most of the Western world and by the end of the century had spurred the rise of a new 'rank' in the middle classes in addition to the Victorian urban 'bourgeoisie': the white-collar workers and junior and middle managers.[35] The American middle class at the dawn of the twentieth century, in addition to wealth, had spare time created by reduced work hours.[36] The new white-collar middle class especially took to themselves "a project of the modernisation of domestic life and leisure through consumerism".[37] The modernisation was achieved through domestic appliances at home, leisure activities (*e.g.*, bicycling and other outdoor activities), participation in 'cosmopolitan urbanism', and expanding mass media (print media and moving pictures).[38] As mentioned earlier, in this process of modernisation, the consumer camera served two purposes: first, that of a domestic appliance representing the modern home and, second, the means of representing that modernity through images.[39]

In this societal context, the Kodak camera and the Kodak photo-finishing service became a success. Unlike the Victorian amateur photographer, whose role models were serious gentleman scientists like Henry Fox Talbot and Charles Darwin, the amateur of the new modern middle class sought amusement rather than enlightenment from hobbies.[40] For these 'non-serious amateurs' (labelled 'dabblers' by the more serious amateurs[41]), photography as a craft did not seem as attractive as the photography offered by the Kodak camera: an easily consumed leisure activity.[42]

However, spending money on photography was not an obvious choice, even for the wealthier middle-class families. Dave Kenyon points out that photography was only one of many outputs for the middle-class family's surplus income in the early 1900s: after paying the rent or mortgage and the servants, income was spent on

---

[33]Calculated on the basis of the Consumer Price Index.

[34]Kenyon 1992, pp. 13–14.

[35]Slater 1995.

[36]West 2000.

[37]Slater 1995, p. 136.

[38]*Ibid.*, p. 136.

[39]*Ibid*; West 2000.

[40]West 2000, p. 42.

[41]*Ibid.*

[42]Slater 1995.

food, and the surplus left was probably spent on things more functional than photography, such as a car, a bicycle, a sewing machine, and other appliances.[43] In other words, photography had to compete with other uses for any surplus money, and some of the other uses were considered more functional and utilitarian.

Kenyon argues that large changes in distribution of wealth in the first half of the twentieth century were more important in diffusing photography to ordinary people than technological innovations were: the increase in spare cash among the lower middle classes and working classes.[44] Once there was spare cash, some of it was spent on photography.

Often the introduction of the Kodak camera in 1888 is described as making photography available to ordinary people. As Kenyon points out, this process was anything but instantaneous. Only after the Second World War did the prices of cameras and film match the surplus income of the working classes.[45] It took half a century for snapshot photography to reach all strata of Western societies.

Nevertheless, within a few years, the number of snapshooters had grown rapidly to outnumber that of both amateurs and professionals alone. By the end of 1905, Eastman Kodak had sold 1.2 million cameras.[46] What kinds of uses did the early snapshooters come up with for the camera and the pictures?

Marketing and advertisement played an important role in shaping how people brought the new technology into use. As the market leader in snapshot photography, Kodak with its advertisements was integral in shaping snapshot practices. Not only was Kodak's market position influential, its marketing budgets were unlike any of its competitors'.[47] To provide people with guidance on what to do with the new camera, the first Kodak included a booklet called the 'The Kodak Primer', explaining the use of the camera and the system for development and printing.[48] Later, Kodak published other promotional material to relay its message, such as the book *At Home with the Kodak* (1922); a magazine, called *Kodakery* (1913); and a radio programme, *The Kodak Hour*, from the mid-1920s.[49] People gladly listened to and read advice on picture-taking and ideas for photographs, and Kodak was more than happy to fulfil that need with its message.

The way in which Kodak introduced its technology to the public almost dictated the use and meanings of that technology, which in the hands of the ordinary person had no strong old conventions – there was no obvious household product preceding the consumer camera. However, as we discussed earlier, the drive for modernisation and related leisure practices of the American middle class of the 1880s were elemental in shaping the design and marketing of Kodak technology. George

---

[43] Kenyon 1992, p. 15.

[44] *Ibid.*, p. 16.

[45] *Ibid.*, p. 16.

[46] West 2000, p. 41.

[47] *Ibid.*, p. 20.

[48] *Ibid.*, p. 48.

[49] *Ibid.*, pp. 24, 27, 51.

Eastman himself was no stranger to that level of society. He was a white-collar bank clerk, although not from an especially wealthy family, and he had taken up photography as a hobby before becoming an entrepreneur in the manufacture of dry plates. The marketing message of Kodak was well attuned to the phenomena, attitudes, and practices of his target market.

Therefore, in the early years of Kodak and snapshot photography, the camera was associated with pastimes and leisure. Especially among the upper and middle classes, photography suited the existing pastimes well. Nancy Martha West points out that at the turn of the century, for decades there had been a major change in progress in the nature, organisation, and perception of work and leisure.[50] Leisure, especially play, was valued as an end in itself, and this attitude was adopted well in the early Kodak advertisements (see Fig. 4.3).[51] The locations and activities in

Fig. 4.3 A Kodak advertisement from 1904 combining leisure time and photography (Unknown artist. Original title: Vacation Days are Kodak Days, 1904. Color Drawing. Wayne P. Ellis Collection of Kodakiana, 1886–1989 and undated, Emergence of Advertising in America, 1850–1920, Duke University Rare Book, Manuscript, and Special Collections Library [http://library. duke.edu/digitalcollections/eaa/]. Republished with permission)

---

[50] *Ibid.*, p. 38.

[51] *Ibid.*, p. 38.

Kodak's advertisements reflect the leisure activities of the American middle classes at the turn of the century: tennis, fishing, camping and other outdoor activities, sailing, picnicking, automobile touring, travelling abroad, and time spent at beaches and fairs.[52] One of the early Kodak slogans advertised: "All out-doors invites you to Kodak." Conveniently, the camera worked best when photographs were taken in the good light conditions to be found outdoors.

The Kodak advertisements in their first two decades promoted the sheer pleasure of taking photographs as part of middle-class leisure. The camera was a device for creating memories of leisure time, to "prolong leisure, allowing consumers to 're-live' their vacations and other pleasurable moments through snapshots".[53]

Kodak's message of snapshot photography as leisure and reliving pastimes shifted gradually toward the privacy of the home. The introduction of the Brownie camera in 1900, which was marketed as a children's camera, was a step toward the domestic indoors. A concrete technical advancement for indoor photography was the introduction of faster film in 1913, which made possible photography inside.[54] Parallel to this technology, Kodak advertisements started to feature home interiors and stress the value of home portraits.[55] According to West, the shift from the out-doors and leisure to the private indoors of the home was complete after the First World War, during which Kodak's advertisement focused even more on presenting photography as a means of communicating domestic events and nostalgia.[56]

Positioning snapshot photography within the privacy of the home resonated with the early-twentieth-century reactions to the modernisation of the world. West describes the antique industry in the Unites States, which "coincided with a new cultural attention to transforming the home into a space of nostalgia".[57] The fascination with antiques was linked to *nostalgia*: an idealised past that was seen as a refuge from the change and uncertainty that modernisation brought at the turn of the century. In the 1910s, the marketing message of Kodak was of nostalgia, and, as West argues, photography and photographs were marketed as antique: the value of photographs growing over time, rhetoric of collection, promotion of the present as already past, and idealising that nostalgic past.[58] In the Kodak marketing rhetoric, the photo album was like an antique in which photographs are transformed into "a timeless, handmade, and personal piece of collection"[59] for telling stories of nostalgia (see Fig. 4.4).

West argues that in its marketing message Kodak actively confined photography's vision to a limited range of meanings and readings: mainly that of a nostalgic record of familial events and relationships with their painful or unpleasant aspects

---

[52] *Ibid.*, p. 38.

[53] *Ibid.*, p. 73.

[54] *Ibid.*, p. 160.

[55] *Ibid.*, p. 160.

[56] *Ibid.*, p. 193.

[57] *Ibid.*, p. 159.

[58] *Ibid.*

[59] *Ibid.*, p. 164.

Fig. 4.4 Nostalgia in a Kodak advertisement from the 1910s (Unknown artist. Original title: The Kodak Album, 191x. Color Drawing. Wayne P. Ellis Collection of Kodakiana, 1886-1989 and undated, Emergence of Advertising in America, 1850–1920, Duke University Rare Book, Manuscript, and Special Collections Library [http://library.duke.edu/digitalcollections/eaa/]. Republished with permission)

systematically erased.[60] In other words, Kodak taught amateur photographers to create the codified and surprisingly similar family snaps we are all familiar with.

West's analysis of the early decades of Kodak advertising emphasises the influence of marketing in shaping the practices for new technology. A camera did not have a place in the everyday life of people prior to the Kodak camera. Once the camera became available, a process of domestication and reconfiguring practices began and Kodak realised the opportunity to shape that process. Not only did Kodak succeed in protecting its business via patents to ensure technological monopoly; it was successful also in shaping people's practices such that what became the snapshot culture was based on its technology and supported its business model.

---

[60] *Ibid.*

With innovative technology and marketing, Kodak planted the seeds of the snapshot culture and shaped its characteristics. One of them, as discussed above, was confining snapshots to the private sphere of the home. This is not surprising, as domestic photography practices before Kodak had a strong familial element: portraits of family members, family albums as records of familial and social networks, and even wedding photos were displayed and valued in an increasingly industrialised society of disperse families. However, absent from the Kodak way of photography was the public element of domestic photography: pictures outside the family context and outside the private domestic sphere. 'Kodakers' did not take photographs for news purposes, to create art, to shape public opinions, to present themselves for a public audience, to sell pictures, or simply to partake in public discourses. The family albums of 'Kodakers' gradually lost the portraits of public figures and purchased stock photographs common in *carte-de-visite* albums of the latter half of the nineteenth century, with the occasional postcard constituting an exception. Only now, in the twenty-first century, are we witnessing changes in snapshot culture in which snapshots and snapshooters are having a clear public role – for example, in photojournalism.

One of the main marketing messages of Kodak was the simplicity of photography. The company wanted to create a clear distinction from glass plate photography, which was difficult, messy, and expensive. In drawing this distinction, Kodak used young women in its advertisements, and after the Brownie in 1900, children as well. Women and children not only emphasised the ease of use of the technology but also distanced Kodak from the male-dominated glass plate professional and serious amateur photography: Kodak was not the kind of photography in which economically independent gentleman hobbyists spent hours in the darkroom.[61]

Kodak also recognised that women were a potential market for its products. Just as collecting *cartes-de-visite* in family albums was deemed suitable for women, so was taking photographs.[62] In Victorian times, the female photographer was not uncommon, and photography was one of the few potentially lucrative professions for middle-class women.[63] The women in Kodak's advertisements were independent young women travelling abroad, driving automobiles, enjoying their leisure time outdoors, and – most importantly – taking photographs. The Kodak Girl in her trademark blue-and-white striped dress soon became the symbol of Kodak embodying the modern New Woman at the beginning of the twentieth century.[64]

In the domestic private sphere, women as mothers were the creators and homemakers of the modern home.[65] In the era of ferment for the snapshot camera, the camera became both the symbol of a modern home and the producer of the modern home: producing pictures of a modern family.[66] Kodak's marketing tapped

---

[61] *Ibid.*, p. 42.
[62] Czech 1996, p. 55.
[63] Kenyon 1992, p. 18.
[64] Holland 2009, p. 140.
[65] Slater 1995, p. 137.
[66] *Ibid.*, p. 137.

into this: the mother of the family as the producer of the modern home through the domestic appliances (the camera) and through photography (representation of the modern home).[67] As the Kodak message shifted from leisure toward the home, the women in the advertisements were more often mothers than before, although the young and independent Kodak Girl was not to disappear for 80 years.[68] A local British newspaper reported in 1905: "Thousands of Birmingham girls are scattered about the holiday resorts of Britain [...] and very large percentage of them are armed with cameras, mainly, of course, of the hand variety. The girls snapshot their sweethearts, the young married women take their young hopefuls [...]. It is as much a feminine as a masculine hobby nowadays."[69]

The role of women in the early decades of snapshot photography gradually was formed into the role of curators of the family photo albums. Both men and women photographed, but the family album was typically left to the mother of the family. These albums contained stories, or the photographs in them were told as stories to viewers and listeners. Deborah Chambers has noted that the album was mainly an oral tradition: there was hardly any text, except for a few captions, and the images were accompanied with spoken narratives.[70] West supports the description of this oral storytelling characteristic by pointing to Kodak advertising wherein the message was that photographs supersede written language as the primary medium for recording personal events and relationships.[71] Kodak was also very active in promoting storytelling as the form of reading and viewing snapshots, and the suggestion that photographs supersede written text was an integral part of the 'Kodak Keeps the Story' marketing campaign.[72]

4.1.2   What Was Captured?

The main change that Kodak facilitated was that in domestic photography the person taking the images was not a professional photographer most often not personally acquainted with the subjects of the photograph. The technology for producing images was given to the consumer of those images. In other words, it was 'user-generated content' over a century ago.

In general, the actual photographs taken in the first half-century of snapshot photography are not that different from the family snaps taken in the second half. Brian Coe and Paul Gates categorise the contents of the snapshots taken between 1888 and 1939 broadly into people, leisure, the seaside, townscapes, life at work, interiors, and events.[73]

---

[67] *Ibid.*, p. 136.
[68] West 2000, p. 12.
[69] As quoted in Coe 1989, p. 65.
[70] Chambers 2003, p. 99.
[71] West 2000, p. 174.
[72] *Ibid.*
[73] Coe and Gates 1977.

Characteristic of these photos was the personal relationship the photographer often had with the locations, people, and events. The snapshots presented photography in general with a fresh approach to capturing relaxed and informal images of people.[74] Also, these categories were not exclusive. Often the photograph was of a familiar person in different settings, such as the seaside or the town.

Early snapshots of people were mostly of family, especially the children of the family. In stark contrast to studio photographs of children, the children in early snapshots were much more relaxed and often literally at home.[75] People were also the main subjects of the other categories, although the main message of the photograph might be a special event or a day at the beach.

As discussed above, leisure and photography were strongly associated with each other in Kodak advertising, and the snapshot camera had an important role as the recorder and symbol of leisure activities.[76] It was taken to picnics, on outings, on automobile or bicycle touring, on hunting trips, and anywhere the early-twentieth-century middle-class man or woman spent leisure time.

One of the most popular leisure locations was the seaside, especially in the UK. According to Coe and Gates, the "seaside ranks second only to the home as a setting for the snapshot".[77] Cars and trains brought the seaside within the reach of more people, and there was often enough light on the seashore for taking photographs. An amateur photography magazine in 1903 wrote: "At the seaside when the sun shines one person in ten carries a Kodak or some other form of hand camera."[78] The seaside also presented photographers with an opportunity to capture the female body in a less clothed form. The *Weekly Times and Echo* wrote as early as 1893: "Several decent young men, I hear, are forming a Vigilance Association for the purpose of thrashing the cads with cameras who go about at seaside places taking snapshots of ladies emerging from the deep."[79]

The urban scene was the background for many snapshots of people, therefore recording buildings and architecture differently from the professional photographs found, for example, on postcards.[80] Coe and Gates list also photographs of people at work, mainly outdoors, as a recurring motif,[81] something that seems to have disappeared from contemporary snapshots, excluding perhaps tourist photographs.

After the introduction of more sensitive films and faster lenses in the 1910s, photography indoors became possible for the snapshooter. And later, in the 1930s,

---

[74] *Ibid.*, p. 12.

[75] *Ibid.*, p. 47.

[76] *Ibid.*, p. 65; West 2000.

[77] Coe and Gates 1977, p. 85.

[78] As quoted in *Ibid.*, p. 85.

[79] As quoted in Coe 1989, p. 63.

[80] Coe and Gates 1977, p. 99.

[81] *Ibid.*, p. 107.

flash photography became an option also. Perhaps not surprisingly, the home was the interior most often depicted in these indoor photographs, which were mostly of children and other members of the family. Events important to the family were also recorded with the camera. The events captured were notable public events, or local happenings, but mainly family events such as weddings, birthdays, or a visit by a relative.[82]

In the decade after the Second World War, the prices of cameras, film, and photo-finishing fell and more people had access to snapshot photography.[83] In the photography industry, the war had significantly hurt German camera and film manufacturers, and also the Japanese photography industry. However, as we will discuss later, the Japanese camera and film industry more than rebounded from the war and in two decades became the world leader in camera technology. The industry was to coalesce around two national industries: the American led by Kodak and the Japanese led by several manufacturers, such as Canon, Nikon, Olympus, Fujifilm, Asahi, Konica, and Minolta.

Although colour film was widely available after the war, it was not until the 1960s that the majority of snapshooters switched away from black-and-white photographs. Other technical changes after the war were the centralisation of photo-finishing: the transfer from local processing to large central laboratories, which could turn film into prints more cost-effectively.

The transfer of snapshots to colour in the 1960s came about while other photographic images were making the most of colour. In particular, colour photographs in magazine and newspaper advertisements, and on the packaging of domestic consumables, depicted a colourful and happy family life to be imitated by colour snapshots.[84] These images in advertisements set the visual standard for depicting a happy family in colour. Colour also entered television, and by the mid-1960s American broadcasters were making full-colour prime-time transmissions.

In the mid-1960s, the baby boomer generation, born during and right after the war, were reaching adulthood. This post-war generation rejected the grey world of their parents, and, according to Geoffrey Crawley, "saw color itself as an expression of freedom and life".[85] The psychedelic colour designs of the 1960s are an icon of that decade when the world literally became more colourful.

The mobility of families, especially in their leisure time, changed because of further motorization of society and found new business as a result of inexpensive tourism. Family holidays in the Mediterranean or on the Canary Islands became the topics of snapshots of more and more European families. In general, the family spent more time outside the home, and these moments were captured on colour film.

---

[82]*Ibid.*, p. 123.
[83]Kenyon 1992, p. 16.
[84]Holland 2009, p. 146.
[85]Crawley 1989, p. 142.

None of these broader social phenomena were missed by camera and film manufacturers. Cameras and film were advertised in connection with vacations and suggested other reasons for people to take photographs.[86] Suggesting a wide range of subject matter for photography, film manufacturers such as Kodak were providing more reasons to consume colour film.

Nevertheless, the technological path set by Eastman's Kodak Company persisted. The business model of selling film and photo-finishing services to consumers did not change. The basic components of that model (a simple camera and roll of film) were made less expensive, faster, more efficient, and more automatic; in other words, the technological development was incremental. The visual contents of snapshots did change as people began to travel more, fashions changed, and the ideal representation of a family changed. However, snapshots were still overwhelmingly in the private domestic sphere, although now the sphere was occasionally extended to sunny holiday locations, and the lessons taught by Kodak marketing were visible on the pages of family albums, under the curatorship of mothers, where familial experiences and memories were physical objects of nostalgia.

4.2 Separation of Public and Private Photographs

In the second half of the nineteenth century, it was not uncommon to have photographs of public figures, events, and locations between the same family album covers as photographs of family members, other relatives, and friends. These *private* photographs, portraits of familiar people, were acquired by exchanges with friends, family, and acquaintances, or posing for a portrait taken by a professional photographer. The *public* photos a nineteenth-century family owned were bought from a news stand, at a bookstore, or in a photography studio, and some may have been exchanged with friends, especially *cartes-de-visite*.

However, the technology for printing photographs and the means of acquiring and seeing images, public and private, changed dramatically at the end of the nineteenth century. The first camera marketed to ordinary people was made public in 1888, and the first newspaper photograph using a halftone was published in 1873. By 1900, there were an estimated 1.5 million roll-film cameras in the world,[87] and the letterpress halftone process had become the dominant process for mass-printing photographs – two technological paths had begun at almost the same time. Roll-film technology and processes would dominate snapshot photography until the late 1990s, and halftone ink-printing would dominate mass-produced photographic publications until the 1960s.[88]

The halftone process applied a glass screen of tiny apertures, which transferred the photographs to a matrix of dots. The size of the dots varied with the intensity

---

[86]Holland 2009, p. 147.
[87]Coe and Gates 1977, p. 21.
[88]Benson 2008, p. 222.

of light in the photograph. The matrix of different-sized dots was chemically transferred to a sheet of copper, and the copper sheet covered with ink and pressed on paper to produce a dot pattern forming the original photograph. The number of dots in the halftone screen produced images of differing resolutions, and from that comes the resolution metric of dots per inch (DPI).

The halftone process was known already to Fox Talbot in the 1840s, but it was not made commercially feasible until the 1880s.[89] The halftone process was inexpensive and easy, and the quality was passable.[90] A key feature in making the process commercially feasible for mass printing came about when the copper plate holding the image could be made thin and curved, and it became possible to mount the plate on a rotary cylinder. As Richard Benson points out, rotation was speed in printing, which brought down the cost of printed photos, and this, again, enabled the production of millions of photographs.[91]

A commercially feasible halftone process meant that all newsworthy and publicly interesting photographs were soon published in newspapers, magazines, and books. The first newspaper to use photographic illustrations in Britain was the *Daily Illustrated Mirror* in 1903.[92] The business of selling individual photographs, or sets of individual photographs, ended with the coming of the halftone process, although stereoscopic images remained an exception. On the other hand, halftone printing gave birth to a new medium for photographs: magazines, which were printed weekly publications with photographic content. Magazines bridged the gap between daily newspapers and the more expensive and permanent books.[93]

At the turn of the century, Western societies had taken a leap in universal literacy, and the advertising industry was growing because of mass production of domestic goods and appliances.[94] Newspapers and magazines reached larger audiences than ever before and created the most important advertising channel of the day. Photography played a key role in this: photographs became more important parts of news material than before, advertisers began to use photographs, and whole new genres of magazines were born because of inexpensive printing of photographs. For example, the photographic celebrity culture born during the *carte-de-visite* craze found a new home in celebrity magazines. The magazines for cinema fans founded in the early 1910s were celebrity magazines that had photographs of movie stars for people to enjoy.

Personal private photographs and publicly appealing photographs became clearly separate within the domestic environment. The personal photographs became, apart from the occasional studio portrait, mainly snapshots taken by the

---

[89]*Ibid.*, p. 218; Peres 2007, p. 6.
[90]Benson 2008, p. 222.
[91]*Ibid.*, p. 224.
[92]Holland 2009, p. 142.
[93]Benson 2008, p. 224.
[94]Holland 2009, p. 142.

person herself or himself, and these snapshots were received as a set of individual pictures from a printing service. Kodak dominated this business and had the leading market share in global film sales for the entire film photography regime. The business model for snapshots was based on the consumption of film.

Public photographs became mainly photojournalism published in printed media, where the photographs were presented alongside text, advertisements, and graphics. This business became the business of media and news companies, who were in no direct competition with Kodak or any other film manufacturer. Public photography business involved selling printed media: newspapers, magazines, and books – and, perhaps most importantly, advertisements.

The public and private photography business were separate already in the late nineteenth century, before Kodak and halftone printing. Private photographs were individually manufactured in studios, and public photographs were mass-produced in specialised 'factories'. However, they had a shared format in the *carte-de-visite* and were often displayed side by side in family albums. Both the public and the private images were individual photographs and not embedded in anything else. And, third, both technologies used the same printing technique (mainly albumen prints).

It is important also to point out that the mass-market logic of halftone images did not fit well with the core business model for snapshot photography. Because the audience for an individual snapshot was limited to a few people only, every film negative was printed only once. This was not a problem for Kodak, because for every printed snapshot there was consumption of film and photographic paper. However, the logic of mass media is that the same content is multiplied thousands or millions of times: a single film negative is the source for numerous printed copies. For Kodak, it made more sense to remain in the 'millions of small audiences'[95] business than enter the 'single audience of millions' business of mass media. George Eastman saw this as an opportunity: his service was processing 7,500 prints a day in 1889.[96] To put it simply, it did not matter that the 7,500 prints were all different, as long as his company was profiting from each one.

The parallel invention of the consumer camera and inexpensive halftone printing created two different technological paths for these two types of photographs: business, technology, legal structures, and practices that kept the two separate for almost a century. Only now, in the twenty-first century, are the two infrastructures converging (public mass media and private 'self-made' media). With the same technical infrastructure used for both private and public photographs (*i.e.*, digital imaging standards and formats, software, and the Internet), we can see snapshots in public media, and public photographs used in the same way as private snapshots. We can also see that business and legal structures are under stress because they were formed around the dividing lines of private snapshots and public media. Print-media companies are forced to reinvent their business logic, and intellectual property rights (mainly copyright and trademark law) are in turmoil amidst attempts

---

[95] Today this model is referred to as the 'long tail'.
[96] King 1984, p. 6.

to adapt to the new technical infrastructure. Also, people's practices are in a process of reconfiguration as the boundaries between private and public media conventions, norms, and uses change.

4.3 Side-Stepping from the Kodak Path

One of our arguments in this chapter is that snapshot photography technology, business, and practice changed surprisingly little in the Kodak Era. Once the technological path of the Kodak model (*i.e.*, selling film to consumers, who would capture images and buy the development of the film and printing of images as a service) was established, neither the consumer technology nor the business model changed. From the snapshooter's perspective, the camera remained an easy-to-use black box where film was loaded and unloaded. To take a picture, the black box was aimed at the subject and a push of a button (or pulling of a string) captured the image. Once the film roll was used, it was taken to a store for developing into prints (*i.e.*, photofinishing). Money exchanged hands when the snapshooter bought a camera, bought the developing and printing service, and bought new film. At the end of the twentieth century, most of the money went into photo-finishing and film: in 1997, photofinishing accounted for 43.5% of the global amateur photo market, film sales 20.0%, conventional camera sales 9.7%, and digital imaging 5.5%.[97]

The Kodak model did not change for a century, and the role of technology in this model changed very little as well. To demonstrate this concretely, let us compare the first Kodak camera from 1888 to an Olympus μ-1 from 1991 (shown in Fig. 4.5). Both are point-and-shoot cameras: the user points the camera

Fig. 4.5 The Olympus μ-1 went on sale in 1991. More than five million were made (© Olli Pitkänen and Risto Sarvas, 2010. Published with permission)

---

[97]Finnerty 2000 (unpublished work), p. 6, quoting the Photo Marketing Association Industry Report of 1997.

and then captures an image with a single push of a button. Both have a roll of film inside on which the images are recorded. The user cannot change the exposure, zoom, aperture, or focus on either one. However, the Olympus has a few features the first Kodak did not: the user can use a self-timer and/or flash; can load and unload a new roll of film; and does not have to advance the film after each exposure, because that is done automatically. And, of course, technically the Olympus produces superb images in comparison to the Kodak, thanks to automation built within the camera. However, on the surface and at the level of user interaction, these two cameras are not very far apart. It is quite probable that a user of the 1888 Kodak would be comfortable using the 1991 Olympus. The original Kodak slogan was still true in 1991: "You push the button, we do the rest".

We do not claim that there were no significant technological advancements in photography technology between 1888 and 1990. There were remarkable innovations and advancements made in camera technology: better lenses, automatic light and distance metering, micromechanics, electronic processing of data, and flash technology, to name a few. The technical differences between photographic film used in 1888 and in 1990 were also substantial: in sensitivity, colour, materials, etc. Third, the technology to automatically develop and print the snapshooters' film advanced as well: for the first Kodak camera, it took more than a week to get the prints; in 1990, it took 1 h to get high-quality prints.

Nevertheless, the technological advancements were all incremental developments based on the technological path introduced by Kodak. All of the research and development work put into consumer snapshot cameras was to make the basic design better: faster, cheaper, more reliable, smaller, more automatic, and better-looking, and to produce pictures of technically high quality. None of the advancements questioned the basic and dominant point-and-shoot camera design: an easy-to-use, small, and mobile camera with minimal functionality (*i.e.*, selecting what to capture and when, with everything else automatic) and minimal interconnections with other technologies (*i.e.*, film roll and battery). To put it simply, the camera was a black box for recording images on a roll of film as easily and effortlessly as possible.

This does not mean that there were no attempts to diverge from the technological path and to disrupt the Kodak model. Perhaps some radical inventions never saw the light of day or have not caught the eye of historians and scholars. Whatever the case, they did not succeed in disrupting the Kodak Path. However, in the following sections we discuss three innovations that had the potential to disrupt or fundamentally reshape the Kodak model: Polaroid instant photography, the 126 film cartridge, and electronic still photography. Although none of the three became a dominant design, they all strongly shaped the history of domestic photography and both the Kodak Path and the Digital Path.

4.3.1 Polaroid and the Automation of Picture Developing and Printing

In 1947, Edwin Land introduced a camera that did not adhere to the Kodak model of photography. The Polaroid Model 95 camera did not require the user to capture a film roll full of images, to send or give the film to an external service, and to receive prints of those images back from the service. The Polaroid camera created the print *instantly* after capture – in 1 min, to be more precise. In other words, it automated the difficult part of the film development and printing process, which George Eastman had externalised into a service.

The first Polaroid images were black and white with a sepia tone. The price of the camera was $89.75[98] (relative worth of $862 in 2009[99]), so this was not for everyone. Nevertheless, the 'instantness' of the process was impressive and simple to demonstrate,[100] although not a completely new idea. A century before Polaroid, the metal plate photographs produced in the daguerreotype, tintype, and ambrotype processes were similarly instant, because they took only minutes to develop. But in 1947 film photography was dominant and the instantness of metal plates was a distant memory remembered only by photo historians and grandparents.

Polaroid cameras became a popular alternative to the film-roll cameras, especially in the United States. Gradually Polaroid was able to shorten the development time, making the photography even more 'instant'.[101] For more than a decade, Polaroid cameras were high-end luxury cameras for snapshooters. They cost over $50 and were, therefore, not a real alternative to inexpensive point-and-shoot cameras. More importantly, as long as Polaroid cameras had high prices, Polaroid could not threaten Kodak's core consumer business of selling film to ordinary snapshooters. This changed in 1963 when Polaroid introduced the Polaroid Swinger (see Fig. 4.6), which cost $14 and was targeted at the teenage baby boomer generation. In 3 years, seven million Swingers were sold, and Polaroid and Kodak had become direct competitors.[102]

In the decade that followed, Polaroid increased its market share among American snapshooters. In 1972, an estimated 20% of the five billion photographic prints made in the United States were Polaroid photographs.[103] In the same

---

[98]Peter C. Wensberg writes that the Model 95 was originally designed to cost $95, but "a late-night crisis of marketing confidence at Polaroid had lowered the camera's price to $89.75" (Wensberg 1987, p. 99).

[99]Calculated on the basis of the CPI.

[100]Wensberg 1987, pp. 99–101.

[101]In 1960, the Polaroid Model 900 had black-and-white film that developed in 10–15 s (Wade 1979, p. 116); however, the famous SX-70 model used film that took around 6 min to develop (Buse 2007, p. 38).

[102]Crawley 1989, p. 142; Olshaker 1978, p. 135.

[103]Life Magazine 1972.

Fig. 4.6 Polaroid Swinger from 1963 (© Olli Pitkänen and Risto Sarvas, 2010. Published with permission)

year, Kodak ended its contract with Polaroid to supply them with film: Polaroid had grown into a significant competitor.[104] In 1983, 46.3% of US households had an instant camera.[105]

In 1973, Polaroid released the SX-70 camera, which came to represent what people often think of when discussing Polaroid cameras.[106] The SX-70 had been in development for years and had consumed vast amounts of the company's revenues. According to Edwin Land, the SX-70 was the camera he wanted to create all along: "Absolute one-step photography" – the full automation of the photography process.[107] The 8 × 8 cm colour images developed in daylight before the eyes of the photographer (previously, it had happened inside the camera), a battery was integrated into the film pack, and there was no paper waste from the process (the paper waste of previous models was considered unfriendly to the environment). The camera was hailed as a technological marvel.[108]

---

[104] Olshaker 1978, p. 144.

[105] Chalfen 1987, p. 14, quoting *The Wolfman Report 1983–84*.

[106] Buse 2007, p. 40.

[107] Buse 2010, p. 217; Lewis 1991, p. 149; Olshaker 1978, p. 170; Wade 1979, p. 127.

[108] Life Magazine 1972.

Without a doubt, Edwin Land's innovations were remarkable technical achievements, and the 'instantness' they enabled was radically different from the Kodak model: the Polaroid was a technological discontinuity in consumer photography that formed a technological side path of its own. With a Polaroid camera, the snapshooter did not have to wait a period of time measured in days to see the captured photograph. In other words, the Polaroid camera combined capture and viewing into consecutive events, which is something digital photography and LCD screens on the back of cameras have achieved again. Peter Buse has listed three main features of Polaroid photography that distinguish it from other forms of photography prior to the digital: speed, the automatic development of the image, and the uniqueness of the print.[109] Buse points out that two of these features are also characteristic of digital snapshots: the speed of seeing the captured image and the automatic development of the image (*i.e.*, there is no need for a darkroom or any processing outside the camera).[110]

How much did these three features shape snapshooters' practices? Perhaps the most significant change from the Kodak model was that the captured image became a physical object almost instantly. No longer was the printed image clearly about the past, as in the Kodak process, where several hours and more often days separated capture from viewing. The Polaroid print was about the present, or, as Nat Trotman describes the Polaroid, "an instant fossilization of the present".[111] Buse discusses the implications of this fossilised present. First he draws attention to the potential of image-capturing becoming more interactive and social in the sense that the captured image becomes a social object and the act of photographing hence a collective pursuit.[112] Second, that the image is not sent to an external service enables new private photographic practices for the snapshooter: "Freedom from the monitory gaze of the photo-chemist means what might have been taboo now becomes picturable."[113] Although, as Graham King points out, the Kodak photo-finishing process became more anonymous in the 1960s as photo-finishing was done in large central laboratories rather than in local shops, the images sent still ran the risk of being seen by someone[114] – unlike Polaroids.

Although Polaroids shaped snapshooter practices, they did not depart radically from the Kodak culture. The context and reasons for photography in Polaroid advertisements followed the path set by Kodak in the early twentieth century: the family in the privacy of the home. One reason for this was that Polaroid wanted to situate its new technology within existing snapshot practices but with the value proposition that its products produced better images and made photography more fun and social[115] – and the added value was based on the instantness.

---

[109] Buse 2007; Buse 2010.

[110] Buse 2010.

[111] Trotman 2002.

[112] Buse 2010, pp. 222–225.

[113] *Ibid.*, p. 225.

[114] King 1984, p. 46.

[115] Buse 2010, p. 222.

From a historical perspective, Polaroid is an example showing how the Kodak model was not the only way in which snapshot photography could have developed. There is no inherent technological reason the Kodak model became dominant, and Polaroid photography provides an example of that – neither technology is inherently better. From the late nineteenth century, the technological developments in image capture had taken the path of celluloid-based film developed and made into prints via an external service. Kodak as the market leader did its best to keep technological development on that path both by taking the leading role in research and development and by actively protecting its intellectual property (*i.e.*, patenting). In the 1950s, Polaroid was too small to raise concerns for Kodak, but, as mentioned above, this changed in 1963 with the introduction of the Swinger, and in the late 1970s, Polaroid was the world's second largest manufacturer of amateur photographic equipment.[116]

However, in terms of consumer business, Kodak and Polaroid were quite similar: profits were made in sales of film rather than on cameras, and, therefore, the role of cameras was to enable easy and effortless consumption of film. At the pinnacle of this simplicity was the Polaroid 1000 (shown in Fig. 4.7), released in 1977 (the 'One-Step Land Camera' in the United States), which was marketed as the "world's simplest camera".[117] The snapshooter using a Polaroid 1000 pushed a

Fig. 4.7 A Polaroid 1000 camera from 1977. This was the best-selling camera (instant or conventional) in the world for 4 years[118] (© Olli Pitkänen and Risto Sarvas, 2010. Published with permission)

---

[116]*Ibid.*, p. 218.
[117]Wade 1979, p. 129.
[118]Kao 1999, p. 119.

single button, and, within a few seconds, the camera ejected a paper print of the captured image – simplicity that has not been matched since.

Maintaining the technological lead in film manufacture and research was increasingly difficult, and competing film producers, such as Ilford, GAF, and Fujifilm, were nipping at the heels of Kodak.[119] In the early 1970s Kodak decided to start its own research and development of instant photography. Polaroid had shown that instant photography was popular, so Kodak decided to follow Polaroid into that market.[120] In 1976, a full 29 years after Polaroid, Kodak introduced its instant cameras: the EK4 and EK6, which used Kodak instant film. However, the decision to start manufacturing instant cameras and instant film angered Kodak's partners in the photo-finishing business, and they started looking for a new partner, primarily the world's second largest film manufacturer, Fujifilm.[121]

Kodak's introduction of instant cameras and film saw the beginning also of a long legal process in which Polaroid accused Kodak of infringing its patents on instant photography. Polaroid was successful, and in 1982 Kodak was ordered by the courts to withdraw all of its instant photography cameras and film from the market.[122] In 1991, Kodak made a settlement and paid $925 millions to Polaroid.[123] The 6 years Kodak was in the instant photography business had cost the company dearly.

Although Polaroid won the legal battle with Kodak, it was not doing well. The company was hit hard in the failure of its Polavision instant movie system in the late 1970s. The development effort and costs of an instant movie film were practically lost as electronic video recorders proved popular and as instant as Polaroid film. In an unwell financial state during the 1980s, the company had few resources to compete and innovate to make an impact on the dawn of digital photography in the 1990s. Finally, Polaroid filed for bankruptcy in 2001, and again in 2008. However, the brand and trademarks ended up with a company that is under the same name doing its best to compete in digital domestic photography. The flagship product of the new Polaroid is a digital camera with an integrated printer.[124]

The saga of Edwin Land's Polaroid photography lasted for over 50 years. Instant photography did not become a dominant design, in the sense that most snapshooters worldwide kept using film rolls and an external photo-finishing service. The instantness of Polaroids did not radically alter people's practices either. However, from the historical perspective on snapshot and domestic photography technology,

---

[119]Olshaker 1978, p. 144.

[120]*Ibid.*, p. 144.

[121]Swasy 1997, p. 25.

[122]Lewis 1991, p. 165.

[123]The New York Times 1991.

[124]In addition to the new Polaroid, there are enthusiasts of the old Polaroid photography who have made Polaroid film available for sale by acquiring the required rights and production facilities. This 'grassroots' initiative is called, appropriately, 'The Impossible Project'.

Polaroid was an example of breaking technological path-dependency: photography did not have to follow the Kodak Path' photography technology was not destined to have an external photo-finishing service.

The history of Polaroid also demonstrates the importance of business factors shaping the technologies made publicly available. Anyone who had bought a Kodak instant camera in the early 1980s learned the hard way that business factors, especially intellectual property rights, have agency in what technology people use to capture their snapshots.[125] Also, Kodak's decision to start manufacturing instant cameras and film was a business decision, and a bad decision in hindsight. The resources spent and lost in instant photography were a factor in the financial troubles Kodak faced in the 1980s, the decade when the seeds of digital photography were starting to grow.

4.3.2 Format Wars in Colour

Kodak's competition with Polaroid in instant photography was not the only war it was waging. In 1963, Kodak introduced colour film for mass consumer use in a new proprietary film format and a new inexpensive series of cameras to go with it: the 126 film cartridge (also known as the 'Kodapak') and the Kodak Instamatic cameras. Kodak's goal was to make snapshooters switch from the 135 film format to the new 126 format as they switched from black-and-white to colour photographs.

Colour film had been in research and development at Kodak and its competitors for decades. Colour photography had been possible already in the first decade of the twentieth century, using the Autochrome process for glass plates, invented and patented by the Lumiere brothers.[126] The challenge of capturing colour on film was the goal of Kodak ever since. This goal was reached in 1935 when the Kodachrome film for 8 mm and 16 mm movie cameras was made available (*i.e.*, the film was positive film that produced transparencies).[127] In the following year, Kodachrome for 35 mm was introduced and also Agfacolor film for 35 mm.[128] 6 years later, in 1942, Kodak introduced 35 mm film for colour negatives, and colour photography took a step toward mass adoption.

---

[125] As mentioned earlier, Kodak was ordered by the courts in 1982 to withdraw all of its instant photography technology from the market. To say the least, this left everyone with a Kodak instant camera 'high and dry'.

[126] Peres 2007. The first colour photograph is credited to the famous mathematician James Clark Maxwell and dates from 1861 (Peres 2007).

[127] Coe and Gates 1977, p. 46.

[128] *Ibid.*, p. 46

It is worth noting that the demand for colour film in the motion picture industry was significant[129] and, therefore, also the potential profit. For that reason, the first colour films were movie films: positive films 8 mm, 16 mm, and 35 mm wide. In the 1950s, the 35 mm film format (*i.e.*, the 135 film cassette) had also become very popular among serious amateurs, partly because of the colour films available in that format.[130] The new 126 film was in reality film 35 mm wide encapsulated inside a plastic cartridge.[131] Inside the cartridge, the film had perforations on only one side, which enabled the usable film area to be 28 mm high in comparison to the 24 mm image height of double-perforated 35 mm film. Also, Kodak made the simplifying decision to make the images square, so that the picture's shape was always the same whether the camera was held vertically or horizontally (*i.e.*, the negative size of 126 film was 28×28 mm).

The investments required to create a colour film for mass production were substantial. The technology of colour film was much more complex than black-and-white photography was, and creating the required processes and processing plants for manufacture required capital that only Kodak and a small number of other companies possessed.[132] Richard Benson summarises the immense investments made in creating colour film: "If we tried to make s single box of 35 mm color film on our own, it would cost millions of dollars."[133]

In 1963, 35 mm colour (negative) film had existed already for 21 years, but snapshooters still used black-and-white film more often than colour.[134] To change that, and to replace the existing snapshot cameras with its new 126-compatible Instamatics, Kodak did more than introduce an inexpensive colour film.

Once again, Kodak relied on *simplicity* as its key sales argument. One of the marketed benefits of the 126 cartridge system was that it was easy to load. The loading of film had been a challenge for snapshooters ever since the introduction of daylight-loading film in 1891. Snapshooters found the loading and unloading of film difficult and laborious: "loading, threading, reeling for unloading, and sticking down the trailer".[135] As a result, many snapshooters left the loading to the photo dealer.[136] With the new cartridge film, all that was required was to drop the plastic cassette into the camera, then pull it out when all of the pictures were taken. To get rid of old cameras, Kodak sponsored retailers' payment for old film-roll cameras when the customer bought a new Instamatic.[137]

---

[129]Collins 1990, p. 268.

[130]*Ibid.*, p. 307.

[131]Coe 1988, p. 224.

[132]Benson 2008, p. 196.

[133]*Ibid.*, p. 196.

[134]Ford 1989, p. 140.

[135]*Ibid.*, p. 141.

[136]Coe 1988, p. 223.

[137]Crawley 1989, p. 142; Collins 1990, p. 309.

Furthermore, promotional campaigns and film given for free ensured that the snapshooter always had film in his or her camera. To maximise the throughput of a photo-finishing laboratory, the consumer had to have film constantly in the camera.[138]

The snapshooters were not the only ones who had to change their equipment to reap the benefits of the 126 cartridge. The new format forced the developing and print services to exchange their machines for new ones, which often turned out to be too expensive for small businesses, such as local chemists or photography shops.[139] The mass shift to colour photography changed the photo-finishing business. Large centralised processing laboratories turned people's colour exposures into prints, and local shops and retailers became collection points from which print orders were forwarded and ready prints collected.[140]

All the marketing and campaigning paid off, and at the end of the decade colour photography accounted for nearly all mass market photography.[141] and over 70 million Instamatic cameras had been sold by the end of the decade (in addition to other 126-cartridge-compatible cameras manufactured under licence).[142] However, although the 126 cartridge had become widely popular, the 135 film format held its ground.

After the Second World War, both the Japanese and the German camera and film industry were understandably facing a challenging situation. The German camera industry had received an especially hard blow in the bombings of Dresden in February 1945. Also, the division of Germany was reflected in the industry, most notably in the division of the Carl Zeiss AG into eastern company Zeiss Jena and western company Carl Zeiss. The German camera industry, considered the best in quality before the war, never fully recovered. However, the Japanese camera and film industry more than recovered. The expertise and knowledge concerning optics and micromechanics from the war were channelled into the manufacture of cameras. Gradually the quality of the cameras came to match that of their American counterparts, then surpassed it.[143] By the 1970s, Japan had become the world leader in production of photo equipment.

The introduction of the 126 cartridge was an episode in this competition between Kodak and the Japanese camera and film manufacturers (mainly Canon, Nikon, Asahi, Fujifilm, Konica, and Olympus). The Japanese camera-makers stood behind the 135 film format. The main argument of the proponents of the 135 was that the larger size of the 35 mm (24×36 mm) produced photographs of higher quality. Kodak, on the other hand, could manufacture smaller and more compact cameras with its smaller 126 format (28×28 mm), and, later on, even smaller cameras with its 110 Pocket Instamatic cartridge format (13×17 mm) introduced in 1972. Accordingly, Kodak invested significantly in producing high-quality small-size film, and the Japanese camera manufacturers invested in miniaturising their 35 mm cameras.

---

[138]Crawley 1989, p. 142.

[139]*Ibid.*, p. 142.

[140]*Ibid.*, p. 142.

[141]*Ibid.*, p. 142.

[142]Collins 1990, p. 309; Coe 1988, p. 223.

[143]The improvement in quality was an explicit goal of the Japanese camera industry, which in 1954 established a national organisation (the JCII) to control quality (Lewis 1991).

However, the size difference between the images of the 135 and the 126 cartridge is less than one tenth (the area of a 126 negative is 91% of a 35 mm). Not until the introduction of the 110 cartridge did the size become significantly different (the image size of a 110 cartridge is 26% of the area of a 35 mm). What seems to have been the underlying issue in the competition between Kodak and the Japanese was that the 126 cartridge was a new proprietary format, unlike the 135 film cassettes in which 35 mm film was contained. The 135 film was an existing industry standard introduced by Kodak in 1934.[144] By 1963, any patents issued in 1934 or earlier would have been in the public domain, making the 135 cassette royalty-free. It is probable that the goal of Kodak was to introduce a new dominant design protected by fresh patents,[145] and the introduction of colour film for the masses was the perfect opportunity. With this taken into account, the opposition of the Japanese camera and film manufacturers is obvious.

However, by the end of the 1970s, it became evident that the Japanese had won the format war. The 35 mm film became the standard for snapshooters and serious amateurs alike, partly because the Japanese manufacturers were able to build inexpensive, pocket-sized, high-quality cameras that took advantage of electronics. Cameras such as the Canon AF-35M (see Fig. 4.8) incorporated within their small dimensions automatic focus, automatic exposure measurement, built-in motor drive, and film rewinding, and they used 35 mm film – all at consumer prices.

By the end of the 1970s, the dominance of Kodak in snapshot photography was no longer obvious. In the early 1980s, Kodak invested in yet another small-size proprietary film format to undermine the dominance of 35 mm film. The Kodak Disc film and compatible cameras were introduced in 1982 (see Figs. 4.9 and 4.10). The Disc had celluloid film within (15 exposures), and the size of the negative was very small: 8×10 mm. The disc shape of the film made it possible to build very flat cameras and, once again, advertise them as being much smaller than cameras for 35 mm film. However, the Disc proved a failure and the Disc cameras ceased production in 1988. Although the research and development put into the Disc format was substantial,

Fig. 4.8 The Canon AF-35M was named the Autoboy in Japan and Sure Shot in the US. Launched in November 1979, it was the world's first lens-shutter 35 mm autofocus camera[146] (© Olli Pitkänen and Risto Sarvas, 2010. Published with permission)

---

[144]Peres 2007, p. 775.

[145]See, e.g., Nerwin 1964.

[146]Canon 2010.

Fig. 4.9 Kodak Disc 4000 and compatible disc film (© Olli Pitkänen and Risto Sarvas, 2010. Published with permission)

Fig. 4.10 From *left* to *right*, a 126 cartridge, a 135 film cassette, and disc film (© Olli Pitkänen and Risto Sarvas, 2010. Published with permission)

the small negative could not compete with the quality of the 35 mm, not even in the relatively small size of snapshot prints.[147] Also, the photo-finishing industry resisted the change in equipment that adoption of the Disc required. The Disc format included automation data to facilitate the photo-finishing process, but the photo-finishers waited for consumer adoption before investing in new processing equipment, and mass adoption of the Disc never took place.[148]

Kodak had made two expensive research and development mistakes within a decade: instant photography and the Disc – both of which cost the company enormously. Not only did Kodak suffer in the research investments lost, its side-steps had angered the photo-finishing industry, who were not enthusiastic about Kodak bypassing them (*i.e.*, instant photography) or making them overhaul their equipment because of a new film format (*i.e.*, the 110 and 126 cartridges and the Disc). This made American photo-finishers more open to the world's second largest film manufacturer, Japan's Fujifilm. In the 1970s, Fujifilm entered the American market and challenged Kodak. In 1981, Kodak lost a symbolic battle on its home turf: the sponsorship of the 1984 Los Angeles Olympics went to Fujifilm. This loss was a clear sign that Fujifilm had become a real threat to the monopoly of Kodak.[149]

---

[147]Crawley 1989, p. 144.

[148]*Ibid.*, p. 144.

[149]Swasy 1997, p. 28.

However, in the early 1980s, the seeds of a more fundamental threat were sown. In 1981, Sony introduced its Mavica camera, which recorded images electronically without any film. The end of film had begun.

4.3.3   No Film Required: Electronic Still Video Photography

A charge-coupled device (CCD) combined with a photoelectric image sensor can transfer light that hits the sensor into an electronic signal, similarly to light that hits photosensitive silver halides and causes a chemical reaction. With advanced technology, the former can record an image as an electrical signal and the latter can record an image as another physical image, most often a negative image on celluloid film.

For a century, the technologies for producing images on celluloid film were perfected to maintain consumer business. Companies produced the film for sale, cameras to aid in creating those images on the film, and a service for turning the images on the film into paper pictures. In the 1980s, Kodak had been the market leader in selling film for almost a century, and 80% of Kodak's profits came from the sales of film.[150]

The first crude invention of digital photography is often credited to Steven Sasson of Kodak.[151] In 1975, he put together a prototype that used digital technology to capture and store an image. The size of the image was 100×100 pixels, and it took 23 s to record the image. According to Sasson, the prototype was found interesting as an example of 'filmless photography' but did not make much of an impact: "It was sort of forgotten. It was a curiosity thing – people looked at it and said, well, that's interesting. Of course it was not nearly the resolution you need for film."[152]

But for consumer electronics manufacturers, the CCD-based technology in imaging was interesting. In the early 1980s, the first consumer video cameras (*i.e.*, camcorders) hit the market, as did the first electronic still cameras. The still cameras used the same technology as the video cameras, and, therefore, they were called 'still video cameras' (SVCs). The Sony Mavica still video camera was introduced in 1981.

Electronic photography and SVCs were seen as an alternative to film in special circumstances, mainly in photojournalism, where the transfer of photographs over long distances was potentially critical. The inferior image quality of electronic images was not seen as a threat to film, not for years.

In the domestic sphere, electronic photography was initially associated with the television, and future visions painted a picture in which the TV was the hub of domestic photography. However, in the 1980s the personal computer (PC) was gradually being introduced to people's homes, and it became evident that the PC would play an important part in photography.[153]

---

[150]Freund 1982, p. 205.
[151]Larish 2008, p. 10.
[152]As quoted in *Ibid.*, p. 12.
[153]*Ibid.*, p. 13.

The rise of 'filmless photography', which in the early 1990s evolved into digital photography, did not happen overnight. The key technology, the CCD, had existed since the late 1960s, and the first imaging prototypes were created in the mid-1970s. And, as mentioned, the 1980s saw the commercialisation of the SVC technology. Not until the early 2000s did digital cameras outsell film cameras. In hindsight, the electronic/digital revolution in photography took more than two decades.

For the flagship company of domestic photography, Kodak, the transition from film to the digital realm was a threat on the core business. The change came at an especially inconvenient time, as the company was facing problems caused by its missteps into instant photography and the Disc format. In the 1980s and 1990s, when it should have been investing heavily in the research and development of future photography, Kodak was forced to restructure its organisation and lay off thousands of its employees. According to Swasy, the company had become conservative, stagnant, and arrogant in the post-war decades: "Executives abhorred anything that looked risky or innovative."[154] In the 1980s and 1990s, Kodak was not in good shape, financially or organisationally, to innovate and react to keep its core business alive. Perhaps the history of digital imaging would be different if the number-one defender of film photography had not been crippled in business wars fought over analogue technology.

Nevertheless, Kodak survived the 'digital revolution' better than some of its rivals did. Polaroid and AgfaPhoto filed for bankruptcy in 2001 and 2005, respectively. According to a Datamonitor market report, Kodak held a 19.50% share, by value, of the global market for photographic products in 2008.[155] This makes it the third largest after Canon and Fujifilm Holdings. However, as we will discuss more in the next chapter, what counts as photography has changed, and drawing the boundaries of domestic photography in a network of interconnected devices becomes ambiguous. For example, it remains unclear whether camera phones are counted as digital cameras in market reports such as the one quoted above. If camera phones count as cameras, mobile phone companies manufacture and sell the most cameras in the world.

4.4 Conclusions

In the history of domestic and snapshot photography, practically the whole twentieth century was dominated by the business model and supporting technology invented by the Kodak company. The way in which ordinary non-professionals captured photographs and made them into paper prints followed this Kodak model: purchase film, consume it by using an easy-to-use camera, give the film to a commercial service, wait, receive paper prints, purchase film, and so on. It is amazing that the model designed by George Eastman and his associates at Kodak in the late 1880s remained practically unchanged for a century. People born at the beginning of the twentieth century would witness technological marvels such as a man

---

[154] Swasy 1997, p. 18.
[155] Datamonitor 2009.

walking on the moon and aeroplanes but see no radical change in photography in their entire lifetime. Cameras, lenses, film, and prints grew less expensive and of higher quality, but the same model would persist. The Kodak model became the basis for the snapshot culture, to which it gave birth, and the role of Kodak and the business interests of Kodak were integral to the practices of snapshooters. No wonder George Eastman said that if his vision became reality he would not change it for the telephone; after all, the telephone industry was not as monopolistic.

However, it is important to bear in mind that Kodak would not have become successful if the model had not resonated with the consumers. In hindsight, there was market demand for simple photography once such a process was available. It was the purchase decisions of 13,000 people in the first year after the release of the Kodak camera that shaped the future of Kodak as much as anything. If these consumers had rejected that camera, history would have been different.

Critical was also George Eastman himself. In the early years, Eastman had a great deal of control over the business decisions of his company, as well as recruitment and marketing. There is little doubt that he had significant agency in shaping domestic photography as much as Daguerre and Fox Talbot had. Eastman's decision to aim for global dominance of the photography business was a bold one. Perhaps someone else would have been content with less, and perhaps then snapshot photography would not have been as homogenous and monopolistic as it was in the twentieth century.

The Kodak Path also brings out the role of the recording medium in the network of technologies that make up photography. Since the invention of photography, the recording medium has changed more than the rest of the camera. Although the basic idea of light-sensitive chemicals was the dominant design until electronic image capture, the medium on which these chemicals react to form a photograph has changed radically: from metal plates and paper into glass plates and celluloid film. It was exactly the recording medium technology (*i.e.*, the manufacturing and photofinishing processes for celluloid film and apparatus using celluloid film) that George Eastman patented and thus monopolised.[156] Therefore, it is no surprise that the Kodak business model was based on easy consumption of film, and the snapshot culture a consumerist culture wherein the consumables were film and paper prints.

Today, in the age of digital photography, both film and paper prints have lost their key role as consumables, but people's practices still follow mostly those on the Kodak Path (*e.g.*, record domestic life by capturing everyday events and special occasions). Therefore, we find ourselves in a situation in which old practices are reconfigured and new ones are invented to fit the technology and businesses that have changed much more rapidly than anyone's photographic practices have. We return to this discussion in Chap. 7, where we look at the future of the Digital Path. However, before that, let us take a critical look at the history of Kodak.

---

[156]The Paris Convention for international protection of patents came into force in the United States in 1887. This allowed George Eastman to patent his inventions abroad as well and effectively enabled more global intellectual property protection than ever before.

The very first decades of Kodak seem to be a textbook example of innovation and the building of a global enterprise. Eastman chose an unpatented new technology (celluloid film) as the basis for his business. Then he designed a consumer product for facilitating consumption of his core technology (that is, his camera). And he came up with a business model that leveraged the technical properties of film and externalised photo-finishing into another revenue flow. Once he had secured his dominance locally, he did not hesitate to expand into a global business, and to sustain that global business he invested heavily in marketing and also in research and development.

Perhaps the dominance of Kodak in the twentieth century was an exception to the rule. In other words, perhaps the success of Kodak will be repeated by no photography company to come. If we look at the Portrait Path, we see that there was no single technology and company as clearly dominant as Kodak. There were several dominant designs (*e.g.*, the daguerreotype, the wet collodion process, and albumen prints) rather than one clear winner. There was no single commercial organisation reaping the majority of the benefits of a technology.

Perhaps Kodak was so dominant because the world at the end of the nineteenth century was such that it allowed corporations to grow as never before (*e.g.*, with global logistics, regulation and deregulation, and mass production technology and ideas). Kodak's contemporaries were such global corporations as Standard Oil, DuPont, General Electric, and BASF. On the other hand, perhaps part of the success was a consequence: everything seems to have fallen into place perfectly for Kodak. The story of Kodak is almost too good to be true.[157]

Whether or not the actual history is as smooth as it seems, the *story* of Kodak's success does influence contemporary thinking about photography: it is not uncommon to discuss and ponder who or what is going to be 'the next Kodak' for the digital age. This line of thinking suggests that a similar homogenous culture of snapshot photography will emerge and there will be a single business model and technology dominating it for a century. As we saw from the Portrait Era, a technological path can consist of several dominant technologies, several commercial organisations that do not remain viable for the full duration of the path, and changes in practices as well. We return in Chap. 7 to the question of how the Digital Path will stabilise and whether there will be a single dominant technology and business model behind domestic photography. Before talking about the future of the Digital Path, however, we need to define the beginning of that path, which is the topic of the next chapter.

References

Benson R (2008) The printed picture. Museum of Modern Art, New York
Buse P (2007) Photography degree zero: cultural history of the Polaroid image. New Form 62(Autumn):29–44

---

[157]It is probably too good to be true. There are few studies of early Kodak that were not sponsored by Kodak or done by the corporation itself. The book by Reese Jenkins (Jenkins 1975) has been the primary source for us in studying the beginnings of Kodak.

Buse P (2010) Polaroid into digital: technology, cultural form, and the social practices of snapshot photography. Continuum 24(2):215–230

Canon Inc (2010) Canon camera museum. Canon Inc. http://www.canon.com/camera-museum/camera/film/data/1976-1985/1979_af35m.html?lang=eu&categ=srs&page=ab&p=1. Accessed 6 Sept 2010

Chalfen R (1987) Snapshot versions of life. Bowling Green State University Popular Press, Bowling Green

Chambers D (2003) Family as place: family photograph albums and the domestication of public and private space. In: Schwartz JM, Ryan JM (eds) Picturing place: photography and the geographical imagination. I.B. Tauris, London

Coe B (1988) Kodak cameras: the first hundred years. Hove Foto, Hove

Coe B (1989) The Rollfilm revolution. In: Ford C (ed) The Kodak museum: the story of popular photography. Century, London, pp 60–89

Coe B, Gates P (1977) The snapshot photograph: the rise of popular photography, 1888–1939. Ash & Grant, London

Collins D (1990) The story of Kodak. H.N. Abrams, New York

Crawley G (1989) Colour comes to all. In: Ford C (ed) The Kodak museum: the story of popular photography. Century, London, pp 128–153

Czech KP (1996) Snapshot: America discovers the camera. Lerner, Minneapolis

Datamonitor (2009) Global Photographic Products – Industry Profile. Datamonitor, New York

Eastman G (1888) Camera. #388850, United States Patent Office

Finnerty TC (2000) Kodak vs. Fuji: the battle for global market share. Unpublished work

Ford C (1989) The Kodak museum: the story of popular photography. Century, London, 184

Freund G (1982) Photography & society. David R Godine, Boston

Holland P (2009) 'Sweet is to scan...': personal photographs and popular photography. In: Wells L (ed) Photography: a critical introduction. Routledge, London, pp 113–158

Jenkins R (1975) Images and enterprise: technology and the American photographic industry, 1839–1925. Johns Hopkins University Press, Baltimore

Kao DM (1999) Innovation/imagination: 50 years of Polaroid photography. H. N. Abrams, New York/London, p 120

Kenyon D (1992) Inside amateur photography. Batsford, London

King G (1984) Say 'cheese'!: the snapshot as art and social history. Collins, London

Larish J (2008) Silver to silicon: a journalist looks back at the changes that have brought us to the era of digital photos. CreateSpace, Seattle

Lewis G (1991) The history of the Japanese camera. The international museum of photography at George Eastman House. Rochester, New York

Life Magazine (1972) A genius and his magic camera. 27 Oct 1972

Nerwin H (1964) Roll Film Magazine. #3138081, US Patent Office

Olshaker M (1978) The instant image: Edwin Land and the Polaroid experience. Stein and Day, New York

Peres MR (2007) Focal encyclopedia of photography: digital imaging, theory and applications, history, and science, 4th edn. Focal, Amsterdam/London

Slater D (1995) Domestic photography and digital culture. In: Lister M (ed) The photographic image in digital culture. Routledge, London, pp 129–146

Swasy A (1997) Changing focus: Kodak and the battle to save a great American company. Times Business, New York

The New York Times (1991) Kodak settles with Polaroid. 16 June 1991

Trotman N (2002) The life of the party – the Polaroid SX-70 Land camera and instant film photography. Afterimage 29(6):10

Wade J (1979) A short history of the camera. Fountain Press, Watford/New York

Wensberg PC (1987) Land's Polaroid: a company and the man who invented it. Houghton Mifflin, Boston

West NM (2000) Kodak and the lens of nostalgia. University Press of Virginia, Charlottesville

Chapter 5
The Digital Path (ca. 1990–)

History is harder to write the closer it is to the present. In particular, socio-technical history of the kind we have been trying to build up in the last chapters begins to lose its coherence in 'eras of ferment'[1] when the dominant design is challenged by new technology and it becomes unclear what will take its place. Consumer digital photography is an era of ferment writ large! Indeed it could be described as the biggest technological discontinuity in photography since the invention of the daguerreotype and the calotype in the 1830s. Based on the replacement of the chemical process for recording an image, electronic (later digital) photography began in 1969 with the invention of charge-coupled devices to convert light intensity into electronic signals. Although most readers will not be familiar with the names of the inventors or the first producers of electronic cameras, the innovation of electronic capture triggered an avalanche of subsequent innovations that have changed the face of domestic photography for good. That the avalanche has not yet come to a stop makes it all the more difficult to summarise what those changes are and point to the new dominant designs and practices that have replaced the old. Ironically, this is despite the increased amount of literature and information about digital photography, which comes with proximity to the present. So we begin this latest path in the history of domestic photography with a new chapter in this book, and a consequent change of tack.

Our aim is still to elucidate the practice of everyday photography and how it has been affected by technological and business factors over time. However, we cannot simply continue to draw on 'milestone' histories of photography and snapshot practice, because these begin to run out in the 1990s with the advent of the first consumer digital cameras. Also, the avalanche mentioned above is still in progress, and, therefore, it is hard to say what technologies and business models are dominant.

In this chapter and the next one, Chap. 6, we use four types of literature as sources of insight into what happened after that and what might happen in the future. First, marketing reports herald the coming of new technologies and their uptake by the masses in different geographies of the world. Second, cultural commentators speculate about the impact of these technologies on our photographic behaviours and our

---

[1] Anderson and Tushman 1990.

R. Sarvas and D.M. Frohlich, *From Snapshots to Social Media - The Changing Picture of Domestic Photography*, Computer Supported Cooperative Work, DOI 10.1007/978-0-85729-247-6_5, © Springer-Verlag London Limited 2011

relationship to the image. Third, social scientists describe studies of transitional practice and popular emergent behaviours. Finally, research and development teams
report on new lab prototypes and how they were used in small-scale experiments and
trials. To pick our way through these bodies of literature and write a first-draft history
of digital photography, we adopt in this chapter the notion of *infrastructure*. By this
we mean the network of devices, software, cables, protocols, screens, file formats,
required to 'do' domestic and snapshot photography in the twenty-first century.

We also divide the examination of the past two decades into two separate chapters.
This chapter continues from where the previous chapter ended: the end of film-based
photography and the beginning of the transition toward mass digital photography. In
this chapter, we go through the *infrastructure* of domestic photography and how each
component of that infrastructure became available for use and adopted. The following
chapter, Chap. 6, focuses on the academic literature on people's practices with the
new technologies and components of the domestic photography infrastructure.

5.1   Digital Photography Infrastructures at Home

The major change in domestic photography in the late nineteenth century was the
Kodak camera and the development and printing service Kodak offered. A key characteristic of this change was that Kodak made it possible for unskilled people to
capture photographs and receive the photographs as prints. As discussed in the
previous chapter, to achieve this, George Eastman of Kodak had to design not only a
new kind of camera but a whole new infrastructure. Prior to Kodak, for one to receive
a photograph of oneself or a loved one, the whole process was bought as a service
from a professional photographer (or perhaps a skilful and wealthy relative had a
camera, a darkroom, and the required chemicals and skills). Kodak offered a camera
and an infrastructure with which the photographs were taken as easily as possible, and
the development and printing (and in the first years also loading and unloading of
film) was externalised to a service – in this case, to a combination of unskilled labour
and specially designed machinery. This business and technology infrastructure was
the 'platform' on which snapshot photography practices were born and built.

Similarly, the introduction of each key element in the digital infrastructure for
domestic photography appears to have generated new behaviours and businesses that
show up across the various types of literature mentioned above. Although the coverage of information about the impact of each element differs, there is enough on most
of the major elements for them to be reviewed separately. Furthermore, there is a
historical order to these elements, which it is possible to plot and follow. This is
summarised in Fig. 5.1, below, and forms the structure for the rest of this chapter.

In contrast to infrastructures for film photography, which tended to be closed
systems dedicated to photography alone, the history of digital photography is a
history of increasing assimilation into a general-purpose, networked computing
infrastructure. Hence, early attempts were made to digitise prints and negatives
with photo scanners for computer manipulation and printing (elements 1, 2, and 5
in Fig. 5.1). Digital cameras followed (3), initially to bring photo 'development'

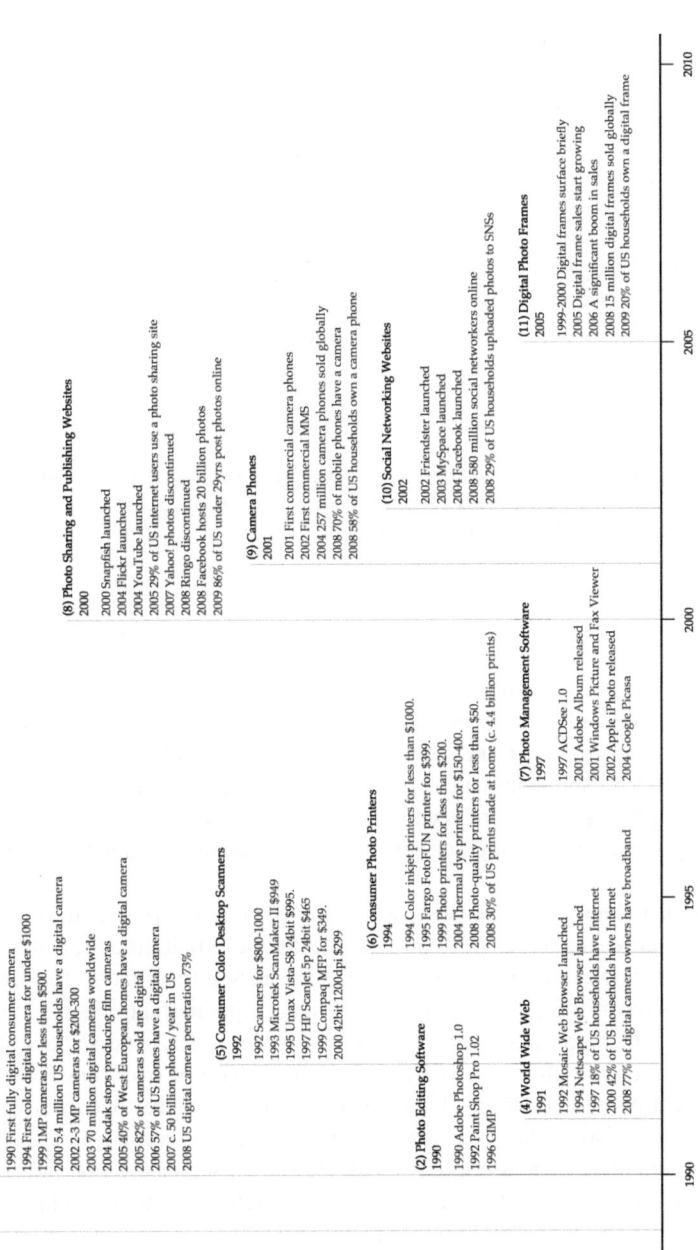

(1) PCs in 15% of households in the US
1989

1993 22.8% US of households have a PC
2000 51.0% of US households have a PC

(3) Consumer Digital Cameras
1990

1990 First fully digital consumer camera
1994 First color digital camera for under $1000
1999 1MP cameras for less than $500.
2000 5.4 million US households have a digital camera
2002 2-3 MP cameras for $200-300
2003 70 million digital cameras worldwide
2004 Kodak stops producing film cameras
2005 40% of West European homes have a digital camera
2005 82% of cameras sold are digital
2006 57% of US homes have a digital camera
2007 c. 50 billion photos /year in US
2008 US digital camera penetration 73%

(5) Consumer Color Desktop Scanners
1992

1992 Scanners for $800-1000
1993 Microtek ScanMaker II $949
1995 Umax Vista-S8 24bit $995.
1997 HP Scanjet 5p 24bit $465
1999 Compaq MFP for $349.
2000 42bit 1200dpi $299

(6) Consumer Photo Printers
1994

1994 Color inkjet printers for less than $1000.
1995 Fargo FotoFUN printer for $399.
1999 Photo printers for less than $200.
2004 Thermal dye printers for $150-400.
2008 Photo-quality printers for less than $50.
2008 30% of US prints made at home (c. 4.4 billion prints)

(2) Photo Editing Software
1990

1990 Adobe Photoshop 1.0
1992 Paint Shop Pro 1.02
1996 GIMP

(4) World Wide Web
1991

1992 Mosaic Web Browser launched
1994 Netscape Web Browser launched
1997 18% of US households have Internet
2000 42% of US households have Internet
2008 77% of digital camera owners have broadband

(7) Photo Management Software
1997

1997 ACDSee 1.0
2001 Adobe Album released
2001 Windows Picture and Fax Viewer
2002 Apple iPhoto released
2004 Google Picasa

(8) Photo Sharing and Publishing Websites
2000

2000 Snapfish launched
2004 Flickr launched
2004 YouTube launched
2005 29% of US internet users use a photo sharing site
2007 Yahoo! photos discontinued
2008 Ringo discontinued
2008 Facebook hosts 20 billion photos
2009 86% of US under 29yrs post photos online

(9) Camera Phones
2001

2001 First commercial camera phones
2002 First commercial MMS
2004 257 million camera phones sold globally
2008 70% of mobile phones have a camera
2008 58% of US households own a camera phone

(10) Social Networking Websites
2002

2002 Friendster launched
2003 MySpace launched
2004 Facebook launched
2008 580 million social networkers online
2008 29% of US households uploaded photos to SNSs

(11) Digital Photo Frames
2005

1999-2000 Digital frames surface briefly
2005 Digital frame sales start growing
2006 A significant boom in sales
2008 15 million digital frames sold globally
2009 20% of US households own a digital frame

1990   1995   2000   2005   2010

Fig. 5.1 Timeline of key technological additions to domestic digital photography (© Risto Sarvas, 2010)

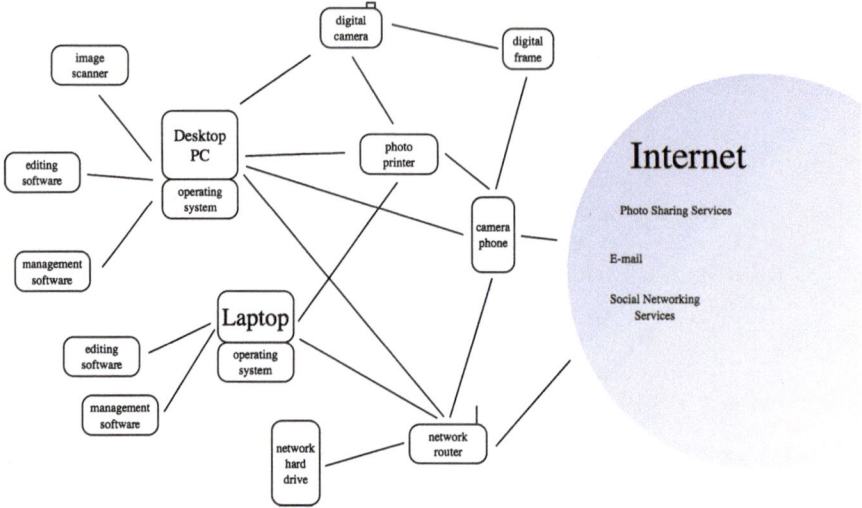

Fig. 5.2 An example of a domestic infrastructure for digital photography. The lines are interconnections, such as USB cable, bluetooth, a memory card, a WLAN connection, or some other specified interface (© Risto Sarvas, 2010)

into the home through local printing. This gave way to more generic computing behaviours involving the management and viewing of home photo collections (7) on the home computer, the incorporation of online photo sharing in existing e-mail and Web publishing activities (4, 8), and the capture and sharing of photographs via mobile phones (9). More recent developments have involved the use of images within social networking services (10) and their presentation on ambient digital displays (11).

Rather than replacing previous elements of this infrastructure, new elements have simply supplemented them, increasing the possibilities for photo 'flow' but also its complexity.[2] The resulting contemporary infrastructure for digital photography, shown in Fig. 5.2, supports a variety of photographic behaviours and businesses, which are more or less integrated with personal and social computing. To understand what these are and how they have evolved over time, we step through different phases in the development of the infrastructure. Because we are dealing here with existing classes of devices and services, we constrain our review to them becoming more or less publicly available for consumer use (*i.e.*, affordable). This largely excludes novel lab prototypes. This literature is referred to in Chap. 7, where we discuss the future of domestic photography.

---

[2]Neustaedter and Fedorovskaya 2009b.

5.2 A Brief History of Digital Domestic Photography

In the late 1980s, all major camera manufacturers, including Kodak and Polaroid, were experimenting with electronic still video cameras for professional use. The new capture technology was marketed mainly to photojournalists, because of their electronic transfer of images, but also to studio photographers for instant viewing. However, consumer photography was showing few signs of change, partly because there were very few affordable SVCs for domestic use and partly because sales of film kept growing. In 1983, it was estimated that amateurs in the US took 11.75 billion stills annually,[3] and 5 years later the estimate was 17 billion.[4] There was no immediate need to make major changes to the consumer business, so Kodak and others continued to make electronic photography products aimed at the high-end market.[5]

The words of Geoffrey Crawley reflect the prevailing belief in film in 1989: "The conventional colour negative process is thus the clear favourite to be the medium of popular picture-taking well into the next century."[6] Probably no-one guessed that in 15 years Polaroid and AgfaPhoto would be bankrupt and Kodak would no longer produce film cameras.

How did the inferior electronic image capture technology overthrow the dominance of the vastly superior film? Step by step, the core technical elements of the domestic photography business were challenged and overtaken by alternative information and communications technology. First, the selling of film and prints was challenged by digital cameras and home computers (PCs) through which it was possible to view photographs without them being made into prints. Second, the resolution of digital cameras and printers combined to enable 'photo-quality prints', which were indistinguishable from those produced through film developing. Third, the need felt for prints was further challenged by the Internet, which enabled people to share digital images over distances. Finally, the camera phone challenged traditional camera sales by integrating the camera into a mobile phone, which made the camera just another aspect of the functionality of a networked and handheld multi-purpose device.

From the perspective of the photography industry, the only change that was evident in the 1980s was the alternative way of recording the image within the camera: using a CCD to translate light into an electronic signal. Characteristic of the early CCD images was that their technical quality (*i.e.*, sharpness, amount of detail, colour representation, etc.) was nowhere near the properties of film. However, SVCs and CCD image capture were relatively mature technology in the sense that the first SVCs had been introduced already in 1981. It probably seemed that electronic photography was going to be contained inside the film photography industry – at least this must have been the goal of the industry stakeholders.

---

[3]Chalfen 1987, p. 13, quoting *The Wolfman Report 1983–84*.
[4]Crawley 1989, p. 153.
[5]Larish 2008, p. 25.
[6]Crawley 1989, p. 153.

The major producers of domestic photography technology envisioned a new domestic infrastructure based on electronic photography, in which photographs were captured with either an SVC or a film camera, and the electronic images were viewed from a monitor or a TV. The images could be printed on paper, and they could be transferred outside the home over telephone lines. Figure 5.3 shows one future vision from 1987, from Kodak's Electronic Photography Division (EPD). The hub of the infrastructure is a 'Still Video Multidisk Recorder' connecting all of the other products together. Peter Sucy, who made the original image reproduced in Fig. 5.3, explains that the image "reflected one point of view within [Kodak], mainly EPD's. The larger corporate view was a strategy to keep people using film as long as possible".[7]

On the one hand, the domestic photo infrastructure envisioned in Fig. 5.3 is a dream that did come true: a central device that connects a printer, a monitor, one or more cameras, a scanner, and a broader network. On the other hand, what this vision does not predict correctly is that the infrastructure was not a photography infrastructure but a general-purpose computing infrastructure. Electronic photography was not contained within the photography industry.

In hindsight, missing from the 1987 vision are the internet, Web photo services and software, and the camera phone. But most surprisingly, or perhaps intentionally, there is no role for the personal computer in the diagram. The PC was already a household

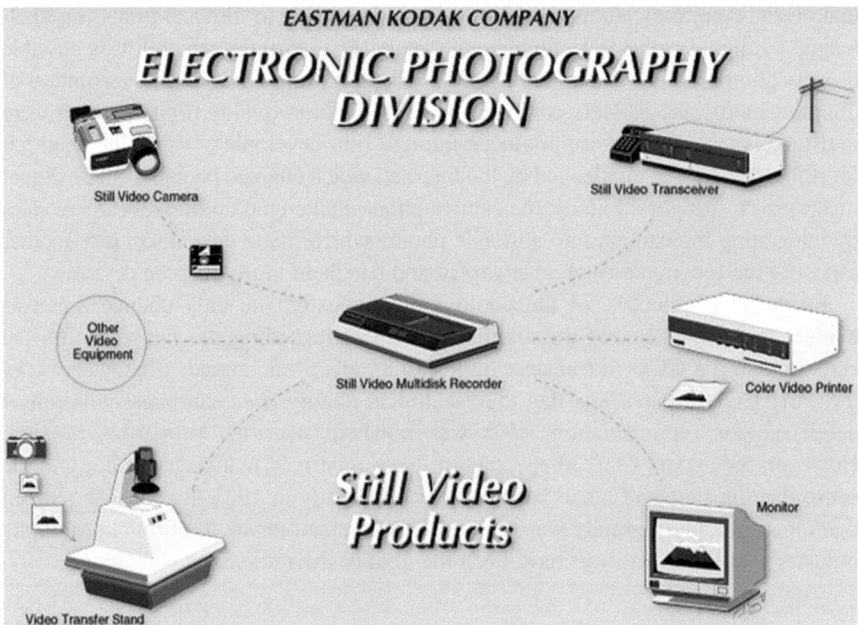

Fig. 5.3 The still video photography infrastructure envisioned in 1987 by Kodak (Original title: Still Video Products. © Peter Sucy, 1987. Republished with permission)

---

[7]Sucy P, 2010, personal communication.

item in the late 1980s, and the numbers were growing. In 1989, for example, 15% of US households had a PC, and the number had almost doubled since 1984.[8] The IBM PC was introduced in 1981, the Commodore 64 in 1982, the Apple Macintosh in 1984, and the Commodore Amiga in 1985, to name a few popular brands.

For whatever reason, the Kodak vision of the electronic photography infrastructure did not include a PC, and this reflects the fundamental change that occurred in the 1990s: domestic photography gradually was moved from a photography-centric infrastructure into a general-purpose information and communications infrastructure not specifically designed for photography. From the perspective of the photography industry, it was exactly this radical change that was a competence-destroying discontinuity for film-based competencies in Kodak, Polaroid, Fujifilm, and Agfa.

5.2.1 The Digital Consumer Camera

In 1990, the PC was no longer news, but that year saw the release of two other components of the new photography infrastructure. The first version of the well-known photo and image editing software Adobe Photoshop was released in 1990. This marked the beginning of image manipulation software for PCs. Although photographs have always been manipulated and edited, the numerical and computational methods made easy to use in photo editing software have significantly changed our perception of what image editing can achieve. The first editing programs were designed and targeted for professionals, but the combination of home PCs and digital cameras opened a new market for them at home. Where snapshots are concerned, easy and automatic editing applications have become common tools for touching up, enhancing, and cropping images.

The second milestone in 1990 was one of the first fully digital consumer cameras, the Logitech Fotoman manufactured by Dycam. 'Fully digital' in this context means that it stored the images captured by the CCD in a digital format (TIFF or PICT). Several cameras at that time stored the image in an analogue format, and viewing or editing the images on a PC required special hardware for digitising the analogue electronic image.[9] The Fotoman had 1 MB of internal memory, which accommodated 32 compressed black-and-white images of 376×240 pixels. The Fotoman cost a few dollars under \$1,000. In contrast, the Kodak DSC-100 announced the same year stored colour images with a resolution of 1024×1280 pixels and cost 30 times more.

It took years before the prices of digital cameras made them widely affordable. The first *colour* digital camera priced under \$1,000 was the Apple QuickTake 100 manufactured by Kodak (640×480 pixels).[10] Two years later, in 1996, Kodak made available its own model, the DC-120, which was the first 1-megapixel (colour)

---

[8]US Census Bureau 2001.

[9]Aaland and Burger 1992.

[10]*Digital Imaging Plus,* Mar 1994.

camera sold for under $1,000. In 2002, consumer cameras with a resolution of 2–3 MP were selling for $200–300.[11] In 2003, there were an estimated 70 million digital cameras worldwide.[12] Soon sales of digital cameras overtook film camera sales, and in 2004, camera phones outsold digital cameras.[13] It had taken more than a decade for the digital camera to replace the film camera in snapshot photography. Then, in 2005, 82% of the cameras sold were digital.[14]

However, the sales of digital cameras did not slow down as more and more households and individuals acquired them. To the benefit of camera manufacturers, people were replacing their old digital cameras with new ones. In 2006, the majority of digital camera buyers were 'repeat buyers'; in other words, they already owned a digital camera but bought a new one nevertheless.[15]

By the end of the decade, in 2010, the price of a digital camera had come down to a fraction of what the Fotoman had cost: a three-megapixel CCD camera could be bought for less than $30. Adjusted in line with the consumer price index (CPI), the cost of a digital camera today is almost the same as the worth of the $1 Kodak Brownie in 1900 (approximately $26.40 in 2009 money[16]). Also, as 70% of mobile phones come with an integrated camera,[17] the price of a camera is perceivably even less.

In 1991, a milestone was reached in the history of the Internet. The World Wide Web (WWW) was made public by Tim Berners-Lee, and in 1992 one of the first graphical Web browsers, Mosaic, was launched. Two years later, the Netscape Web browser was introduced. The Web did not become popular overnight. For example, it took over a decade for Internet connections to reach half of the households in the US.[18] Nevertheless, for those households the Web did reach, self-made HTML homepages viewable by Web browsers were a channel to publish digital photographs and share them with friends, family, or anyone happening to stumble upon the Web page. Another convenient method of sharing photographs, and a more popular one, was e-mail, which was an integral part of the Internet since its beginning. For the first time in the history of domestic photography, it was possible to show and view personal photographs quickly over long distances. Later, this activity (*i.e.*, photos shared via e-mail and on homepages) would spur the beginning of photo sharing Web services, which specialised in providing an easy way to share and publish photographs online. But before photo sharing Web sites, three photography technologies became available and affordable for the home infrastructure: image scanners, photo printers, and photo management software.

---

[11] CNET News, 1.3.2002.

[12] Larish 2008, p. 135.

[13] Strategy Analytics 2005.

[14] IT Facts, 2005.

[15] Shankland 2007.

[16] Calculated via tools at http://www.measuringworth.com/.

[17] Hsu 2009.

[18] US Census Bureau 2001.

5.2.2 The Home Lab: Scanning, Printing, and Organising

A few years before photo printers, colour flatbed scanners became affordable for consumer use. In 1992, flatbed desktop scanners cost between $800 and $1,000, but gradually the prices came down, and in 1997 a 24-bit scanner cost $465. By 2000, colour scanners with 1200 ppi (pixels per inch) were sold for $169–349. At the end of the 1990s, so-called multi-function peripherals (MFPs) or all-in-one devices (AIOs) were introduced. These were integrated printer–scanner–copier devices that acted as PC peripherals. Some versions also plugged in to the phone network and served as fax machines. The relatively low pricing of these multi-purpose machines made them attractive items for home use (*e.g.*, a Compaq MFP cost $349 in 1999), so a photo printer and an image scanner entered the domestic infrastructure, sometimes at the same time.

Inkjet technology brought photo printers for home printing to the consumer market in the mid-1990s. In 1994, one could buy a colour inkjet printer for less than $1,000, and in 1995, for example, a Fargo FotoFun printer cost $399.[19] These printers did their best to make people print their digital photographs at home rather than take the memory cards to commercial services (retailers) for printing. The photo printers were marketed as an integral part of the 'home photo laboratory', where photographs captured by digital cameras and edited by special software were then 'developed' into prints by the printer. This can be seen as a reversal of the old film snapshot philosophy wherein everything between capture and prints was either automated (Polaroid model) or externalised (Kodak model). With the combination of a digital camera, a PC with editing software, and a photo printer, the snapshooter had the opportunity to be in charge of the development process. Whether or not more control was what snapshooters wanted, it nevertheless came with the cost of greater complexity, as now more components and activities were required to produce a print.

As digital cameras were adopted increasingly for home use, people's personal collections of digital photographs started to accumulate. Soon a need was felt for easy-to-use technology for organising and managing one's collections on the computer. In the late 1990s and early 2000s, a new type of photo management software emerged, which was not primarily about editing and manipulation (*e.g.*, ACDSee in 1997, Adobe Album in 2001, and Apple iPhoto in 2002). Some of this software was bundled with cameras, printers, or scanners. Some applications came as a built-in of Windows or Mac operating systems (*e.g.*, Apple iPhoto and Windows Picture and Fax Viewer), and some were standalone third-party programs. Those that came with the operating systems became very popular automatically.

---

[19]PR Newswire 1995.

5.2.3 Photographs on the World Wide Web

As domestic Internet connections got faster, photo management software was integrated more and more often with a photo sharing Web site (*i.e.*, an online photo service) so that selected and searched images on the home PC could be shared easily. But at the beginning of the new millennium, digital photographs were most often shared in e-mail messages as attachments, and the growing size of the cameras' CCDs made the image files bigger. Sharing a dozen photographs as e-mail attachments ran the risk of the mail's rejection or deletion by mail servers for being too large, or filling the e-mail inbox of the recipient. Also, e-mail programs (*i.e.*, e-mail clients) were not ideal for viewing photographs and discussing them. Ofoto, Shutterfly, and Snapfish were some of the first so-called photo sharing Web sites, where people could share their photographs with others, often for free.

In the decade that followed these, different business models were tried on various photo sharing Web sites to cover the costs of running the service: a membership charge, Web advertising, and charging for high-definition downloads, to name a few examples. By the end of the decade, some of the photo sharing Web sites had not made a profit and were terminated. For example, the photo and video sharing Web site Ringo shut down in 2008, and it informed its users that they had a month to download their photographs from the service before they would be deleted. Ringo provided no way to retrieve the users' uploaded videos, because they were hosted by a business partner who did not provide the technology required for retrieval.[20] In the case of Ringo, not only were videos lost, but so were all comments, captions, and discussions about the photographs. The Kodak Gallery photo sharing Web site made the possibility of deletion of its users' photographs an incentive to cover the costs of the service. In 2008, it started requiring its customers to make "a minimum annual purchase" from its Web site or face possible deletion of the photographs.[21]

However, photo sharing Web sites have now become a common component of the home photography infrastructure. In 2009, the combined number of photographs on some of the most popular Web sites was estimated to be 50 billion (with about 325 million unique visitors to these Web sites in February 2009).[22] The Web site with the most photographs was the social networking service Facebook, although the company does not profile that Web site as a photo sharing service. A report by TechCrunch (2009)[23] compared the number of unique photographs on popular services: 20 billion for Facebook, the same for ImageShack, 7.2 billion on Photobucket, 3.4 billion on Flickr, and three billion for Multiply.[24] In July 2010, Facebook was reported to have 48 billion unique images and 500 million users.[25]

---

[20] Hernandez 2008.

[21] Kodak Imaging Network Inc. 2009.

[22] TechCrunch 2009.

[23] *Ibid.*

[24] *Ibid.*

[25] Time Magazine 2010; Zuckerberg 2010b.

Ringo and Kodak Gallery are examples of the risk of losing one's photographs, videos, and related data because of the commercial enterprise behind the Web site changing its terms of use or shutting down altogether. Transferring the social interaction around photographs into a commercial service integrates people's photography practices into the business and profitability of the service at hand. Often the service provider reserves the rights to change the end-user licence agreement (EULA) as it sees fit.

5.2.4 The New Class of Camera: The Camera Phone

But before the introduction of the so-called social networking sites and services to the domestic photography infrastructure, a significant new component emerged from the telecommunications industry: the camera phone. The first commercially available camera phone is credited to Sharp's model J-SH04 from 2001. Later the same year, Nokia released its first camera phone model, the 7560. Advancements in image sensor technology had made it feasible to integrate a camera into a mobile phone. The low power consumption and small size of CMOS (complementary metal-oxide–semiconductor) image sensors made them ideal for the mobile phone. The integrated camera became a sales argument for new models of mobile phone, and soon more and more phone models had a camera, whether the buyer wanted one or not (*e.g.*, in 2008, 70% of mobile phones had a camera[26]). For the first time in the history of domestic photography, snapshooters had a camera device the primary purpose of which was not to capture images, and it was not made by a traditional camera manufacturer. And as we mentioned earlier, in 2004, more camera phones were sold worldwide than digital cameras.[27]

One of the advertised features of the camera phones was the ability to send images to other phones. In Europe, the dominant standard was MMS (the Multimedia Messaging Service), which was a built-in functionality in all GSM-compatible phones. The first commercial MMS system was launched in 2002. The idea was to send picture messages to other phones much like the popular text messages. However, this was not adopted as quickly and widely as the phone network operators had hoped.[28] From the perspective of domestic photography, the MMS approach enabled sharing and sending photographs directly from the camera. It demonstrated that the camera phone was effectively a networked camera, and this made phone network operators concrete stakeholders in the business of photography.

---

[26] Hsu 2009.

[27] Strategy Analytics 2005.

[28] Humphries 2004.

5.2.5   Social Networking Services

At the same time as camera phones were becoming popular and the Multimedia Messaging Service was introduced, the first social networking Web sites and services started to emerge, among them Friendster in 2002 and MySpace in 2003. Characteristic of these Web sites was that they facilitated connecting people and making these connections (*i.e.*, social networks) explicit. Users of social networking Web sites each had a profile, which could be connected to other profiles on the Web site. The network of profiles then acted as a communication channel, and the profiles themselves as representations of the user. Similarly to HTML homepages in the late 1990s, people using the social networking Web sites used their own name rather than a pseudonym. Also, the connections were dominantly social ties that already existed outside the Web site: friends, family, colleagues, and friends of friends. In contrast to the open WWW, the domain of a diverse range of HTML homepages, a social networking Web site as a closed system had more control over the features and functionality provided to its users. The social networking Web sites provided an easy way to construct an online representation and connect it with acquaintances. In 2004, the Facebook social networking Web site was launched, and in 5 years it had become the most popular in that field. As mentioned above, Facebook had 500 million users, worldwide, in July 2010.

From the perspective of domestic photography, social networking Web sites are important in two respects. First, they seem to serve two of the main purposes of domestic photography: to strengthen and reify social bonds and to demonstrate cultural and group membership. Second, and perhaps because of that first factor, a significant amount of photographic content is shared on these social networking Web sites. As mentioned previously, Facebook in 2009 hosted more personal photographs than any other Web site, even more than Web sites focusing explicitly on photo sharing.[29] Facebook, as a commercial enterprise, has access to personal photographs paralleled by no other business in history. We will discuss in detail in Chap. 7 how the role of social networking Web sites is central in shaping the future of snapshots and domestic photography.

5.2.6   The Latest Component: A Digital Frame

As our final component in the contemporary domestic photo infrastructure we have the digital photo frame. A digital photo frame is an electronic display approximately the size of a traditional photograph frame for paper prints. These kinds of frames were briefly available at the turn of the millennium but did not see enough

---

[29]Data Center Knowledge 2009.

demand. Therefore, they were almost absent from the consumer market until 2005.[30] Then, 2006 proved to be a turning point for the sales of digital photo frames, and in 2008, 15 million frames were sold, globally.[31] According to a market research conducted by PMA, every fifth US household owned a digital frame in 2009.[32]

A typical photo frame has a memory card reader and some internal memory for storing the photographs and showing them on the display. Some advanced ones can show videos and are connected to the home network wirelessly. The digital photo frame is an alternative display screen to the PC, the television, mobile phones, and laptops. As a traditional photo frame can, it can be used as an ambient display, or it can be picked up and used to scroll through images stored in the frame or on a memory card. The digital photo frame as a product is currently under much research and development in an attempt to differentiate and add functionality to it (*e.g.*, automatic downloads from the Internet, connectivity with mobile phone data networks, and display of videos). Time will tell what functionality and features will be part of a typical frame and whether it will become a more popular item for display and viewing.

5.3 The Characteristics of Digital Photography Technology

Replacing the recording medium inside the camera may seem like a minor change in photography. However, the short history above shows that this is not the case, as the new recording format had enormous repercussions for the whole infrastructure of domestic photography technology. In hindsight, we can identify a few technical characteristics of the new image format (*i.e.*, of the storing of numerical values in a digital file format) that constituted a significant difference from the previous format (*i.e.*, a chemically formed image on celluloid film) and were significant also in a historical context. In our discussion of these characteristics, we apply Lev Manovich's principles of new media: numerical representation, modularity, automation, variability, and transcoding.[33]

5.3.1 Reproduction: Costless, Errorless, and Endless

The possibility of reproducing digital images infinitely and without loss of quality is one characteristic that in the context of history is unprecedented. Although having several copies of personal snapshots was technically possible on the Kodak Path, it had its costs and required extra effort. An exception was the quite common offer of

---

[30] Wang 2007.
[31] Wang 2009.
[32] PMA 2009a.
[33] Manovich 2002.

photofinishers to provide 'doubles' (two prints of each exposure on film) for a small fee or for free.

The possibility of making an exact copy of a digital image at the push of a button has enabled sharing and publishing of photographs in a new way. Giving a digital photograph to another person does not mean that there is one photograph fewer in the giver's collection. Perhaps this has diminished the value of a photograph as a gift, because there is hardly any uniqueness and singularity associated with a digital image.

The possibility to have endless copies of an image makes it possible also to archive the images while they are still used for other purposes. Backups and remote archives are a copy of a set of images, and if any of the other copies is destroyed, recovering the lost image is possible. However, the easy copying of images also makes fragmentation of one's image collection possible. As images are copied to other devices, the Internet, and different hard drives, it becomes a difficult task to keep track of whether all the images are in one place or they are distributed over a network of devices and digital storage spaces.

Third, the easy reproduction means that a single photograph can have parallel life cycles and several meanings in different contexts. After capture, one copy of the image can end up on a 'photo blog', another copy is made to the photo archive on a PC, a third copy is edited and printed on paper, and perhaps a fourth copy of the same image ends up being deleted. On the Kodak Path, and even more with the Portrait Path, once a photograph was captured, it often had only one instance, perhaps two. Several copies were made of only very special photographs, such as photographs sent with, or as part of, Christmas cards. On the Digital Path, it is almost impossible to keep track of the life cycle of a captured photograph.

5.3.2   Transferability: Bridging Time and Space

The numerical representation of the image captured by the camera makes it possible to transfer the image over electronic networks at unprecedented speeds. Needless to say, to take full advantage of this technical characteristic, the transfer infrastructure has to be in place and accessible. Therefore, the Internet and the other networks connected to it (*e.g.*, the mobile phone network) are critical.

The possibility of sending or receiving an image immediately after its capture was present in the instant photography introduced by Polaroid in 1947. However, in contrast to Polaroids, the image sent is a copy of the original (see above), and, perhaps more significantly, the image can be immediately sent over vast geographic distances. For example, an image captured on a camera phone can be sent as an MMS message to another part of the world, and it will reach the recipient in a matter of seconds.

Not only can images be sent over distances in very little time; they can also be found and viewed independently of time and space. Someone can put photographs on display on the Web, and the viewer of those images does not have to look at them at the same time as the other person or from the same location.

5.3.3   Storage: No Physical Space Required

The numerical representation of the image means that storing that information electronically requires very little physical space. Again, if one is to be able to take advantage of this characteristic, there need to be technologies to store vast quantities of digital data in very little physical space, such as hard disk, memory card, and optical disk technologies.

A hard disk the size of a shoebox can hold a few terabytes of data, which means several hundred thousand digital images (if each image has ca. 14 megapixel resolution and is about 10 megabytes in size). In practice, this means that all of a household's digital photographs can fit into a relatively small space. Second, because of the continuous advances in storage technology, acquiring more storage space will not be a major investment (in early 2010, a two-terabyte external hard drive cost less than €100, which is roughly the price of an inexpensive point-and-shoot digital camera).

The minimal physical storage means also that hundreds of images can be stored on the camera before they have to be transferred elsewhere to free space for new photographs. In practice, this means that people can take a few hundred photographs at a single event, or even of a single subject, without running into limitations on the camera. The ability to transfer the images to even larger storage spaces than those of the camera does not encourage people to delete any of the photographs. As a result, people are accumulating personal photography collections the size of which (as measured by number of photographs) is unprecedented in domestic photography. By some estimates, 50 billion photographs were taken (presumably by Americans) in 2007.[34] In comparison to the 17 billion in 1988,[35] the increase was from 70 to 200 photographs a year[36] per person, and the number is probably growing. However, because of the easy copying and transfer of images, people's image collections include also photographs shared with them or given to them. This increases the number of photographs 'used' in domestic photography, and some of them probably end up in personal archives as well.

5.3.4   Editing: Cropping, Filtering, and Automatically Enhancing

As we mentioned briefly earlier in this book, the numerical representation of the captured images enables editing of the image by means of computation – namely, algorithms and mathematical formulae. Software tools have made these editing

---

[34] Shankland 2007.

[35] Crawley 1989.

[36] Population estimates from U.S. Census Bureau 2010.

algorithms easy and simple to use, and many of the algorithms are automatically executed without the photographer even knowing about it. For example, a digital camera executes a set of algorithms on the captured image data prior to storage in the camera's memory.

Some of the editing tools are simple to use but significantly different from what Kodak Path film photography allowed. Replacing red eyes with pixels of other colours, for example, is a task that would have required some skill on the Kodak Path in order to yield realistic results. Now, reasonably good editing of red eyes can be done automatically. Similarly, automated algorithms can enhance the colours, contrast, sharpness, and lighting of a digital photograph at the push of a button. However, part of the skill that separated the serious amateurs from the snapshooters used to be editing, and this has not changed in the digital era. The algorithms, tools, and methods for digital editing are numerous, and to master them requires skills.

Not all editing of digital photographs is directly related to the image. Practically all digital photographs are edited to adhere to standard formats and quite often also edited for compression of their storage size.

5.3.5   Convergence: It Is All Ones and Zeroes

The numerical representation of a photographic image turns the image into binary data like any other data for computers. The same can be said about computer files: an image file is very much like any other file on a computer. This means that there is technical convergence of photographs with any other computed data. This similarity is at the core of the change in photography infrastructures. The same devices, protocols, cables, software, operating systems, processors, etc. can be used to handle photographs and any other data. The technology becomes multi-purpose technology rather than being specific technology, such as the photography specific technology of the Kodak Path.

The convergence of the technologies also encourages convergence of practices and new combinations of data. People read news on the Internet with the same device they use to view photos on a Web site; perhaps these activities will be combined in practice such that news-reading is done at the same time as viewing personal photographs. Photographs can now be combined with location data (*e.g.*, geographic co-ordinates), which has enabled practices such as location-based browsing of images.

All of these technical characteristics of digital photography depend heavily on the surrounding and supporting infrastructure of technologies. Digital image capture was invented in the 1970s, but for the rest of the domestic technology to support the key characteristics of that technology it took almost a quarter of a century. For this reason, we pay attention to the infrastructure of domestic photography rather than the individual devices as separate technologies.

5.4 Conclusions

The objective of this brief historical overview is to show how much the infrastructure at home for snapshot and domestic photography departed from the Kodak Path. The main components of the film-based infrastructure were the camera, the film roll, the external photo-finishing service, the paper prints, albums, and perhaps a few frames for some special prints. This simplicity has given way to heterogeneous complexity. Not only are the main components for digital photography different, but also the ways in which they can be combined are numerous. For example, the PC can be connected via an operating system to photo editing software, which can be connected via a USB cable to a printer, which can be connected via Bluetooth to a camera phone, which can be connected via GPRS to a photo sharing Web site, which can be connected via home broadband to a digital photo frame, which can be connected via a memory card to a digital camera, which can be connected via HDMI cable to a television set, and so on.

The heterogeneity and complexity of devices and interconnections means that no two constellations of photography technologies in a home are the same. This also means that no technology provider can know beforehand what the end user's technical environment will be. In trying to adapt to the situation, technology providers have to update their technologies to better interconnect with other technologies, and for the snapshot photographer this means updating device drivers and/or firmware, changing software versions, or buying a new product – in other words, maintenance work that was not required on the Kodak Path.

The monetary costs of snapshooting were relatively easy to measure with the Kodak Path: the purchase of a camera (more or less a one-time cost), the price of a roll of film, and the price of the photo-finishing service. A consumer could estimate the price per captured photograph relatively easily by dividing the cost of a film roll and its development and printing by the number of exposures (24 or 36). In contemporary domestic digital photography, the cost of a single photograph is very difficult to measure. Also, the cost of photography in general becomes hard to estimate because there are a myriad of ways in which to capture and use photographs, and the devices used for photography often have other uses as well.

There is no simple way of estimating the costs of 'doing' snapshot photography. All we can say without a detailed study is that there are significant one-time costs, such as those of a PC, a printer, photo editing software, a scanner, a camera, a memory card, and so on, and there are some running costs, such as for home broadband service, mobile phone data service, and a photo Web site subscription fee. If one is to be able to participate fully in snapshot photography culture on the Digital Path, the costs of acquiring hardware and software, and the costs of services, seem to be much higher than the costs on the Kodak Path.

The contemporary domestic photography infrastructure also shows that, in comparison to the Kodak Path, there are new business stakeholders in snapshot and domestic photography. Domestic photography has become predominantly information and communications technology (ICT), and most of the businesses involved in people's photographic practices are from that industry. There are software and device manufacturers who are directly involved in photography: photo management and editing software developers, digital camera manufacturers, digital photo frame manufacturers, photo printing and photo product services (*e.g.*, photo books or photos on mousepads), photo printer and scanner manufacturers, and so on. In addition, there are non-photography-specific businesses that also have a stake in snapshot and domestic photography: mobile phone manufacturers and carriers, operating system providers, memory card manufacturers, social networking services, Internet service providers, hard drive manufacturers, and search engine providers, to name a few.

In contrast to the Kodak Path, there is no dominant business model here for making a profit on snapshot photography. The business stakeholders are as numerous and heterogeneous as the technologies involved. Whether there will be a dominant design and a dominant business model in snapshot photography remains to be seen. In the year 2010, we are still living in an 'era of ferment' that began in the 1980s with the introduction of electronic photography.

In the next chapter, we take a closer look at the practices of snapshot photography and how user- and human-centric research in computer science (*i.e.*, human–computer interaction, computer-supported co-operative work, and interaction studies) has studied the practices of the past decade.

References

Aaland M, Burger R (1992) Digital photography. Random House, New York

Anderson P, Tushman M (1990) Technological discontinuities and dominant designs: a cyclical model of technological change. Adm Sci Q 35(4):604–633

Chalfen R (1987) Snapshot versions of life. Bowling Green State University Popular Press, Bowling Green

Crawley G (1989) Colour comes to all. In: Ford C (ed) The Kodak museum: the story of popular photography. Century, London, pp 128–153

Data Center Knowledge (2009) Facebook now has 30,000 servers. Data Center Knowledge. http://www.datacenterknowledge.com/archives/2009/10/13/facebook-now-has-30000-servers/. Accessed 19 Mar 2010

Digital Imaging Plus (1994) Apple quicktake 100. Mar 1994

Hernandez V (2008) Ringo photo sharing Website bows out of cyber space by end of June. All Headline News. http://www.allheadlinenews.com/articles/7011151890. Accessed 19 Mar 2010

Hsu J (2009) The worldwide mobile phone camera module market and Taiwan's industry, 2009 and beyond. Market Intelligence & Consulting Institute (MIC), Taipei

Humphries M (2004) MMS not popular in EU. Geek.com. http://www.geek.com/articles/mobile/mms-not-popular-in-eu-20040513/. Accessed 19 Mar 2010

IT Facts (2005) Film sales drop by 20% every year. IT Facts. http://www.itfacts.biz/film-sales-drop-by-20-every-year/4889. Accessed 6 Sept 2010

Kodak Imaging Network Inc (2009) Terms of service at Kodak gallery. Kodak Imaging Network Inc. http://www.kodakgallery.com/gallery/footerLinksContent.jsp?pageID=600010. Accessed 29 Apr 2010

Larish J (2008) Silver to silicon: a journalist looks back at the changes that have brought us to the era of digital photos. CreateSpace, Seattle

Manovich L (2002) The language of new media. MIT Press, Cambridge, 1st MIT Press pbk

Neustaedter C, Fedorovskaya E (2009) Understanding and improving flow in digital photo ecosystems. In: Proceedings of the graphics interface 2009, Kelowna. ACM, New York

PMA (2009) U.S. households make photo books for family keepsakes. PMA. http://pmaforesight.com/?p=40. Accessed 2 Sept 2010

PR Newswire (1995) Fargo introduces FotoFUN!: Digital color photo printer comparable to a photo lab. 8 Aug 1995

CNET News (2007) Cameras: shipments rising, but prices falling. 19 Sept 2007

CNET News (2002) Toshiba crops digital camera price. 1 Mar 2002

Strategy Analytics (2005) Camera phone sales surge to 257 million units worldwide in 2004. Strategy Analytics. http://www.strategyanalytics.com/default.aspx?mod=PressReleaseViewer&a0=2354. Accessed 19 Mar 2010

TechCrunch (2009) Who has the most photos of them all? Hint: it is not Facebook. Techcrunch. http://techcrunch.com/2009/04/07/who-has-the-most-photos-of-them-all-hint-it-is-not-facebook/. Accessed 19 Mar 2010

Time Magazine (2010) How Facebook is Redefining Privacy. 31 May 2010

US Census Bureau (2001) Home computers and Internet use in the United States. Aug 2000

US Census Bureau (2010) U.S. and World population clocks. U.S. Census Bureau. http://www.census.gov/main/www/popclock.html. Accessed 16 Sept 2010

Wang H (2007) Digital Photo Frames: Picture a Good Year. Parks Associates, Dallas

Wang H (2009) Digital Photo Frames: Annual Global Market Analysis and Forecasts. Parks Associates, Dallas

Zuckerberg M (2010) 500 million stories. The Facebook Blog. http://blog.facebook.com/blog.php?post=409753352130 Accessed 6 Aug 2010

Chapter 6
Digital Photo Adoption

Given the unfolding of the digital photography infrastructure over the last 20 years, as described in Chap. 4, we now turn to its practical use by Western families as described in the research literature. We draw mainly from work in HCI and interaction design, since that provides the most detailed empirical insights on technology mediated practice. Our interest in reviewing this here is in whether and how the traditional values of film photography are changing, and what new social and business practices are emerging to characterise domestic photography. In Chap. 2, we pointed to three primary values of domestic photography, related to memory, identity, and communication (after work by Chalfen and Musello[1]). In Chaps. 3 and 4, we showed how these were played out in differing combinations, salience, and forms in the development of film photography as people learned what could be done with a camera and a photograph, and how it might be archived and shared. In this chapter, we consider whether the same values are still realised through the properties of digital photographs and our interaction with them, or whether the digital revolution has changed the very nature of photography and why we perform it.

We also examine the interplay between technology, business, and practice factors as this changes with the introduction of each new element of the digital photography infrastructure. This broadly follows the timeline shown in Fig. 5.1, in the previous chapter. Because of the lack of early papers on the use of individual products such as digital scanners, cameras, and photo printers, we begin with an examination of what we call the home photo lab, before moving on to cover the home archive, the camera phone, online photo sharing, offline photo sharing, and current photo ecologies.

---

[1]Chalfen 1987; Musello 1979.

R. Sarvas and D.M. Frohlich, *From Snapshots to Social Media - The Changing Picture of Domestic Photography*, Computer Supported Cooperative Work, DOI 10.1007/978-0-85729-247-6_6, © Springer-Verlag London Limited 2011

6.1   The Home Photo Lab

The first studies of digital photo adoption in the home began to be published after the millennium year, 2000. This was at least 10 years after the introduction of the first digital camera to the consumer market, in 1990, indicating the typical time lag between the release of a new technology and empirical studies of its adoption. Prior to that time, there was growing speculation in the media studies area about the possible impact of digital imaging on visual culture in general. This was captured most succinctly in a collection of essays by British scholars on the photographic image that was edited by Lister 1995,[2] including one by Don Slater on domestic photography and digital culture.[3] We begin with this essay as a preface to the first three empirical studies of digital photo adoption, as it sets the scene for those studies and raises issues we will return to later in the chapter.

Slater argues that domestic photography has always been bound up with family narratives and identity, as well as with home entertainment and leisure. Somewhat paradoxically, photography equipment and snapshots are forms of consumer goods enjoyed in leisure time, which is itself the main subject of images depicting family life. Snapshots typically capture the family at play rather than at work, and domestic photography is something done in 'play time', either on holiday or at family gatherings and rituals. This situation is sometimes illustrated graphically by snapshots showing a snapshooter at work. Digitisation of photographs, according to Slater, did not appear to threaten these kinds of capture activities, but it did appear to interact with related forms of visual, sound, and textual media being introduced into the home through cable TV, digital games, and multimedia computing in general. In 1995, this appeared to Slater to create opportunities for combination of private still images with other media and with public images of other kinds:

> However, as already noted, looked at from the present moment, and without engaging in ungrounded prediction, it is not at all clear that domestic photography – in the sense of snapshooting – has been transformed in the slightest by digital technology. What certainly has been transformed is the domestic context in which snapshots exist, a transformation in the domestic economy of images: digital technologies patently involve a major extension in the volume and complexity of flow of public images through domestic time and space.[4]

On the basis of other trends in domestic image consumption, Slater then speculates about the potential of digital images to liberate family members from their idealised representation in the family album, and empower them to tell their own stories in the moment:

1. The pinboard or 'photographic wall' may become a more dominant metaphor for domestic photography than the family album. This builds on the practice of creatively assembling photos of the moment as *"acts of* practical communication rather than reflective representation".[5]

---

[2]Lister 1995.
[3]Slater 1995.
[4]*Ibid.*, p. 131.
[5]*Ibid.*, p. 139.

2. Individual family members may use digital photos to tell their own stories to themselves and to others.
3. Practice in self-presentation and representation through images may demystify portrayals in public media and call into question their realism.
4. Self-produced representations may challenge the dominant media, act as instruments of local democracy, and become "part of the rebirth of civil society in which our private cultures have real public meaning".[6]

As we shall see, these issues turned out to be remarkably pertinent, especially as subsequent waves of (Internet) technology unfolded to support the wider flow of snapshots into and out of the home. However, this was not immediately apparent from the first empirical studies of domestic digital photography, which focused very much on the home photo system and the parallel use of analogue and digital photographs.

The first three studies published on home digital photography originated in the corporate research labs of Hewlett-Packard and AT&T, both giants in their respective fields: personal computing and telecommunications. Competing photo management systems were under development in both labs, FotoFile at HP[7] and Shoebox at AT&T,[8] together with related lightweight communication tools dating back to the early 1990s (e.g., Deskslate,[9] Montage,[10] Voicefax,[11] Telenotes,[12] and informal video[13]). Following the development of FotoFile at Palo Alto Labs in 1997, the technical team partnered with the second author (Frohlich) at HP Labs Bristol to conduct a more basic study of photo organisation and sharing in 1998.[14] This was carried out with 11 digital-camera-owning families in Northern California. AT&T researchers independently conducted a field trial of Shoebox in the spring and summer of 2000 with 13 individual staff from their Cambridge, UK, labs.[15] A second AT&T team, based on the west coast of the United States, replicated aspects of the HP study with 10 teenagers from high schools in northern California.[16] This supported their parallel investigation and development of instant messaging technology.[17]

Early preoccupations then were with the issues of archiving, retrieving, and *printing* digital photographs from home collections, and with sharing them over the Internet. Contrasts with 'legacy' practices based on photographic prints were

---

[6]*Ibid.*, p. 145.
[7]Kuchinsky et al. 1999.
[8]Mills et al. 2000.
[9]O'Conaill et al. 1994
[10]Tang et al. 1994.
[11]Frohlich and Daly-Jones 1995.
[12]Whittaker et al. 1997.
[13]Isaacs et al. 1997.
[14]Frohlich et al. 2002.
[15]Rodden and Wood 2003.
[16]Schiano et al. 2002.
[17]Isaacs et al. 2002a, b.

inevitable since all participants in these studies were users of existing prints and film cameras. The default assumption of most of the computing industry at that time was of digital photography replacing film photography through a 'digital whiteroom' or 'home photo lab', in which families could capture, edit, print, and store their own photographs at home without recourse to external photo-processing or storage services. This was especially true of HP, who were a leading manufacturer of home printers as well as home computers. A competing view was adopted by Kodak, who aimed to digitise their photo-processing services and make them the preferred outlet for printing all home photographs, of both analogue and digital origin. Unfortunately, this print-centric vision of digital photography never was realised and was challenged immediately by findings from each of the above-mentioned studies.

Frohlich et al. (2002) re-purposed Johansen's (1988) groupware framework[18] to step through the use of four forms of 'photoware', or groupware for photographs (see Fig. 6.1). These activities included co-present sharing of images, remote sharing, archiving, and sending. Insights into each activity came from in-depth family interviews conducted in homes, as well as analysis of diaries and recorded conversations related to photo sharing episodes taking place over 3 months after

	SAME TIME	DIFFERENT TIME
SAME PLACE	Prints Slides & projector **CO-PRESENT SHARING** *Photo viewing software & devices*	Shoeboxes Albums & frames **ARCHIVING** *CD-ROM* *PC filestore* *Photo website*
DIFFERENT PLACE	Telephone **REMOTE SHARING** *Application sharing* *Instant messaging* *Video conferencing*	Mail **SENDING** *Email attachment or website reference* *Internet photo frames*

Fig. 6.1 Dimensions of photoware (Reproduced from Table 1 in Frohlich et al. 2002. Original title: Dimensions of photoware. Republished with permission)

---

[18]Johansen 1988.

the visits. Digital photographs had not replaced analogue photographs as the primary record of family life, but they had supplemented them as a means of easy transmission to family and friends. Face-to-face sharing was still done largely through printed photographs, because of the difficulty of sharing on fixed desktop computer screens, and *selected* digital photographs were printed for sharing and incorporation into traditional print albums and frames. Parallel archives of print and digital photographs were kept by families in roughly the same state of disarray, although families believed that their digital photographs would be easier to find and manage in the future. The difficulty of remote photo-conferencing was identified as an opportunity for new technology, as was the creation of contextualised mini-albums (stories) and community photo Web sites for sharing. Perhaps more important than the individual findings and recommendations was the call to support *photo-ware* for family and friendship groups. This term eventually came to mark an identifiable shift in domestic photography with digitisation, away from a focus on memory, toward a focus on communication.

Similar findings were reported by Schiano et al. (2002) in a brief poster write-up of the teen study. Printed photos still dominated accounts of face-to-face photo sharing and display, even though some participants reported early experimentation with PC, TV, and camera LCD screens for this purpose. Fewer digital photos seemed to be printed by teens as compared to families in the Frohlich et al. study, leading to divergence of print and digital collections and more extensive online posting and sending of digital snapshots by teens. The authors also recommended better photoware for supporting the "social/conversational aspects of photo viewing and sharing", and easier methods for annotation, browsing, and retrieval of digital images from a collection.

The Rodden and Wood (2003) study effectively tested three examples of the latter methods, including thumbnail browsing, audio annotation/transcription, and content-based retrieval. Participants were given digital cameras for a 6-month period and copies of the Shoebox application in which to store their digital images on a family computer. Analogue and digital photo management practices were compared. As in the two previous studies, participants all attempted to create printed photograph albums from film-based snapshots, with mixed success, falling behind with the task for more recent photographs but enjoying the result and aspiring to keep up. In contrast, they rarely attempted to make digital photo albums inside or outside Shoebox, and they limited their manual photo organisation activities to making time or event-based folders (known as 'rolls' in Shoebox) in which to keep their photo sets. Annotation of individual photographs was deemed unnecessary and time-consuming, so users tended to browse the collection manually, using thumbnails and folders arranged chronologically. This preference persisted despite the possibility of recording annotations in speech and having them automatically transcribed to text (with some errors). Some participants were too self-conscious to record their own voice, while others felt that the transcription was too inaccurate. In general, all participants took many more digital than analogue photographs, because of the lack of cost penalties, and prioritised the immediate sharing of images over organising and archiving them.

6.2 The Home Archive

Although printing turned out to be a less important component of the home photo lab than expected, storage emerged as central. Freed from the constraints of having to pay for each photograph taken, families began to use the digital camera in a more professional way, 'bracketing' events with greater coverage by photographs and taking multiple images of the same thing to achieve the perfect shot. Coupled with the proliferation of cameras themselves, this led to an exponential rise in image capture, with the associated need for high-capacity storage and retrieval. This need was anticipated by the industry in the late 1990s, as indicated by the photo management systems mentioned above. However, consumers were slower to recognise it, as shown in the Frohlich et al. (2002) study, where they displayed misplaced faith in the power of digital technology to help them organise their images. In an internal presentation to HP from this work, we predicted a serious consumer storage problem in about 5 years' time from 2001. This problem manifested itself in a number of ways and became the subject of a new round of studies, aimed at understanding and addressing it.

Hence, in 2006, Microsoft Research published a new study of home photo organisation and retrieval, picking apart the various elements involved.[19] These included selecting, discarding, editing, filing, backing up, and assembling photographs in a cycle of activities following capture but before sharing. These are illustrated in a framework reproduced in Fig. 6.2. Activities are referred to as 'photowork', to distinguish them from various forms of 'phototalk' as described by Frohlich et al. (2002). Insights on photowork were derived from in-depth home interviews with 12 digital camera users who had more than 1,000 digital photos in their collection. Findings covered each stage in Fig. 6.2 and showed the diversity of reasons and contexts for reviewing images and manipulating them in various ways. Typically, participants would review images and delete bad pictures from the camera before downloading them in a batch to a home computer. These would be filed with minimal effort in default folders, which were occasionally duplicated or supplemented with others. Half of the group also worked on the images at this point to modify their composition or correct red-eye effects. Apart from occasional backup activity, the next context for photowork was as a prelude to sharing. This involved correcting and selecting the best images and assembling a mini-collection to print or share. Although selected images were still printed for incorporation in albums or home displays, and to give to others, participants did not generally create digital photo albums or slide shows. That most of these activities were performed for recently captured images indicated that participants did not often search for specific target images across the whole collection. They did not therefore report a problem with retrieving and managing images, despite the growing size of their collections and counter to the prediction above.

---

[19] Kirk et al. 2006.

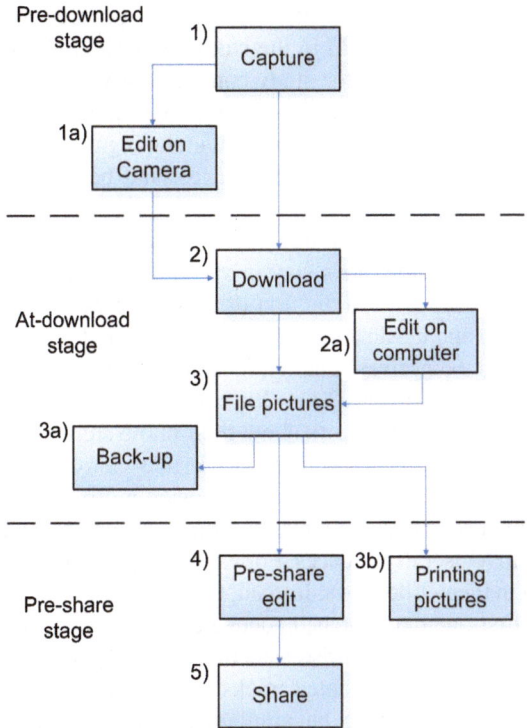

Fig. 6.2 The photowork life cycle (Reproduced from Fig. 2 in Kirk et al. 2006. Original title: The photowork lifecycle. Republished with permission)

These findings are challenged by a more recent study of photo retrieval, using a different methodology. Eighteen parents of young families using digital cameras and home computers were interviewed at home about their photo management practices.[20] In the first part of the interview, they were asked to name significant family events from more than a year ago that they had photographed digitally. In the second part, they were asked to find a photograph from between three and five of these events before discussing the retrieval experience. Participants were surprised to discover that they could find only 61% of the target images. The reasons for this included having too many pictures to search through; having distributed storage of images across different folders, directories, computers, hard drives, and storage media; using minimal hierarchical organisation of folders; and doing minimal revision and maintenance of the photo collection over time.

The average size of participants' photo collections in this study was 4,475 digital pictures, and, as in previous studies, very few of these were organised into digital photo albums. This means that people were effectively searching through 'loose' photographs organised in digital 'packets' likely to contain many more than the

---

[20]Whittaker et al. 2010.

traditional 36 prints from a roll of film. While this appeared to be sufficient for finding photos less than a year old in the study by Kirk et al., it was not enough for finding older photographs in the study conducted 4 years later on significantly larger photo collections. There is no single solution to this problem, but Whittaker et al. suggest a range of measures to address it, including retrieval by event, manual rating and automatic content analysis of images, and better use of metadata for indexing and presentation.

A final series of studies in this area begins to turn this work on its head and reveal an *advantage* to losing one's way in very large media collections, for both private and social reminiscing. In the first of these studies, findings on organising and navigating photo and music collections were compared.[21] The researchers from Motorola Labs found themselves conducting similar studies of photo and music use in the winters of 2002–2003 and 2004–2005 respectively. In the photo study, six participants were interviewed at work about their photo storage and sharing behaviours. In the music study, 13 participants were interviewed at home about their music consumption habits and asked to select music for different scenarios. Various inefficiencies in their search and organisation strategies across media were reported and linked to positive user experiences. For example, participants rarely looked for one specific item in their collections. Instead, they looked for a certain kind of thing and selected the first one that matched adequately. This behaviour is called 'satisficing' and often results in a surprise selection that is 'good enough' for current purposes. Skipping through unwanted tracks from a random music shuffle is an extreme example of this for music, but similar behaviour was observed with photographs, where folders were opened speculatively with a view to finding something 'interesting'. Such interest could be piqued by the automatic presentation of photos by a computer screensaver. Participants also reported frequent occasions of sidetracking, where they started out looking for one kind of thing and ended up selecting another. This was especially likely when they came across old media that hadn't been seen or heard for a long time, such as pictures of a child now several years older. These experiences often led to enjoyable excursions into forgotten territories of a music or photo collection. Within the constraints of the interviews, participants were sometimes observed to have these experiences and launch into spontaneous storytelling to the researchers, from either medium.

Further findings on the serendipitous discovery of old and new music from random shuffle have been reported by Leong and colleagues in Australia.[22] Interestingly, this effect is enhanced by the size of the music collection over which the shuffle operates. Back in the photographic domain, Hilliges and Kirk have tried to support serendipity over an entire photo collection, using a novel photo visualisation and control interface to a tabletop display.[23] The interface, called *PhotoHelix*, allows users to spread out multiple images for an event from a spiral-shaped calendar on the display, using a cylindrical control knob placed anywhere on the display surface. They show how it can lead to surprises and side-tracking in photo-talk

[21] Bentley et al. 2006.
[22] Leong et al. 2005; Leong et al. 2008.
[23] Hilliges and Kirk 2009.

between pairs of people, reviewing material together on the display. The same sort of side-tracking has been observed in more naturalistic interactions around printed photographs or those displayed on a shared computer screen.[24] Typically they occur in what Frohlich et al. (2011) call 'collaborative photowork', where photos are discovered and discussed among members of the family whilst being sorted or prepared for sharing.

While many of these practices apply to printed photo archives, others are specific to digital ones, which are easier to duplicate, edit, and distribute between devices and people. From the perspective of ordinary families, the full photo archive consists of a mixture of printed and digital photographs with interesting connections to other home media such as music, books, and video. The exponential increase in digital photo capture does not seem to have affected short-term photo storage and retrieval but is leading to a paradoxical mixture of frustration and delight in longer-term use as families forget what photographs they have taken and where they have put them, only to find them again via accidental browsing and discovery.

6.3 Camera Phone Use

Around the time Frohlich and colleagues were examining digital camera use by UK and US families (in 1998), a group of European researchers were examining the combined use of digital cameras and mobile phones by four Finnish boys and an Austrian family of seven.[25] This work pre-dated the launch of the first camera phones by Sharp in 2001 and Nokia in 2002 (discussed in Chap. 5) and consequently involved a different methodology. Instead of monitoring the uptake of commercial technology, the team ran a field trial of a prototype camera phone. This took the form of a large digital camera tethered to a laptop in a backpack, with software and hardware supporting image editing, combination, and transmission to similar prototype devices via GSM. The study was part of a European Union project called *Maypole*, investigating the future of family communications between 1997 and 1999. Nokia was a partner in the project, as were IDEO, Meru Research, the Centre for Usability Research and Engineering in Austria, and the Netherlands Design Institute. An overview of findings was reported in a special issue of *Interactions Magazine* at the end of 1999, in which there was a palpable sense of excitement.[26] Seppo Kari from Nokia was quoted in an interview as referring to wireless imaging as the next step in mobile telephony, involving a shift in emphasis 'from ears to eyes'.[27] Describing the camera phone trial, Kay Hofmeester, the project manager of Maypole, said this: "It worked! The results we saw gave us the feeling that we had stumbled on a phenomenon that was much broader and more interesting than we had dared expect".[28]

---

[24] Frohlich et al. 2011.

[25] Mäkelä et al. 2000.

[26] Hofmeester 1999.

[27] Seppo Kari quoted in Staal 1999, p. 65.

[28] Hofmeester *Ibid.*, p. 10.

They were right. From a photographic point of view, the addition of mobile communication to a digital camera gave consumers the opportunity to share images and experiences remotely in real time – speeding up the sharing process, which was already becoming the driver for digital photography in the home. From a mobile communication point of view, the addition of a digital camera allowed consumers to illustrate their conversations or messages with images – extending the communicative flexibility of the phone. Both values and behaviours were evident in the field trial. Unlike traditional snapshots of special occasions and holidays, trial participants took photographs of everyday life and sent them to each other to establish more frequent connections over the course of each day. Many images were deliberately playful and often combined together in sequences to form photo narratives. For example, the 12-year-old boys created visual jokes or fictitious movie scenes such as a murder. They also sent around pictures of their pets or girls they had seen. One boy even took screenshots of a computer game to help describe it to his friends. The parents in the Austrian family had less time and inclination to communicate like this but appreciated being sent images showing what their children or distant parents were doing. One parent, a grandmother of the children, had more time and crafted artistic images of her garden and life to share with her grandchildren. Most participants complained about the lack of text or sound-recording by which to explain the images to recipients, and this was recommended by the researchers as a design suggestion. Many of the prototype features were endorsed among these recommendations, including a review screen for local sharing, image editing facilities, multi-photo messages, and printing.

Many of the recommendations were taken up immediately in two follow-up studies by Ilpo Koskinen and colleagues at the University of Art and Design Helsinki. These were supported by Nokia again and Radiolinja, Finland's main mobile phone operator at the time. The first study, titled 'Mobile Image', conducted with 20 participants in 1999–2000, was a field trial of another prototype camera phone, in the form of a Casio digital camera and a Nokia Communicator 9110 mobile phone with infrared connection.[29] Software on the phone allowed images to be attached to e-mail messages sent to other phones by GPRS. The second study, Radiolinja MMS, conducted with 25 participants in 2002, was a field trial of the Nokia 7650 mobile phone with integrated multimedia messaging (MMS) incorporating pictures, sound, and text.[30] Hence these studies extended the original Maypole work by looking at the combination of photographs with text and sound, as used by a larger number of young adults.

In the Mobile Image study, participants exhibited the same kind of playful use of photographs as in the Maypole study to maintain social connections within groups of five friends. Humour and fun were intrinsic to many of the exchanges and involved friends teasing each other with pictures of attractive partners and activities, or staged and manipulated images of fake experiences. More details emerged on the

---

[29]Koskinen et al. 2002.
[30]Koskinen 2007.

Fig. 6.3 A picture message from Italy, sent in the Mobile Image study. The associated text reads as follows: "Terde, at 1100 metres +25C. Stuffed my face with pizza, birra and grappa" (Koskinen et al. 2002. Original title: A picture message from Italy. Republished with permission)

interactive features of image exchanges, in part because of the conversation-analytic orientation of the analysis. Almost all images were framed by text commentary in the e-mail body. For individual images, this comprised a greeting and sign-off with a brief reason for sending in between. When sent from a holiday destination, these had the character of a postcard, as shown in the message reproduced in Fig. 6.3. More typically, they were sent from everyday places, made to sound exotic. Individual messages were tailored to the interests and knowledge of the recipient, such that the same image received different text annotation for different recipients. Collections of images were often sent together as a photo narrative with interspersed text, or generated across the group in themed responses. 'Theming' was extremely common and involved replying to a photo with a photo concerning a similar topic, such as pictures of current boyfriends circulated in a group of five females.

In the Radiolinja study, the same style of image-based communication was observed but with additional features. Participants introduced third-party contacts, used pictures of hand and body gestures to signal to each other, took photographs of TV programmes to discuss, and circulated riddles and jokes. The capability to add sound to a message led to additional findings on sound–image–text combinations.[31] In general, sound was used much less frequently than text was with an image. Text was almost always used, whereas sound was used in only 13% of the 543 sampled messages. This meant that participants treated sound as an adjunct to an image+text message, which was the usual form. In fact, it appeared to be one particular group in the Radiolinja study who discovered the value of sound together and tended to use it in their photographic exchanges. Typical uses included verbal greetings, imitations of animal and human sounds (such as snoring), recordings of particular ambient sounds such as baby noises, and paralinguistic items (including singing, shouting, and laughing).

---

[31] Koskinen 2005.

These sounds appeared to add emotional depth to the messages rather than substantial linguistic content, which was left to the text portion. For example, in one multimedia message (Message 5.1) a birthday message in text was attached to a picture of flowers and combined with a badly sung rendition of 'Happy Birthday to You'. Koskinen also argued that ambient background sounds in each of the recordings provided additional cues to the location and context of the sender, which may have been important for the subsequent interaction. These findings were contrasted with those of Frohlich (2004) on audio–photo combinations recorded on audio-capturing cameras.[32] Whereas sound from a camera appeared to support the *memory* associated with an image and its discussion with others, sound on a camera phone appeared to support the *message* created from the image+text and its interpretation by others. This is not surprising, given the prominence of text messaging in MMS creation. The interface of this prototype has been carried forward into modern mobile phones and has involved the addition of secondary image and sound elements to a primary text message.[33] This introduces additional steps in the process of adding sound to an image and privileges text as the primary form.

All these early studies of camera phones were done as field trials of prototypes given out to small groups. As commercial camera phones became more common, a new set of more naturalistic studies was conducted, looking at the capture and sharing of images with off-the-shelf equipment and infrastructure. Two key studies in this category involved interviews with ordinary consumers in Japan, the UK, and the US. Here, Okabe and Ito at Keio University interviewed 15 people in Tokyo during the autumn of 2003.[34] In contrast to the field trial results reported above, Okabe described a much stronger personal use of camera phones for capturing more casual mementoes of everyday life. The images were less stylised than traditional family snapshots and depicted more mundane subjects, such as pets, landscapes, social events, and work scenes. But they were taken with the same intention of remembering intimate personal experiences in the future. These same photographs were often shown to others on the LCD display of the camera phone rather than sent remotely, although sharing was not the original motivation for capture. A new behaviour was visual note-taking for practical purposes, such as taking a photograph of a book to remember to buy it later. Some of the same playful exchanges of messages observed in the camera phone trials were described by Japanese camera-phone-owners. These included pictures of food, unusual objects, and events that were sent in the moment by e-mail or MMS to close family and friends. This appeared to extend a text messaging practice of establishing distributed co-presence by sending (picture) messages telling recipients what one is currently doing.

About 9 months later, in the summer of 2004, Kindberg and colleagues at HP and Microsoft interviewed 19 camera-phone-users in the UK's Bristol and Cambridge,

---

[32] Frohlich 2004.

[33] Koskinen, 2010, personal communication.

[34] Okabe and Ito 2003.

and 15 others in the San Francisco Bay area of the US.[35] They found similar practices to those seen with the Japanese consumers. In particular, e-mail and MMS sending of images was rare in comparison to sharing locally on the camera phone screen, and half of the images (51%) were taken for personal use. Those taken for social reasons were often to share with people who were with them at the time, as well as with absent family and friends, and there was a general split between photos taken for their affective and their functional value. This led the authors to propose a taxonomy of six reasons for image capture on a camera phone. These are listed below, with their definitions and examples from the paper:

1. **Individual personal reflection**: Affective images used for personal reflection or reminiscing. Example: Picture of a gift received.
2. **Individual personal task**: Functional images used to support some future task not involving sharing. Example: Picture of a car registration number after an accident.
3. **Social mutual experience**: Affective images used to enrich a shared, co-present experience. Example: A celebration in a pub.
4. **Social absent friend or family**: Affective images used to communicate with absent friends or family. Example: Picture of muddy boots at a music festival.
5. **Social mutual task**: Functional images shared with people co-present in support of a task. Example: Picture of a plumbing problem for diagnosis.
6. **Social remote task**: Functional images used to accomplish a task by sharing with remote family, friends, or colleagues. Example: Picture of a goldfish for the recipient to remember to feed.

At the time of this study, nine of the 34 participants were able to record video clips on their camera phones. However, these people took three times as many photos as videos and most activity was related to still image use. Later work reviewing the use of short video clips on camera phones and digital cameras is worth mentioning here in the context of digital photography. As it turns out, short video clips seem to be used like photographs to support some of the six values above, but in far fewer numbers than photographs themselves.

For example, in an attempt to understand *videowork* as well as *photowork*, Kirk and colleagues interviewed 12 families and seven teenagers in the UK to discuss their use of digital video.[36] This broke down into two forms of video use, 'lightweight' and 'heavyweight', based, respectively, on the *ad hoc* capture of short video clips on a camera / camera phone or the more deliberate capture of home video footage on a digital camcorder. Lightweight video use was characterised by spontaneous capture and consumption on the device itself to enhance a shared event (value 3 above) or share with absent family and friends later (value 4). Sometimes the later sharing would be done by uploading the video clips to a Web site, but more often than not it was done locally on the camera or camera phone. A further study of lightweight

---

[35] Kindberg et al. 2005.

[36] Kirk et al. 2007.

video use was conducted by Lehmuskallio and Sarvas in spring 2007 with 13 Finnish participants.[37] Users were interviewed at home about photo and video use, and seven were given camera phones for an 8-week period in which to capture new photo and video material. By comparing photo and video content and practices in this group, the authors were able to show that brief video clips were effectively used as 'living photographs' rather than as narrative forms of film. They called these clips *snapshot video* and showed how their content was similar to snapshots but captured in situations where sound and movement added to the memory or affective impact of the recording. Snapshot video clips were also stored, shared, and treated as snapshot photos are, leading to recommendations for integrating them with media editing, archiving, and sharing tools – including photo/video Web sites. These findings also gel with those on audio-photographs, which were captured very much in a point-and-shoot mode to enhance the atmosphere of a photograph with sound.[38] Further findings on camera phone use have been collected in the context of online and offline sharing of photos, and these will be mentioned in Sects. 6.4 and 6.5, below.

6.4 Online Photo Sharing

The earliest forms of electronic transmission of digital photos were made possible in the latter half of the 1990s via e-mail attachment and publication on self-made Web sites. These came to be supplemented by multimedia messaging on camera phones and through the use of commercial photo-oriented Web sites around 10 years later (see again Fig. 5.1). The launch of photo Web sites and camera phones on the consumer market at around the same time, in 2000 and 2001, respectively, led to a delayed burst of studies in the mid-2000s on their combined use.

Hence, the first studies of online photo sharing were a pair of independent field trials of prototype camera-Web systems for 'mobile image sharing'. We report on these here since they indicate styles of online photo sharing observed in later studies of commercial photo Web sites. *MobShare* was a Finnish system for adding camera phone images to an organised Web album[39] and sending notifications of these to selected recipients, while *MMM2* was an American system for doing the same thing with some implementation and interface differences.[40]

In general, both systems extended the functionality of the mobile blogging systems available at the time, by prioritising images and adding sharing features for group notification and access. For example, *MobShare* allowed users of the mobile phone part of the system to put newly captured images in folders for sharing. Contacts from the address book could then be associated with folders before sharing was performed by upload of the folder to a Web site and notification of

---

[37]Lehmuskallio and Sarvas 2008.
[38]See again Frohlich 2004.
[39]Sarvas et al. 2004b.
[40]Davis et al. 2005, and the predecessor MMM1 (Sarvas et al. 2004a).

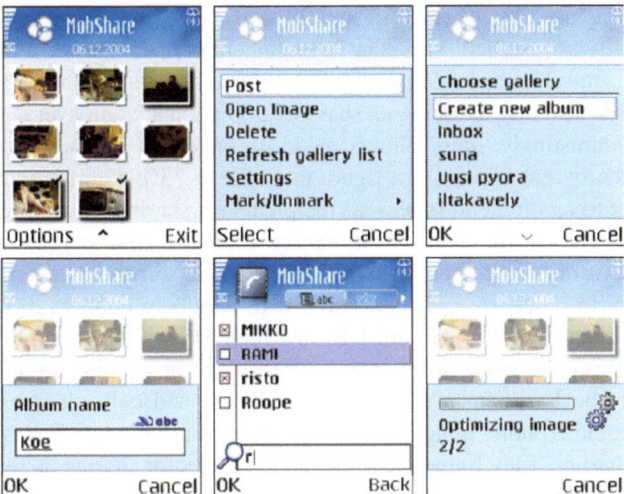

Fig. 6.4 The process for Internet photo sharing from a mobile phone running MobShare (Figure 1 in Sarvas et al. 2004b). Original title: MobShare screen shots. Republished with permission

contacts of the URL by SMS text message (see Fig. 6.4). Because of the limitations of mobile Web browsing at the time, users were expected to use an Internet-connected PC to browse and view the photos. Discussion of the images was also supported through text annotation of the original photos and subsequent text responses in the Web-based gallery. A similar process was used in *MMM2*, which allowed captioning of individual photos and sharing with a checklist of recipients via a Web site. After every capture, senders were asked whether they wanted to upload images, and recipients were informed of the destination URL by an e-mail message containing a thumbnail of the image.

Both systems were tested locally, in Finland and the US. MobShare was used for 5–6 weeks by five friends who were familiar with e-mail, Web browsing, and SMS but had not owned a camera phone before.[41] Each participant recorded an average of 24 photos a week (589 in total for everyone) and shared 89% of these with each other or any of 48 additional users in their contact lists. Most pictures (84%) were shared within 3 days of capture and commented on within 6 days of posting to the Web site (95%). This reflects the importance, found in other studies, of **recent** image sharing but shows that sharing was not always done immediately, even from camera phones equipped for this. In general, the sooner recipients visited a gallery after posting, the more likely they were to leave a comment. Discussion of photographs ranged from responses to initial comments and questions, personal perspectives on a shared event, observations on an unfolding drama (such as the birth of a dog), and thanks for a photo or social event.

---

[41] Sarvas et al. 2005.

MMM2 was used by 40 students and 20 staff at the University of California at Berkeley.[42] It was installed on Nokia 7610 camera phones that were in service for 5–9 months, from November 2004.[43] Analysis of student data from the first 6 weeks of the trial showed that participants shared 1,500 photos, at an average rate of one per day.[42] Interestingly, these photos made up only 57% of the total number of pictures taken by participants – a figure that rose to 75% with the introduction of an algorithm to recommend (guess at) recipients for sharing. Both figures are substantially lower than those in the *MobShare* trial, and they indicate that the US participants were taking more personal photographs on their camera phones or sharing them in other ways. This accords with Kindberg et al.'s (2005) survey of camera phone users in the US and UK, in which 51% of photographs were taken for personal use and many were shared face-to-face on the display of the camera itself. As in the Kindberg et al. study, Van House and colleagues examined the content of camera phone images with participants, but this time it was to infer the reason for sharing. They found the same range of uses for sharing as for capture, as shown in Kindberg et al.'s taxonomy, given in Sect. 6.3. However, to these they added self-expression and self-presentation, referring to the sharing of artistic images and self-portraits, respectively. This pointer to the sharing of images related to **identity** turned out to highlight a key behaviour observed on some commercial photo Web sites and social networking sites.

The first commercial photo Web sites, such as Snapfish and Kodak Gallery, were launched in the early 2000s and designed as online archives for family photographs. In fact, there was a debate in the industry at this time about whether families would move all their digital photographs from the home PC to the Web for long-term storage, whom they would trust to look after the images, and how much they would pay. Consequently, the facilities provided by these Web sites were more primitive than those of MobShare and MMM2, and simply allowed collections of images to be assembled in folders or albums for joint viewing by family and friends. Internet connection speeds tended to limit the sizes of images that could be conveniently uploaded to and downloaded from the Web, and also the effectiveness of additional features such as slide-show creation and sharing. This may also have been a factor contributing to families' tendency not to move their photo collections to the Web, although a bigger factor is likely to have been the volatility of Web companies and photo Web site services, which sometimes went out of business and could not be trusted with priceless memorabilia. These companies struggled to make money from hosting photographs and still rely on income from advertising and online printing services, which compete with offline print shops, public kiosks, and home printers. Nevertheless, they continue to be used by large numbers of people for simple online photo sharing and exchange. Along with e-mail photo attachment, simple posting to a gallery Web site from a computer may account for the majority of online photo exchange in the world today. This was indirectly confirmed in a

---

[42] Van House et al. 2005.

[43] Van House and Ames 2010 (unpublished work).

small-scale study by Miller and Edwards of online photo sharing, featuring Flickr as an example of a new class of social networking Web site.[44]

Flickr is essentially a gallery of sorts but supports the tagging of photos and photo elements with multiple keywords and phrases. This means that users can express who is in their photos and what the photo content is, and use these tags to browse through their own and other people's photo collections in a more flexible way than fixed folders and albums allow. They can also make comments on photographs, leading to threaded discussions and blogs on photo content. This functionality brings more of the social interaction that traditionally took place verbally around printed photos into the online domain and fixes it there as a record of interaction for others to see and add to over time. An example screenshot from a typical Flickr page is shown in Fig. 6.5 for reference.

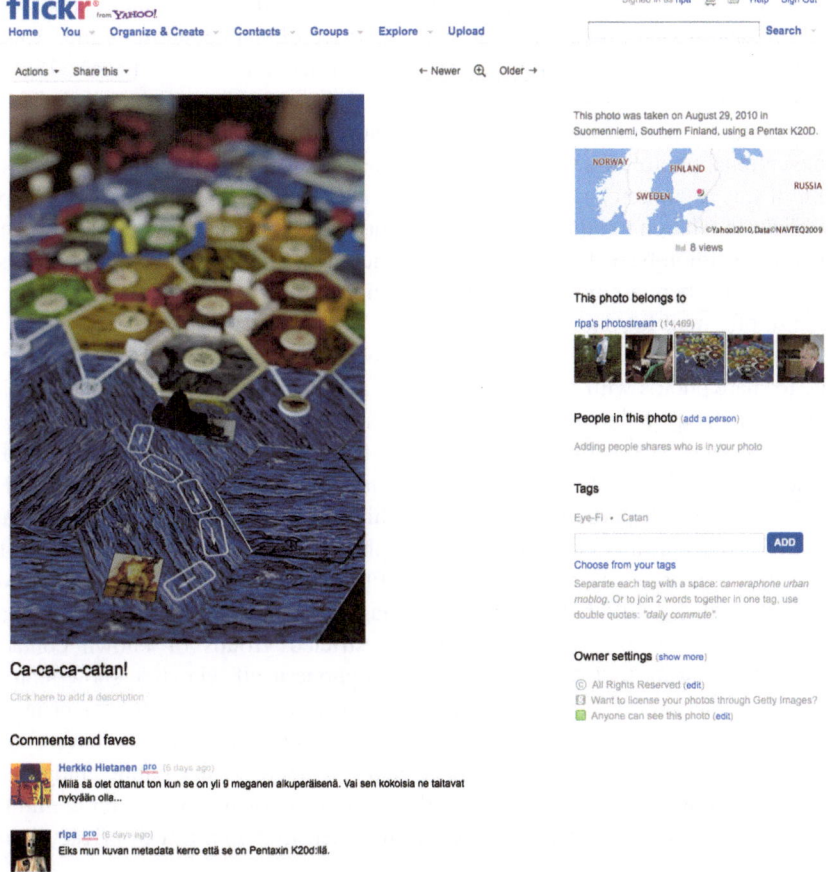

Fig. 6.5 A screenshot from a Flickr photo collection (Reproduced with permission of Yahoo! Inc. © 2010 Yahoo! Inc. YAHOO!, the YAHOO! logo, FLICKR and the FLICKR logo are registered trademarks of Yahoo! Inc.)

---

[44]Miller and Edwards 2007.

In the US study by Miller and Edwards, 10 people from Atlanta, Georgia, aged between 30 and 50, were interviewed in 2006 about their digital photo practices. Five participants were recruited from a Flickr group and reported photo sharing behaviours quite different from others'. The rest exhibited classic 'Kodak Culture' behaviour and shared digital photographs with family and friends primarily by e-mail but also by means of prints and a variety of photo Web sites, depending on their costs and benefits. Those recruited through Flickr were referred to as 'Snaprs' and shared digital photos with strangers as well as family and friends, primarily through Flickr and its tagging mechanisms. This group shared an interest in the artistic properties of photographs and appeared to use Flickr as a kind of online camera club for viewing and discussing photographs, some of which were taken on 'photo-strolls' with local Flickr users. The photographs in this case were used to reflect the photographic abilities of authors and reinforce their identities as amateur photographers. These two groups had quite different attitudes to photo annotation, sharing, and privacy. The Flickr group were more organised, more willing to tag, and more open to sharing their photos without restriction.

Subsequent work has explored Flickr use and tagging in more detail, leaving a noticeable absence of research on the more mundane but pervasive practice of using conventional photo Web sites and e-mail attachment for online sharing. An indication of this asymmetry is given by recent statistics on the number of photographs in Flickr in relation to other Web sites. In April 2009, the ImageShack Web site had 20 billion, Photobucket had 7.2 billion, and Flickr 3.4 billion unique images.[45] Despite this, there are no published studies of Photobucket or Snapfish use, nor of the use of e-mail for photo sharing.

Further work on Flickr has shown that Kodak Culture people are now using the site to share photos with restricted groups of family and friends for communication and relationship maintenance, if not for memory archiving. This conclusion was based on interviews with 12 Flickr users in the US.[46] A more recent study by the same author and her colleagues confirmed this finding in a 3–5-month field trial of Flickr with 26 US participants.[47] In fact, this work replicated the MobShare and MMM2 trials with Nokia N80 camera phones and commercial software for uploading and browsing mobile images on Flickr (ZoneTag and Zurfer). It showed that, although only a sub-set of captured images were uploaded to Flickr, the main benefit of doing so was to share with restricted groups of known contacts. Additional sharing took place on the camera phone itself, via slide-show features built in to the gallery function of the device or provided on Zurfer for browsing Flickr remotely. Further studies of tagging in Flickr and ZoneTag have shown interest by early adopters in tagging to help members of the public find posted images, although most tags are designed for personal organisation or for communication with family and friends.[48] Users remain sensitive to a raft of privacy issues

[45] TechCrunch 2009.

[46] Van House 2007.

[47] Ames et al. 2010.

[48] Ames and Naaman 2007.

connected with expanding access to their personal photographs, and they worry about new dilemmas such as how to control images of them taken by others.[49]

The final chapter to date in the story of sharing photos online concerns the introduction of social networking sites such as MySpace, Facebook, and Twitter. All of these sites integrate text messaging, media sharing, and contact management in the same application.[50] Photos can be posted as personal profile images or associated image collections but serve in either case to support text-based communication as the primary function. This reverses the situation in Flickr and other photo Web sites containing text annotation and commentary, where photo sharing is the primary function. While much has been written about the network structures and social behaviours associated with these kinds of sites, their use as a means of photo sharing remains un-researched. For example, photographs are mentioned as a subsidiary motive for using Facebook, but their use within the system has yet to be examined.[51]

6.5 Offline Photo Sharing

Given all the media and research attention on the World Wide Web and its transformative effect on social communication, one might be forgiven for thinking that most digital photos are shared online today. This is not true. Online photo sharing is an important component of contemporary domestic photography in the West, as shown above, but offline photo sharing is equally important and probably more pervasive. Indeed, conventional methods of displaying printed photos in domestic settings are historically more established and are better supported than ever before with digital printing technology. Families can now order a wide range of printed photo products in person or over the Web, ranging from posters and photo books to t-shirts and coffee cups. They can also print variable-sized photographs and collages on inexpensive or portable printers of their own. Furthermore, as the infrastructure for digital photography has grown, there has been a proliferation of options for the display of images on screens. These range from the LCD screen on the back of a digital camera or camera phone to every imaginable shape and size of screen on desktop, laptop, and handheld computers, as well as on television sets, game devices, and media players. Add to these the growth of digital photo frames since 2005 and current developments in pico-projectors and tabletop displays, and we begin to see a rich paper-and-screen landscape for the display and sharing of images *locally*, as well as globally over the Internet.

The importance of co-located social practices surrounding photos has been underscored recently in a special issue of that name in the *International Journal of Human–Computer Studies*.[52] We begin with two key papers from that issue to

---

[49] Ahern et al. 2007; Besmer and Lipford 2009.

[50] Boyd and Ellison 2008.

[51] Joinson 2008.

[52] Lindley et al. 2009.

introduce what is known about offline photo sharing from these and other studies. In many ways, this behaviour is the most complex aspect of domestic photography to summarise, because of the number of technological options available and the absence of research on many of them. The tendency in the literature is to study the latest and most novel of options first, preferably ahead of their market launch. This is the opposite of what we need in this review to describe the ongoing or modified practices of families 'doing photography' under very new technical and social conditions. For this purpose, studies of the most popular and resilient commercial technologies are often the most instructive. We will return to this issue at the end of the chapter and book, but for now we turn to two studies that take a broad view of offline photo sharing and how it is done in the family home.

Van House (2010)[53] draws on four studies of family photography conducted with colleagues between 2004 and 2007 to outline a range of co-located sharing practices in US households. These span the use of most of the paper- and screen-based technologies mentioned above, placed and prioritised within their varying social contexts. For example, loose prints and albums are still valued as aids to storytelling and continue to be proudly displayed in frames and *ad hoc* collages around the home. Participants were aware of the memorial value of displayed images and of how they can act as 'conversation pieces' with visitors to the home. The availability of additional ways of sharing photos on-screen appears to have both extended these behaviours and made them more selective. Digital prints are likely to be fewer and more 'special' than analogue ones, and supplemented by digital photo sharing mainly on capture devices and computers. Camera phones in particular often contain collections of recent images that are brought out in conversation to illustrate a point. Larger collections are shown at home on desktop computer screens or laptop computers. Laptops are often preferred within the home because of the flexibility with which they can be positioned when compared with desktops, which may be in inconvenient locations for sharing. Families reported viewing photographs from remote online galleries such as Flickr as well as from local filing systems, giving further flexibility to the location of sharing. There was also some evidence in a minority of families of co-ordinating digital slide shows or creating digital stories. These practices echo the analogue slide shows of previous years, in which a sequence of images is shown with accompanying spoken narrative. Digital storytelling can be seen as a kind of recorded digital slide show containing the narrative normally delivered live to a co-present audience. This creative and performative potential of digital photography was stressed in the discussion of findings, and it emerged again in the following study.

Durrant and colleagues (2009a)[54] at the University of Surrey and Microsoft Research reveal conflicts in eight UK family homes over the management and display of their photograph collections. Using a creative photo selection task and phenomenological analysis of responses, the authors examine long-term practices of photo

---

[53] Van House 2009.

[54] Durrant et al. 2009a.

curation in the home rather than short-term practices of photo sharing. The findings show that the traditional domestic order of mothers taking responsibility for organising, displaying, and distributing family photographs is being undermined by digital technology. This appears to benefit teenage children in photo organisation and sharing, both inside and outside the home. Hence more family members in the study were able to take digital as compared to analogue photographs, including surprisingly young children who had never had access to film cameras before. Furthermore, older children and teenagers were able to file and use the images with more skill and creativity than their mothers, who felt frustrated and disempowered by digital technology. Teens assisted and collaborated with their parents in determining how they and the family were portrayed on computer displays within the home. However, they also used the technology for personal expression through printed photo collages and online photo sharing, free of parental control. This reveals a new complexity to the management of multi-author photo collections within the family, and the need for more careful design attention to the *politics* of photo display.

Together, these studies show the importance of two key factors in the organisation of offline photo sharing: the physical properties of the photo display and the span of time over which display is managed. Physicality can be broken down crudely into paper- versus screen-based representation, although many refinements of each category can be made. Temporality can also be split into long-term curation and short-term sharing, although these are relative terms with gradations within and between categories. The interaction between the two factors gives rise to four kinds of co-present sharing, shown in Table 6.1. Paper- and screen-based forms of SHARING and CURATION will now be considered in turn, as a way of structuring the literature pre-dating the above-mentioned studies and filling in details of the behaviours they describe.

Printed photo sharing is remarkably under-researched, given its importance as a commonplace form of storytelling in conversation and a source of design inspiration for screen-based photo sharing. It was first examined in detail as part of the photoware study by Frohlich et al. 2002,[55] although only a summary of findings was presented in that paper. More detailed findings on the dynamics of a corpus of 80 audio-recorded photo sharing episodes spanning 15 h of photo-talk are reported in Chap. 7 in Frohlich's 2004 work.[56] The full analysis was led by Steven Ariss from

Table 6.1 Four types of offline photo sharing

	Sharing	Curation
Paper	Printed photo sharing	Printed photo curation
Screen	Screen-based photo sharing	Screen-based photo curation

[55] Frohlich et al. 2002.

[56] Frohlich 2004.

the University of York, using a conversation-analytic approach. This involved looking at the turn-by-turn organisation of utterances in collections of transcribed episodes, for systematic patterns and dynamics. Although physical movements and photographs were missing from the audio-recordings, it was nevertheless possible to identify verbal references to images and the way in which these functioned in the activity.

Three significant discoveries were reported in the longer write-up. First, a striking difference could be heard between two types of photo-talk. This hinged on whether some or all of the participants shared the memory of the photographs being discussed. If all did, this resulted in what was called *reminiscing* talk (60% of episodes), characterised by mixed-initiative dialogue in which everyone chipped in comments, often in overlap and usually to remark on the physical characteristics of the images and identify the time or context in which they were taken. If only some of the participants shared the memory, this resulted in *storytelling* talk (29% of episodes), dominated and led by the photograph-owners to convey photo-stories and meanings to the others. Mixed groups were also found in the corpus, comprising two or more people who were present when the photos were taken, sharing them with one or more people who weren't. This resulted in a mixture of storytelling and reminiscing talk (11% of episodes) characterised by collaborative storytelling, such as observed by Edwards and Middleton (1986) in group discussion of films.[57] A second major finding was that audiences were very active participants in steering the course of the talk itself. In fact, the word 'audience' did not really apply to participants in reminiscing talk, who were empowered by their knowledge of the photographs to remark on any individual feature or association. In storytelling talk, where the audiences were those without knowledge of the photographs, they still interjected questions and expressions of interest in particular images, which served to trigger stories or steer their elaboration and closure. This interaction tended to result in the telling of stories about individual images and sometimes led to the telling of *reciprocal stories* by audiences. Finally, by examining multiple sharings of the same photos with different people, it was clear that storytellers tailored their stories to the audience at hand. This is called *recipient design* and involves attention not only to audience talk but also to the relationship between storyteller and audience member, and the impression the story is intended to make. This did **not** extend to the telling of different stories concerning the same photos, but it did affect the wording and emphasis used.

Using video-recordings of two printed photo sharing sessions from UK families, Crabtree et al. (2004)[58] point out features of the visual conduct not available in Frohlich's audio data. In the first session, four adult members of an extended family share a loose set of prints with each other and two of their young children. The photos are passed between some of the participants and also picked up freely from the pile at will. This results in distributed control of which photo is discussed at any moment, and in changing orientations and distances from which it is viewed by each person.

---

[57] Edwards and Middleton 1986.

[58] Crabtree et al. 2004.

In the second session, two adult members of a family are shown old family photos assembled by a third. Questions about the identity of people in the photographs are resolved and answered with the aid of various pointing and circling gestures over the images. The authors suggest that such complex behaviours are enabled by the physical properties of printed photos and will be difficult to support on-screen or at a distance. This point is also underscored by Frohlich (2004), who shows how poorly the linear 'slideshow model of photo-talk', used in most screen-based photo viewing applications, stacks up to the non-linear and interactive forms of printed photo sharing he observed.

Screen-based photo sharing was investigated directly by Lindley and Monk (2006).[59] In interviews with six individuals from four UK families in 2005, they discussed the pros and cons of various screen-based options for photo sharing. In general, screen display of photos was valued for being large-scale when compared to 6" by 4" prints, enabling image details to be seen more easily by a group. As Van House[60] did, they found that desktop computers were not always in the most sociable or convenient locations for photo sharing, leading to seating or standing arrangements wherein audience members had to 'hover' behind the photographer. The preferred arrangement was in a 'huddle' beside the photographer. This was reported to be possible with prints or a laptop when only two or three people were involved. Laptop screens were criticised for their narrow viewing angle, as was slide-show software for inhibiting conversation. As predicted by Frohlich, mentioned above, photographers reported frustration with trying to fit commentary to the speed of slide transition, while audiences complained of having to view too many photos with similar shots of the same thing. Looking at photos on a television screen from a physically connected digital camera was viewed more favourably, apart from the lower image resolution and short lead, which meant that the photographer often had to crouch on the floor beside the TV set. The authors also noted a contrast between control of printed and screen-based photo sharing, such that prints and albums were often passed to an audience whereas mouse or camera control of screen-based photos was not.

Seating and control factors were subsequently explored further in two follow-up experiments.[61] In the first experiment, groups of three friends discussed 12 photographs from a near-vertical tablet PC display, in a semi-circle or triangle of chairs (see Fig. 6.6). The photographers always sat nearest the display, and photographs were varied across reminiscing sessions (where the event depicted was known to all parties) or storytelling sessions (where it was not). Conversation measurements were taken throughout, and participants filled in user experience rating scales between conditions. Reminiscing talk contained more turns and overlaps than story-telling talk did, irrespective of seating arrangement, as observed for printed photo sharing.[62] However, sitting alongside the photographer led to significantly more

[59] Lindley and Monk 2006.

[60] Van House 2009.

[61] Lindley and Monk 2008.

[62] Frohlich 2004.

Fig. 6.6 Two seating arrangements for screen-based photo sharing (Reprinted from Fig. 3 in Lindley and Monk 2008. Original title: Two seating arrangements for screen-based photo sharing. Republished with permission)

equal and free conversation and an experience reported as better, than did sitting behind the photographer. Side-by-side seating also resulted in about twice as much socially directed gaze (i.e., time spent looking at each other), creating greater awareness of audience reaction and overall audience engagement. Similar findings emerged in a second experiment, on shared control of screen-based photographs, using three remote-control units in semi-circular seating around a TV screen, rather than one. In addition, there was more overlapping talk in the shared-control condition and participants reported a stronger element of fun when they had their own remote controls. This was mainly due to zooming in and out on details of the photos rather than reversing or advancing the photograph sequence. Conversely, a photographer holding the only remote control felt as if he was giving a formal presentation.

Related work on the vertical and horizontal orientation of workgroup displays shows that each has different affordances for collaboration and conversation.[63] Vertical displays could accommodate larger groups, which could change in size, and ensured that everyone could maintain a similar viewing angle. Horizontal displays were better for collaboration within smaller groups and facilitated more fluid conversation and role-switching. Combining these insights on working document displays with those on (vertical) PC and TV photo sharing above suggests that multi-touch tabletop displays may be optimal for screen-based photo discussions, as long as the photographs can be easily reoriented on the table. These displays are starting to be explored by a number of groups to good effect and are likely to change the landscape for live domestic photo sharing as their cost decreases (see, e.g., Apted et al. 2006 and Kirk et al. 2010).

A final development in the emerging practice of photo sharing on screens is suggested by work on handheld photo viewers. Stelmaszewska and colleagues[64] report the findings of interviews with 11 adults from the UK about *where* they shared a selection of digital photographs taken on their camera phones. While the home was said to be one of the most convenient places in which to share photographs, several

---

[63]Rogers and Lindley 2004.
[64]Stelmaszewska et al. 2008.

other locations were mentioned also as popular sharing sites. These included bars and cafés, which were noisy but sociable; restaurants, where circumstances were calmer and more organised; and parties in other people's homes or public venues, which were highly interactive. Camera phones were said to be shown to others or passed around groups in all of these places, often with attempts to swap photos phone to phone via Bluetooth. This was said to work well with small numbers of close contacts in quiet surroundings but not for sharing with a larger group of mixed contacts. Participants were concerned about the privacy of their personal data, the security of their phones, and the inability to explain their photographs in these conditions, leading the authors to recommend lockable folders and Bluetooth broadcast to a collection of selected phones. A variation of this idea using Wi-Fi multicasting has been explored recently in an experimental setting.[65] The authors found that groups of four friends could effectively share a photo set by simultaneously browsing it on four phones, as long as control rested clearly with one person. In an alternative approach, Balabanović et al. (2000) explored the usefulness of a single handheld tablet for collaborative photo sharing and storytelling.[66] This was tested with seven pairs of US participants, in a study in which a primary user showed photos to a secondary user and later recorded a digital story for sending to a hypothetical recipient. The larger screen allowed both members of a pair to view and point to images clearly, but the weight of the device led to its use on the knees of one participant. It was usually held and operated by the primary user, although there were some instances of shared operation and passing of a device to the secondary user. Storytelling was organised as either commentary on each photo in turn ('photo-driven') or a verbal story illustrated with related photographs ('story-driven'). Audio-recording was performed only for remote recipients and usually after all the relevant images had been assembled. As we now know, tablet viewers of this kind have not become common in the 10 years since this study was conducted. However, the new range of electronic photo frames and the recent launch of the iPad from Apple both provide new platforms from which this kind of photo sharing could increase.

Printed photo curation in family homes appears to be just as complex as printed photo sharing is. Again there is relatively little research on the topic, but such research as there is reveals a range of practices making use of the versatility of printed photographs for being displayed in different ways. Drazin and Frohlich (2007)[67] refer to these as *framing* practices because they relate to the material form in which printed photos are displayed and located for particular audiences and purposes. In a study of nine UK families in 2002, they examined framing practices as part of a more general discussion of photo sharing and annotation. Four kinds of framing were discovered. *Disposable photographs* were loose prints that were never put on display but never really disposed of either. In some ways, these were

---

[65] Kun and Marsden 2007.

[66] Balabanović et al. 2000.

[67] Drazin and Frohlich 2007.

Fig. 6.7 A rogues gallery of photographs and other reminders (Reprinted from Fig. 2 in Drazin and Frohlich 2007. Original title: A rogues gallery of photographs and other reminders. Republished with permission)

photographs in a default unframed state, stored away in forgotten corners of the home. *Rogues gallery* photographs were loose photographs displayed in informal collections on corkboards, fridge doors, and walls. They were often displayed alongside hand-written notes, postcards, letters, and bills, as in Fig. 6.7. This indicates their transient nature and practical purpose in serving as iconic reminders of people to keep in touch with, replies to send, or actions to perform. *Album* photographs were those selected, combined, and positioned in book form with a view to 'long-term future remembering'. Mothers were usually the creators and curators of albums. Although the latest albums were kept out and shown to visitors, older albums were archived for future reference by members of the family. *Framed* photographs were those given the most formal and prominent display, in cardboard, wooden, plastic, or metal frames. These were often of individual people and were hung on the wall or placed on a shelf near other types of objects, such as ornaments or trophies. Like these, framed photos appeared to mark and commemorate relationships, times of life, or achievements of lasting significance in the life of the owner. While photographs are usually thought of as direct triggers to remembering the past, the authors argued that photograph displays of all these kinds act as more or less public triggers for 'remembering to remember' in the future. In this respect, they announce an *intention to remember*, and never forget, the subjects featured in the photographs.

More recent work by Swan and Taylor (2008)[68] confirms and extends these findings with greater attention to the location and arrangement of particular images. From home tours and interviews with six families in London, they report collections of family relations on a mantelpiece, wedding photos on a sideboard, family portraits on a 'family wall', *ad hoc* events represented on a bookcase, and a collage of children's art in a home office. Many of these areas are said to have a shrine-like quality and were treated with considerable respect.

Screen-based photo curation is a natural extension of paper-based curation but requires a form of *situated* display that can present and refresh photographic material over sustained periods of time (cf. O'Hara et al. 2004[69]). The new class of wireless electronic photo frames, such as those by Kodak, are highly suitable for this purpose, as they provide a new and dedicated display for photographs in the home and can be fed from a variety of sources. These include a USB stick, camera memory card, or local computer, as well as a remote Web site or even a remote mobile phone. Screensavers on existing computer screens or TVs might also serve this purpose but suffer from primary use for other purposes. Surprisingly little work has been done on situated photo displays in this context, and we can find no studies examining the uptake of commercial displays in the home.

One early paper on smart digital photo frames, by Kim and Zimmerman (2006),[70] outlines the possibility of a context-aware photo frame that reacts to the presence of different users of a display to adjust its content to their interests. However, this does not seem to have been subsequently built and tested by the authors. In a development of their previous work on printed photo curation, Taylor, Swann and Durrant go on to speculate about a network of photo displays designed to work together in different ways, using photos from a shared home archive.[71] Three possible displays are introduced in this work as design suggestions, on the basis of findings about paper photo curation in 15 UK families:

- **Photo mesh** – a circular touchscreen collage that cycles randomly through photos from the home collection and responds to direct selection. It can also function as a point of upload to the collection.
- **Photo switch** – a rectangular photo display with a sliding door for presenting one photo at a time from two photograph collections. Sliding the door over one side of the display obscures a photograph from one collection, which fades to black and changes randomly after 15 min.
- **Photo illume** – a light-sensitive frame for single photo presentation that fades to black and moves on to a new image if not stimulated by light.

Each of these displays was subsequently built and exhibited in 2008, when Photoswitch was also trialled.[72] Mothers and daughters from four UK households

---

[68] Swan and Taylor 2008.

[69] O'Hara et al. 2004.

[70] Kim and Zimmerman 2006.

[71] Taylor et al. 2007.

[72] Durrant et al. 2008; Durrant et al. 2009.

put 12 photos each into the device and lived with it for about a month. In addition to seeing more of their digital photos displayed in the home, the participants valued showing each other their selected photos of self and family. This triggered conversation between them and others in the family about the reasons for selection and the photos themselves. This included disagreements on preferences for certain photographs, and corresponding behaviour to cover them from display or defend them from disappearing. The device was also effective in eliciting views about the relationship between the content and location of displays, the duration of image display, and the balance between manual and automatic control over photographs. Although this work does not suggest an emerging new practice for screen-based photo curation in the home, it does indicate the 'play of possibilities'[73] for more interactive, dynamic, and automatic presentation of photos than people are used to with paper prints.

6.6   Current Photo Ecologies

So far in this chapter, we have reviewed the way in which the infrastructure for digital photography has been built over the last 20 years and been adopted, piece by piece. What started as a home photo lab designed to put 'development' and printing in the hands of families themselves has ended up becoming a veritable home photo *factory* (see again Fig. 5.2, in Chap. 5). This is centred on the home computer and allows family members to capture, edit, store, distribute, and display photographs across a variety of devices both within and outside the home. Keeping the factory going is now a maintenance and upgrade job in its own right, as Norman has recently pointed out for all forms of computing infrastructure.[74] He recommends spending more time on understanding and designing the infrastructure, before it gets too complicated to manage and use. Two final pieces of work are beginning to do this, and these are described here as a way of attending to infrastructure issues in family photography and opening up the ensuing discussion of its effects on photographic practice and visual culture in general.

In a recent analysis of the everyday use of objects, Shove et al. (2007)[75] examined the adoption of digital photography by a variety of individuals in the north of England. By focusing on the photography *careers* of amateur family photographers, the authors avoid an overemphasis on particular devices and show how existing film/print skills and routines transfer to new digital/screen context and technologies. At one extreme they cite John, who simply substitutes a Kodak Easyshare C300 for his film camera and takes its memory card for processing and printing at a popular chemist's.

---

[73] Anderson 1994.

[74] Norman 2009.

[75] Shove et al. 2007.

At the other extreme is Louise, a teenager who, because of the cost of film and processing, has never really been encouraged to take analogue photos. Like other teenagers in the study, she has been enabled to take and share photos on her camera phone and the family's compact digital camera, which she borrows from time to time. The importance of the computer for the storage and online sharing of images privileges Louise, and others like her, who have existing computer skills they can now apply to photography. At the same time, it created barriers for some of the older members of a camera club in the study, who had to invest in new computer equipment, editing software, and associated learning in order to reap the benefits of the image manipulation previously done in a darkroom. Some became evangelistic converts, but only after considerable time, effort, and persistence that was lacking in more casual snapshot photographers.

Switching to a family unit of analysis, Neustaedter and Fedorovskaya (2009)[76] discussed patterns of photo flow through 'digital photo ecosystems', as revealed by one or more informants in each of 22 US families. They found that family members adopted different roles in family photography, according to their age, expertise, and gender. Families were able to point to individual members acting as primary capturer, organiser, and display manager, and these were different people in the majority of households. The roles were usually taken by the adult parents of each family, with more mothers than fathers across the sample. This imbalance was lowest for primary capturers (14:5) and highest for primary display managers, all of whom were mothers. The fact that different people often took these roles in each family was important for photo management because it meant that the knowledge of what photos had been taken, where they had been stored, and for whom they had been shared and displayed was distributed between individuals. This was accentuated by the fact that there could be several family members in *secondary* roles, also taking photographs, storing them, and displaying them.

This arrangement grows even more complicated when one considers the path along which individual photos travel. The authors distinguished between primary and secondary paths, which could be digital (in electronic format) or print. Somewhat surprisingly, they found that the majority of households (13) used a primary path that involved printing most of their photos. Eight of these families printed via a computer to a home printer, kiosk, or online print service, while five printed straight from the camera. The remaining nine families kept the majority of their photos in digital form, using a variety of devices on which to store and display them. This led to distributed storage of photos across devices, with considerable duplication and redundancy. The authors went on to explore a set of design concepts for ubiquitous collection, ubiquitous sharing, and automatic updating of displays, as mechanisms for unifying and automating various aspects of home photo flow. The first two concepts met with the most positive reactions but revealed additional requirements for privacy, selection, and control of images within a single collection.

---

[76] Neustaedter and Fedorovskaya 2009b.

6.7 Discussion

We have seen from this review that many of the same processes of innovation, marketing, and assimilation of technology as were present in the film era of photography have been evident also in the digital era. The introduction of new technologies such as the digital camera, the home photo archive, the camera phone, the photo Web site, and electronic photo displays has in each case presented families with new ways of taking and using photographs that they have had to learn, accept, or reject in relation to what they did before. The affordability of each technology and its fit with existing practices and abilities have been as important as its functionality and design in determining success in the market. Some technologies, such as the home photo printer, have met with less success than expected, because of the cost of paper and ink as compared to the negligible cost of display on-screen. Other technologies, such as the camera phone, have seen more success than expected, by extending the range of contexts in which images can be captured and making them easier to share. Even here, issues of cost and complexity have affected how images are shared, mitigating against extensive use of multimedia messaging in favour of local sharing on the camera phone screen or uploading to computers and Web sites. The current complexity of photo ecosystems and of the flow of images around them continues to provide new opportunities for family photography and support for photographic 'careers' that can grow and change over time. A major effect of all these options has been to democratise photography within the family, involving many more, younger and older, members than before and increasing the total number of photographs captured. This is also personalising photography, whereby each family member is beginning to take more control of his or her own photographs and to share them more widely outside the family, in both private and public spheres.

Given such heterogeneous technical and social context for digital photography today, it is hard to point to a single dominant design that is emerging as the replacement for the film camera and printed snapshot. The digital camera and camera phone have become the surrogate gatehouses to a network of technologies and activities that now allow images to be used in a myriad of ways. Individuals are still coming to terms with the options that suit them best as members of friendship and community groups, as well as members of their local and extended family. Hence the 'era of ferment' for digital photography is still very much with us, with little prospect of subsiding in a traditional way. Indeed, the nature of this domain casts doubt on the model of technology adoption proposed by Anderson and Tushman[77] as outlined in Chap. 2. This is something we will discuss further in the next chapter, along with how the Digital Path is likely to stabilise.

For now, we wish to note simply that the use of photographs for memory, communication, and identity is evident in all of the digital photography activities reviewed above and continues to underpin the value of these images in a domestic context.

---

[77] Anderson and Tushman 1990.

Although the new possibilities for image assembly, combination, and annotation have led some authors to suggest *creative expression* as a new value for digital photography today,[78] we believe this can be seen as an extension of the identity value for the representation of self. We therefore agree with Van Dijck (2008)[79] that memory, communication, and identity still provide the motivation for digital photography but in different degrees than for film photography, and with very different manifestations.

Our review suggests that communication has surpassed memory as the primary function of domestic photography, and that identity is now fighting for second place. Whereas the family album was the intended end result of family photography in the film era, the digital home archive has taken its place as a source of family memories. Online photo archives serve as memory sources for more distributed communities. Inspection of the content of these archives and the way in which they are shared reveals a large number of casual and mundane images used to show someone or other a fleeting glimpse of the *present*. From playful camera phone jokes to tagged images of pets or street signs on Flickr, many of these images have no lasting value beyond their use for immediate communication and are in sharp contrast with album snapshots selected for posterity. The practice of tagging and discussing such content reinforces its ephemeral nature: time-stamping and fixing interpretations that were once ambiguous and fluid. Ironically, the original use of the album to house *carte-de-visite* images of visitors and friends has resurfaced on social networking sites such as Facebook. Young users now craft profile images of themselves to convey changing identities and affiliations, and they collect those of friends they want to see and be seen with.

Returning to Slater's speculations about the impact of digitisation on family photography,[80] we can now see that he was right about the stability of photography's values but also about the importance of the integration of photography into a new 'economy of images'. Photo flow is now part of a new photo ecosystem, extending beyond the boundaries of the home, and is beginning to mix private with public images as Slater predicted. Individual family members can now take their own images and tell their own stories, unmediated by parental control or children's censorship. New forms of online and offline photo display allow temporary 'acts of practical communication' with images, replacing the album metaphor with a kind of rogues gallery corkboard or photograph wall for the digital age. Freedom from both the constraints of the family album and reliance on traditional mass media may ultimately lead to more democratic accounts of domestic, local, and global events, as Slater also suggested.

In the next chapter, we look back over the entire history of the snapshot to continue this speculation and make some predictions of our own. This also allows us to draw out some general lessons for the study of domestic photography in HCI, science and technology studies, and visual culture and to consider how these approaches could work together in future research.

---

[78] Van House 2009.

[79] Van Dijck 2008.

[80] Slater 1995.

References

Ahern S, Eckles D, Good NS, King S, Naaman M, Nair R (2007) Over-exposed?: privacy patterns and considerations in online and mobile photo sharing. In: Proceedings of the SIGCHI conference on human factors in computing systems, San Jose, 2007. ACM, New York, pp 357–366

Ames M, Naaman M (2007) Why we tag: motivations for annotation in mobile and online media. In: Proceedings of the SIGCHI conference on human factors in computing systems, San Jose, 2007. ACM, New York, pp 971–980

Ames M, Eckles D, Naaman M, Spasojevic M, Van House N (2010) Requirements for mobile photoware. Pers Ubiquit Comput 14(2):95–109

Anderson R (1994) Representation and requirements: the value of ethnography in system design. Hum Comput Interact 9(2):151–182

Anderson P, Tushman M (1990) Technological discontinuities and dominant designs: a cyclical model of technological change. Adm Sci Q 35(4):604–633

Apted T, Kay J, Quigley A (2006) Tabletop sharing of digital photographs for the elderly. In: Proceedings of the SIGCHI conference on human factors in computing systems, Montreal, 2006, pp. 781–790. ACM

Balabanović M, Chu L, Wolff G (2000) Storytelling with digital photographs. In: Proceedings of the SIGCHI conference on human factors in computing systems (CHI '00), The Hague, 1 Apr 2000. ACM, New York, pp 564–571

Bentley F, Metcalf C, Harboe G (2006) Personal vs. commercial content: the similarities between consumer use of photos and music. In: Proceedings of the SIGCHI conference on human factors in computing systems, Montreal, 2006. ACM, New York, pp 667–676

Besmer A, Lipford H (2009) Tagged photos: concerns, perceptions, and protections. In: Proceedings of the 27th international conference on human factors in computing systems, Boston, 2009. ACM, New York, pp 4585–4590

Boyd D, Ellison N (2008) Social network sites: definition, history, and scholarship. J Comput Mediated Commun 13(1):210–230

Chalfen R (1987) Snapshot versions of life. Bowling Green State University Popular Press, Bowling Green

Crabtree A, Rodden T, Mariani J (2004) Collaborating around collections: informing the continued development of photoware. In: Proceedings of the 2004 ACM conference on computer supported cooperative work, Chicago, 2004. ACM, New York, pp 396–405

Davis M, House N, Towle J, King S, Ahern S, Burgener C, Perkel D, Finn M, Viswanathan V, Rothenberg M (2005) MMM2: Mobile media metadata for media sharing. In: Proceedings of the CHI '05 extended abstracts on Human factors in Computing Systems, Portland, 1 Apr 2005. ACM, New York

Drazin A, Frohlich D (2007) Good intentions: remembering through framing photographs in english homes. Ethnos 72(1):51–76

Durrant A, Taylor AS, Taylor S, Molloy M, Sellen A, Frohlich D, Gosset P, Swan L (2008) Speculative devices for photo display. In: Proceedings of the CHI '08 extended abstracts on human factors in computing systems, Florence, 2008. ACM, New York, pp 2297–2302

Durrant A, Frohlich D, Sellen A, Lyons E (2009a) Home curation versus teenage photography: photo displays in the family home. J Hum Comput Stud 67(12):1005–1023

Durrant A, Taylor A, Frohlich D, Sellen A, Uzzell D (2009b) Photo displays and intergenerational relationships in the family home. In: Proceedings of the 23rd BCS conference on human computer interaction, Cambridge, 2009. British Computer Society

Edwards D, Middleton D (1986) Joint remembering: constructing an account of shared experience through conversational discourse. Discourse Process 9(4):423–459

Frohlich DM (2004) Audiophotography: bringing photos to life with sounds. Kluwer, Dordrecht/ London

Frohlich D, Daly-Jones O (1995) Voicefax: a shared workspace for voicemail partners. In: Proceedings of the Conference companion on Human factors in computing systems, Denver, 1995. ACM, New York, pp 308–309

Frohlich D, Kuchinsky A, Pering C, Don A, Ariss S (2002) Requirements for photoware. In: Proceedings of the 2002 ACM conference on computer supported cooperative work (CSCW '02), New Orleans

Frohlich DM, Wall S, Kiddle G (2011) Re-discovery of forgotten images in family photo collections. Submission to HCI journal special issue on Designing for Personal Memories

Hilliges O, Kirk DS (2009) Getting sidetracked: display design and occasioning photo-talk with the photohelix. In: Proceedings of the 27th international conference on human factors in computing systems, Boston, 2009. ACM, New York, pp 1733–1736

Hofmeester K (1999) Introduction. Interactions 6(6):8–10

Isaacs E, Whittaker S, Frohlich D, O'Conaill B (1997) Informal communications re-examined: new functions for video in supporting opportunistic encounters. In: Finn K, Sellen A, Wilbur S (eds) Video-mediated communication. Lawrence Erlbaum Associates, Mahwah

Isaacs E, Walendowski A, Ranganathan D (2002a) Mobile instant messaging through Hubbub. Commun ACM 45(9):68–72

Isaacs E, Walendowski A, Whittaker S, Schiano DJ, Kamm C (2002) The character, functions, and styles of instant messaging in the workplace. In: Proceedings of the 2002 ACM conference on computer supported cooperative work, New Orleans, 2002. ACM, New York, pp 11–20

Johansen R (1988) Groupware: computer support for business teams. The Free Press, New York

Joinson AN (2008) Looking at, looking up or keeping up with people?: motives and use of Facebook. In: Proceedings of the twenty-sixth annual SIGCHI conference on human factors in computing systems, Florence, 2008. ACM, New York, pp 1027–1036

Kim J, Zimmerman J (2006) Cherish: smart digital photo frames for sharing social narratives at home. In: Proceedings of the CHI '06 extended abstracts on human factors in computing systems, Montreal, 2006. ACM, New York, pp 953–958

Kindberg T, Spasojevic M, Fleck R, Sellen A (2005) I saw this and thought of you: some social uses of camera phones. In: Proceedings of the CHI '05 extended abstracts on human factors in computing systems, Portland, 1 Apr 2005

Kirk D, Sellen A, Rother C, Wood K (2006) Understanding photowork. In: Proceedings of the SIGCHI conference on human factors in computing systems CHI '06, Montreal, 1 Apr 2006. ACM, New York, pp 761–770

Kirk D, Sellen A, Harper R, Wood K (2007) Understanding videowork. In: Proceedings of the SIGCHI conference on human factors in computing systems CHI '07, San Jose, 1 Apr 2007. ACM, New York, pp 61–70

Kirk DS, Izadi S, Sellen A, Taylor S, Banks R, Hilliges O (2010) Opening up the family archive. In: Proceedings of the 2010 ACM conference on computer supported cooperative work, Savannah, 2010. ACM, New York, pp 261–270

Koskinen I (2005) Sound in Mobile Multimedia: a mobile design challenge. In: Proceedings of the designing pleasurable products and interfaces 2005 (DPPI 2005), Eindhoven, 2005

Koskinen IK (2007) Mobile multimedia in action. Transaction, New Brunswick

Koskinen I, Kurvinen E, Lehtonen T-K (2002) Mobile image. Edita, Helsinki

Kuchinsky A, Pering C, Creech M, Freeze D, Serra B, Gwizdka J (1999) FotoFile: a consumer multimedia organization and retrieval system. In: Proceedings of the SIGCHI conference on human factors in computing systems: the CHI is the limit CHI '99, Pittsburgh, 1 May 1999. ACM, New York

Kun LMA, Marsden G (2007) Co-Present photo sharing on mobile devices. In: Proceedings of the 9th international conference on human computer interaction with mobile devices and services, Singapore, 2007. ACM, New York, pp 277–284

Lehmuskallio A, Sarvas R (2008) Snapshot video: everyday photographers taking short videoclips. In: Proceedings of the 5th Nordic conference on human–computer interaction: building bridges, Lund, 1 Oct 2008. ACM, New York, pp 257–265

Leong TW, Vetere F, Howard, S (2005) The serendipity shuffle. In: Proceedings of the 17th Australia conference on computer-human interaction: citizens online: considerations for today and the future, Canberra, 2005. Computer-Human Interaction Special Interest Group (CHISIG) of Australia, pp 1–4

Leong T, Howard S, Vetere F (2008) Choice: abdicating or exercising? In: Proceedings of the twenty-sixth annual SIGCHI conference on human factors in computing systems CHI '08, Florence, 2008. ACM, New York, pp 715–724

Lindley S, Monk A (2006) Designing appropriate affordances for electronic photo sharing media. In: Proceedings of the CHI '06 extended abstracts on human factors in computing systems, 1 Apr 2006, Montreal. ACM, New York

Lindley S, Monk A (2008) Social enjoyment with electronic photo displays: awareness and control. Int J Hum Comput Stud 66(8):587–604

Lindley SE, Durrant A, Kirk D, Taylor AS (2009) Editorial: collocated social practices surrounding photos. Int J Hum Comput Stud 67(12):995–1004

Lister M (1995) The photographic image in digital culture. Routledge, London

Mäkelä A, Giller V, Tscheligi M, Sefelin R (2000) Joking, storytelling, artsharing, expressing affection: a field trial of how children and their social network communicate with digital images in leisure time. In: The SIGCHI conference on human factors in computing systems CHI '00, The Hague. ACM, New York, pp 548–555

Miller A, Edwards W (2007) Give and Take: a study of consumer photo-sharing culture and practice. In: Proceedings of the SIGCHI conference on human factors in computing systems CHI '07, San Jose, 1 Apr 2007. ACM, New York, pp 347–356

Mills TJ, Pye D, Sinclair D, Wood KR (2000) Managing photos with AT&T shoebox (demonstration session). In: Proceedings of the 23rd annual international ACM SIGIR conference on research and development in information retrieval, Athens, 2000. ACM, New York, p 390

Musello C (1979) Family photography. In: Wagner J (ed) Images of information: still photography in the social sciences. Sage, Beverly Hills, pp 101–118

Neustaedter C, Fedorovskaya E (2009b) Understanding and improving flow in digital photo ecosystems. In: Proceedings of the graphics interface 2009, Kelowna, 2009b. ACM, New York

Norman D (2009) Designing the infrastructure. Interactions 16(4):66–69

O'Conaill B, Geelhoed E, Toft P (1994) Deskslate: a shared workspace for telephone partners. In: Proceedings of the conference companion on human factors in computing systems, Boston, 1994. ACM, New York, pp 303–304

O'Hara K, Perry M, Churchill E (2004) Public and situated displays: social and Interactional aspects of shared display technologies (Cooperative Work, 2). Kluwer Academic Publishers, Norwell

Okabe D, Ito M (2003) Camera phones changing the definition of picture-worthy. Jpn Media Rev

Rodden K, Wood K (2003) How Do people manage their digital photographs? In: Proceedings of the SIGCHI conference on human factors in computing systems CHI '03, Fort Lauderdale, 2003. ACM, New York, pp 409–416

Rogers Y, Lindley S (2004) Collaborating around vertical and horizontal large interactive displays: which way is best? Interact Comput 16(6):1133–1152

Sarvas R, Herrarte E, Wilhelm A, Davis M (2004) Metadata creation system for mobile images. In: Proceedings of the 2nd international conference on mobile systems, applications, and services, Boston, 2004. ACM, New York, pp 36–48

Sarvas R, Viikari M, Pesonen J, Nevanlinna H (2004) MobShare: controlled and immediate sharing of mobile images. In: Proceedings of the 12th annual ACM international conference on multimedia, New York, 2004. ACM, New York, pp 724–731

Sarvas R, Oulasvirta A, Jacucci G (2005) Building social discourse around mobile photos: a systemic perspective. In: Proceedings of the 7th international conference on human computer interaction with mobile devices & services mobileHCI '05, Saltzburg, 1 Sept 2005. ACM, New York

Schiano D, Chen CP, Isaacs E (2002) How teens take, view, share, and store photos. In: Proceedings of the computer supported cooperative work (CSCW 2002), New Orleans, 2002

Shove E, Watson M, Hand M, Ingram J (2007) The design of everyday life. Berg, New York

Slater D (1995) Domestic photography and digital culture. In: Lister M (ed) The photographic image in digital culture. Routledge, London, pp 129–146

Staal G (1999) Strategic outlook: from ears to eyes. Interactions 6(6):64–67

Stelmaszewska H, Fields B, Blandford A (2008) The roles of time, place, value and relationships in collocated photo sharing with camera phones. In: Proceedings of the 22nd British HCI group annual conference on HCI 2008: people and computers XXII: culture, creativity, interaction – vol 1, Liverpool, 2008, pp. 141–150

Swan L, Taylor A (2008) Photo displays in the home. In: Proceedings of the 7th ACM conference on designing interactive systems (DIS '08), Cape Town

Tang JC, Isaacs EA, Rua M (1994) Supporting distributed groups with a montage of lightweight interactions. In: Proceedings of the 1994 ACM conference on computer supported cooperative work, Chapel Hill, 1994. ACM, New York, pp 23–34

Taylor A, Swan L, Durrant A (2007) Designing family photo displays. In: Proceedings of the 10th European conference on computer-supported cooperative work (ECSCW 2007), Limerick, 2007. Springer, pp. 79–98

TechCrunch (2009) Who has the most photos of them all? Hint: it is not Facebook. TechCrunch. http://techcrunch.com/2009/04/07/who-has-the-most-photos-of-them-all-hint-it-is-not-facebook/. Accessed 19 Mar 2010

Van Dijck J (2008) Digital photography: communication, identity, memory. Vis Commun 7(1):57–76

Van House N (2007) Flickr and public image-sharing: distant closeness and photo exhibition. In: CHI '07 Extended abstracts on human factors in computing systems (CHI '07), San Jose

Van House N (2009) Collocated photo sharing, story-telling, and the performance of self. J Hum Comput Stud 67(12):1073–1086

Van House N, Ames M (2010) The social life of camera phones. Unpublished work

Van House N, Davis M, Ames M, Finn M, Viswanathan V (2005) The uses of personal networked digital imaging: an empirical study of cameraphone photos and sharing. In: CHI '05 extended abstracts on Human factors in computing systems (CHI '05), Portland

Whittaker S, Swanson J, Kucan J, Sidner C (1997) TeleNotes: managing lightweight interactions in the desktop. ACM T Comput Hum Interact 4(2):137–168

Whittaker S, Bergman O, Clough P (2010) Easy on that trigger dad: a study of long term family photo retrieval. Pers Ubiquit Comput 14(1):31–43

Chapter 7
The Future of Domestic Photography

A colleague told us the following story. She had given her 9-year-old son a disposable camera to take with him to a camp. This was an ordinary one-time-use disposable film camera that needs to be given to the photo-finishing service for development and printing. When her son came back from his trip, he threw the camera on the floor as if to throw it away. Her mother stated that surely he had dropped the camera by accident, and he should take it to a photo-finishing provider for development and prints. The son did not understand what his mother was talking about. She had to explain that the camera had film inside and that, for one to see the images, the film had to be developed and the images printed on paper. This was all new to her son, who said that he'd thought the camera was digital.

It is not surprising that a person born less than a decade ago had no experience with film photography or film cameras and therefore had not understood how the camera works. Perhaps more surprising in the story is that no matter what technology the camera used, the son threw it away. He obviously thought that the camera had served its purpose and now was supposed to be disposed of. He had not seen any of the images captured (although he had used the camera at camp) and was quite content with that. For the son, the camera was a device used in the moment at the time of capture. It was a piece of equipment to mark an event, people, and locations as important and meaningful. In other words, taking the camera out, interacting with people to frame a good shot, and pushing the button on the camera served the purpose of social bonding and marking the moment as special. The actual images that were captured on film were secondary and, in this case, disposable. If this was not the case, why did the son throw the camera away?

In this chapter, we turn our gaze to the future and make our predictions as to what will influence future snapshot photography. Our starting point is what we discussed in Chap. 5: in the past two decades, the infrastructure of domestic photography has changed from a film-based one into a general-purpose information and communications technology infrastructure. As our story above shows, the technological change is such that the youngest generations have very little knowledge of film photography. However, our story also suggests that not everything has changed. The son took the camera to camp and used it to capture images of people,

R. Sarvas and D.M. Frohlich, *From Snapshots to Social Media - The Changing Picture of Domestic Photography*, Computer Supported Cooperative Work, DOI 10.1007/978-0-85729-247-6_7, © Springer-Verlag London Limited 2011

locations, and events that were important for him and his friends. His mother probably had done exactly the same at the age of nine. On the other hand, the story also demonstrates that something has changed in the functions and values that people assign to snapshot photographs: the son had no desire to see the actual photos; the value was in the capture, not in the images. The son had no burning desire to see the images, put them in an album, and reminisce about them with his friends – something that older generations, such as his mother's, would find the most natural thing to do with photographs.

Domestic photography is in a state of change, or, to use the term coined by Anderson and Tushman,[1] it is in the middle of an *era of ferment*. A technological discontinuity emerged in the late 1980s and early 1990s in the form of digital photography, and that discontinuity disrupted the existing regime, the Kodak Path. Today, in hindsight, the disruption is obvious: film is no longer dominant and some of the biggest businesses in film photography have gone bankrupt. However, the dust has not yet settled from the disruption. There is no obvious dominant design such as the former symbiosis of cameras, film, and photo-finishing, and no homogeneous practice and culture like the snapshot culture of the twentieth century. The Digital Path has clearly begun, but the relationships among the actors have not stabilised to form a distinct technological path (i.e., a dominant design).

In the discussion below, we summarise what we see as the most important changes that have occurred in domestic photography in the past two decades: the sheer number of pictures and cameras; the possibilities for editing photographs; the new ways of sharing, archiving, and storing digital photographs; and – given a brief look here – the changes in the 'domestic sphere'. We also discuss changes in the social functions of photographs, the organisation of personal photographs, new domestic cameras, and the division between public and private photographs. After that, we cast our gaze into the future and discuss what we see as the main actors shaping the Digital Path. In other words, we ask what can be found as key business models, discourses, legal actions, and other actors that should be taken into account in thinking about the future of domestic photography. In the final section, we summarise our view of the issues soon to face the ICT infrastructure that forms the environment of photography technology.

7.1   What Has Changed?

As we have pointed out, the major disruptions in the history of domestic photography are not changes in the camera but changes in the recording medium for the images created inside the camera. The transition to digital imaging has practically overhauled the whole photography infrastructure and industry. Domestic photography has become one of the many functions for the devices, software, cables, displays,

---

[1] Anderson and Tushman 1990.

connections, service contracts, networks, subscriptions, protocols, etc. that make up the home ICT infrastructure. In comparison to the Kodak Path, the move to ICT has made the technologies that people use for photography heterogeneous and the providers of those technologies (i.e., businesses) fragmented. The major change in domestic photography technology reflects the transformation in the photography industry in general: there is no longer an unambiguous network of commercial organisations that can be called 'the photography industry'. The list of business stakeholders in domestic photography is long and diverse: camera manufacturers, phone manufacturers, phone network carriers, broadband service providers, developers of photo editing software and of photo management software, photo game developers, display manufacturers, storage media manufacturers, cloud storage services, computer manufacturers, operating system developers, manufacturers of network technology, GPS unit manufacturers, positioning services, Web search services, online photo publishing and sharing services, social networking services, photo product providers (e.g., offering coffee mugs, t-shirts, calendars, mouse pads, photo books, and prints), printer and ink manufacturers, newspapers and news services, game console manufacturers, and all other technology providers who have photo-related functions in their technology or otherwise do business using people's snapshots.

If the technology and business have changed significantly, how much have people's practices, the ways in which people 'do' domestic photography? As Shove et al. discuss, people's 'careers' as photographers are in transition and old practices are reshaped and reconfigured in this transition to fit and shape the new technology and business models.[2] On the one hand, people are still sharing, editing, publishing, storing, copying, posting, commenting upon, liking, printing, and displaying photographs – as in the days of the Kodak Path. On the other hand, the technologies for performing these activities are different from those of the Kodak Path, and so must be the ways in which these things are done. In the sections that follow, we summarise the changes in practices and uses of the photography technology we discussed in Chap. 6.

7.1.1 More Pictures and More Cameras

One of the obvious changes facilitated by digital technology is that people take more photographs than ever before. In 2007, the number of photographs taken annually in the US was estimated at between 420 and 670.[3] In addition to captured photographs, people receive digital photographs via e-mail, on CDs or DVDs, through online Web services, and so on.[4] The change in the number of images

---

[2] Shove et al. 2007.

[3] Shankland (2007).

[4] According to a study by PMA Foresight, 37% of US households received digital images in 2008 (PMA 2009c).

circulating globally is significant. The Kodak Annual Report in 1998 reported that 2.2 billion rolls of film were consumed globally in 1997, which means roughly 53–79 billion photographs for both professional and non-professional purposes (approx. 9–14 photographs per person, globally[5]). Measuring the current number of photographs captured globally is much more difficult, because there is no measurable consumable such as rolls of film. To give some indication, in May 2010, the social networking service Facebook was reported to be receiving 1 billion unique digital photographs weekly[6] (i.e., roughly 52 billion images a year). In other words, the most popular social networking service manages almost the same number of photographs annually as was the global number 13 years ago.[7]

The uses for the camera have changed as well. People take photographs for clearly utilitarian purposes – for example, to copy a bus schedule, to compare prices, or for insurance purposes. Photographs are also taken for immediate distant communication, such as to relay a feeling of togetherness with people who may be at distant locations.[8] Taking images for gaming is a new use for cameras that mobile phone technology in particular has enabled. Also, camera phones have made candid photography easier, as it is difficult to distinguish between picture-taking and other user interaction.

The number of cameras has influenced people's practices. Camera phones have supported picture-taking in situations where people seldom have a camera with them, because people carry their mobile phones with them most of the time outside the home.[9] The integrated cameras in mobile phones have also increased the number of cameras in a household – in particular, the number of children who have a camera of their own. No longer are the children in the family dependent on the 'family camera'; they have their own device for capturing and sharing images.

7.1.2   Editing

In addition to the possibilities and technologies for capturing photographs, the editing of photographs has departed significantly from the Kodak Path. The possibilities for editing snapshots on the Kodak Path were limited when compared to the opportunities today. Once the image had been captured, the snapshooter could

---

[5]The world population in 1997 was estimated at 5.8 billion (United Nations 2000).

[6]Fletcher 2010.

[7]It is good to bear in mind that photographs on Facebook are predominantly non-professional (in contrast to the Kodak statistic from 1997 that includes professional use), and that images on Facebook are only a subset of all images captured in the world. In other words, the comparison is not unproblematic.

[8]Nancy Van House discusses the concept of "distant closeness" that is achieved by capturing and immediately sharing photographs (Van House 2007). See also Kirk et al. 2010.

[9]According to Hsu 2009, 70% of mobile phones in 2008 had a camera in them.

choose the size of the print from a small number of options (often a non-default size would add extra costs), perhaps there was a choice between matte and glossy prints, and later in the 1980s and 1990s there was often a choice of getting 'doubles' or even 'triples' for a small extra fee. Any control over the actual image was beyond the snapshooter. On the other hand, the process was very simple and the technical problems with the developing and printing process were taken care of by the photo-finishing service.

The possibilities for an ordinary snapshooter to edit photographs with the Digital Path are much more diverse and complex than with film photographs. Perhaps most dramatically, right after the capture of the image, one can delete the image, which is something that was not easily done with film technology. After capture, it is also possible to edit the shape, size, lighting, colours, contrast, sharpness, tones, etc. with a variety of tools, ranging from automated 'wizards' on camera phones to full-scale image editing software on desktop computers. Because home computers have become widespread and the price of professional editing software is within the reach of non-professionals, the possibilities to edit personal photographs are almost endless.

However, the ability to edit personal photographs has not turned every snapshooter into a photography artist. First, the possibility of editing photographs has added to the overall complexity of digital photography. Compared to the snapshooting process on the Kodak Path, the process on the Digital Path is more complex, partly because there are so many opportunities to edit the captured image. Second, mastering the image editing tools requires new skills to be learned and equipment to be bought. For example, to be able to use a desktop editing tool, the snapshooter must have a personal computer, technical skill in using the computer and transferring the images from the camera to the PC, and enough skill in using the editing program. If basic desktop editing of digital snapshots is becoming the norm, basic snapshooting requires these skills and pieces of equipment. Therefore, the range of possibilities that editing enables has the risk of excluding people from practising digital domestic photography – specifically, those who do not have the skills and the equipment or the money to acquire both. We return to this potential 'digital divide' in domestic photography later on in the chapter.

7.1.3   Sharing Photographs

Sharing photographs online typically utilises technologies and services such as e-mail, multimedia messaging, instant messaging, social network services, and Web page galleries. The ability to make photographs available for viewing on the Internet has enabled the sharing of photographs independently of time and location. The person sharing the images does not have to be in the same physical space at the same time as the recipient viewing the photographs. A person in Finland can share a photograph on Tuesday, and a recipient in England can view it Thursday. This is, of course, something that traditional mail has allowed for over a century, but the difference with the Digital Path is that now there is a location on the Internet (i.e., a Web address) that one or more people can view, making it possible for a group of people to share and discuss the same photographs without regard to time (i.e., asynchronously) and location (i.e., as long as they can access the Internet in their physical location). To put it simply, sharing photographs online enables social interaction around and about photographs over long distances and at different times.

Sharing photographs online has also made it possible to show photographs to audiences that were not probable or possible on the Kodak Path. It is possible to have relatives living in different parts of the world 'gather together' around photographs published in a Web service. Or let otherwise separate social groups (e.g., family and colleagues) view and comment on the same photographs. On the other hand, it is also possible to share images with people with whom there is no social connection. Personal photographs can be made visible to anyone with access to the Internet, which makes it possible to have viewers who are not a coherent group and/or to have viewers in numbers that were practically impossible on the Kodak Path.

Web services for sharing photographs online provide tools for helping people to promote their own images and to find images that might be of interest. One of the most popular tools is 'tagging'. A 'tag' is a keyword attached to an image, but, unlike a static keyword, a tag is often a Web link as well, and clicking on a tag activates a search for other images that have been tagged with the same keyword. For example, tagging an image with the keyword 'hamster' makes the image potentially easier to find for people looking for images of hamsters. And, as the hamster example implies, tagging an image also serves the person searching for hamster images.

Adding a tag for a photograph does not necessarily suggest passively waiting for someone to search for images with that specific tag. For example, tagging can mean naming a person in a photograph, with the naming triggering a message to the person being named. In this case, tagging is a message sent to the recipient about the photographs in the service.

Tags are of commercial value in three main ways. They provide information about the contents of images, which makes it possible, for example, to target advertisements better. Tags also connect photographs (and other media objects) together, which makes it possible to infer commercially valuable information, such as who has been where and at what time. This information can be used for advertising but also for design of products and services. Third, tags can be used to create switching costs for the user of a system. In other words, the effort required to switch to another system might be too much if the tags in the system cannot be transferred as well.

Tagging and the different ways it is used are an example of a new and popular combination of technologies, business opportunities, and people's practices in domestic photography. Tagging had its predecessor on the Kodak Path – namely, written annotations on the backs of paper prints or text in a photo album. The familiarity with old practices has probably been crucial in the uptake of tagging as a practice. However, the technical and business infrastructure in which tagging has been implemented is very different from writing keywords on the back of a paper print.

Sharing photographs on the Internet has not replaced sharing of photographs that is *dependent* on location and/or time – we call this kind of sharing offline, in contrast to online. It is still possible to take (or upload) digital images to a photo-finishing service and receive prints. However, the low cost of photo printers has made them popular devices in homes, and, according to a marketing study, 30% of photo prints in the US were made at home in 2008.[10] The printing has, of course, changed, because the prints no longer are the only way to see the images. Printing has become selective: not everything is printed. That is reserved for only a selected few. In other words, printed photographs have become more of a luxury product made only for special occasions or specific purposes, such as gift-giving.

Another print product has gained popularity as the traditional photo print has lost its dominance: the photo book.[11] Photo books are printed books that a person can create on his or her computer, using his or her own photographs. Often, photo books have ready templates into which the user can 'drag and drop' his or her photographs, so little graphical design work is required. According to another marketing statistic, people in the US make these books mainly as family keepsakes and, secondly, simply for displaying photographs or as a gift to family.[12] Again, photo books can be seen as an extension of the over-a-century-old photo album practice in which prints were 'dragged and glued' onto the blank pages (or placed in ready-made sleeves) of albums. The transfer of this practice into an ICT context has shaped the practice, and, for example, people can give several photo books as gifts because reproduction is no longer a problem.

In addition to physical prints, offline sharing includes creating CDs or DVDs full of photographs and sharing (or giving) them. It is precisely the physicality of CDs, DVDs, photo books, and prints that make them potential gifts, unlike images shared online. The gift-giving traditions and practices related to photographs are also in flux, as the uniqueness and physicality of photographs have changed in the last two decades.

However, not all offline sharing is about giving gifts. As we discussed in the previous chapter, digital photo frames are gaining popularity. These we consider to be 'offline', although they can be connected to the Internet. They are 'offline' in the sense that they are separate from ordinary 'Web surfing' with computers and mobile phones, and often even those frames connected to the Internet are passive displays. The change in comparison to the traditional non-electronic picture frame is mainly that more than one image can be displayed, and if the frame has a network connection, the images on display can be changed remotely.

7.1.4   Archival and Storage

The digital nature of personal photographs has changed storage and archival. On the one hand, digital images take very little physical space, unlike paper prints. On the other hand, digital images are very fragile in the sense that tens of thousands of photographs can be deleted very easily without any effort. Also, the digital format of

---

[10] In 2008, 61% of digital-camera households in the US made paper prints from their digital images and 45% of all US households made prints from digital images (PMA 2009a, b).

[11] According to PMA (2009c), the photo book market was expected to reach $340 million in 2009. The source is not clear as to whether this is the global or the US market.

[12] PMA 2009a.

photographs is dependent on existing standards and technology supporting those standards: it is much more probable that a paper print can be viewed in 20 years' time than a digital image in JPEG format.

We return to archival and storage in the next section; therefore, here we only say in summary that the sheer number of photographs is changing not necessarily the ways in which people archive photographs (traditionally, paper prints were notoriously left unorganised in shoeboxes) so much as the ways in which people can access old photographs. These are changing dramatically because photos are so numerous and their storage is distributed.

7.1.5 Changes in the Family

In the term 'domestic photography', the nature of the domestic has changed radically over the last two decades, at least in Western Europe and the USA. What it means to be a family is now different in those locations. Although we have not looked in detail at the changes in family structures, values, and constellations, we do see the importance of such changes in shaping domestic technology. For example, Abigail Durrant has looked at intergenerational power dynamics between parents and teenagers in the context of photography.[13] Gillian Rose has studied the maternal obligations in family photography in the digital age and discusses how domestic photography is still a gendered activity.[14] Barbara Harrison draws attention in her studies to how family representation in contemporary domestic photography has been supplanted by self-presentation,[15] and this is also emphasised in the democratisation process in family life as described by Anthony Giddens.[16] Giddens draws attention to the political climate in Britain for its increased emancipation of junior family members living at home, and Durrant points out the importance of this cultural environment in the context of family photography and teenage photography.[17]

7.1.6 The Social Functions of Domestic Photography

Although practices and activities have changed in the past century, the reasons and motivations of people for 'doing' domestic photography have remained surprisingly constant. Looking at people's photographs today, we can identify the same values

---

[13]Durrant et al. 2009; Durrant 2010.

[14]Rose 2003.

[15]Harrison 2002.

[16]Giddens 2000.

[17]Giddens 1998; Durrant 2010.

and social functions that have been dominant throughout the history of photography: social bonding and communication, demonstration of cultural and group membership and identity, and preservation and retention of memories.

For example, in Figs. 7.1 and 7.2 on the left is a family portrait taken in a photographer's studio in 1846, and on the right is a social networking profile picture taken by the person himself in 2008. The images are visually quite different, the recording medium is different, and the cost of the image was different. Nevertheless, both served the same social functions: emphasising the social bonds between the people in the photograph, demonstrating membership in the family as ideal at that time, and preserving a memory of a specific time in the history of the family.

The visual differences reflect the family values of the time. In 1846, the solemn faces and clothing would suggest to a viewer a respectable middle-class family that has enough wealth to acquire a photographic portrait. The setting is formal, and the people wear probably their best clothes. Creating an image of the family in 1846 was a serious matter. In 2008, the faces, the clothing and equipment (the backpack), and the outdoor setting suggest to a viewer a happy and sporty father who enjoys spending time with his son. The feeling is not of formality and seriousness but of love, laughter, and intimacy. Creating an image of family life in 2008 is fun and spontaneous. Also, the photograph from 2008 is without the mother, which suggests a modern father who takes an active role in the children's upbringing. A missing mother in the portrait from 1846 would have raised questions.

Figs. 7.1 and 7.2 Constructing an image of oneself and family relations in 1846 (*left*) and in 2008 (*right*) (*Left Figure*: Unknown photographer. Original title: Adams family portrait, with man, woman, and baby girl, 1849. Daguerreotype. Library of Congress Prints and Photographs Division, USA [Reproduction Number LC-USZ6-2017]. No known restrictions on publication. *Right Figure*: © Frode Skarstein, 2008. Published with permission)

However, the functions these people had for the photograph are, broadly speaking, the same: communicating an ideal familial image and reifying the familial bonds, and also preserving a memory of a specific time. This suggests that the functions for which photography was domesticated in the 1840s have persisted for almost 170 years. This persistence is perhaps more obvious when set off in contrast to new cameras in the domestic sphere that have been domesticated for different purposes, such as surveillance and logging. We return to the domestication of new cameras later in this chapter.

The social functions have not remained unchanged, as we discussed in Chap. 6. Although the social functions and values for domestic photography have not significantly changed in the past two decades, the balance between them has shifted. Snapshots today are captured and shared more for social bonding, communication, and demonstrating a specific identity than preserving memories. Domestic photographs have become more transient than on the Kodak Path, where a dominant motivation was to capture images for future reminiscing. Today, a typical photo album is shared via a Web service on the Internet, and once it has been viewed and commented upon, it is almost forgotten.[18] Archival and long-term storage are not typical activities in the current 'fermentation' of the Digital Path. Partly this is due to new uses for photography that are enabled by camera phones and the Internet – uses that have little to do with building a visual history of a person's life. It is possible to capture an image and send it immediately to other people as a message, which is then consumed within seconds, minutes, or hours. Also, images are captured for more utilitarian purposes, as in the example of photographs of bus schedules or price tags. These images are not taken to preserve and retain memories for future reminiscing.

Another change is in children's camera ownership. On the Kodak Path, children and teenagers often could not afford a camera of their own, but today parents often sponsor and even insist on their children having a mobile phone, and that phone more often than not has a camera. As a result, there is a generation of young people who have had a camera of their own rather than a shared family camera, and their uses for the cameras and images are of interest for photography studies. However, perhaps focusing on young people's habits also over-emphasises any decline in the long-term-memory value of photographs. Often, uses by teenagers and young adults are reported as new, emerging practices.[19] Typically, young people have less interest in reminiscing on their past than older people do, and this is reflected in the uses for images. In relying on teenagers and young adults as indicators of future practices, there is a risk of overlooking that people in their teens are in a special phase in life. It is probable that today's teenagers will retain something of their current photography practices as they grow older, but it is as probable that life changes such as parenthood or moving out of the childhood home will shape those practices toward preserving memories for the future.

---

[18] See, e.g., Sarvas et al. 2005.
[19] See, e.g., Van Dijck 2008.

When we also take into account that the most popular social networking service, Facebook, which is the one holding the most photographs (an estimated 48 billion photographs, from 500 million users[20]), was originally designed for university students (i.e., mainly young adults), it becomes understandable that the service does not strongly support long-term preservation of memories but, rather, emphasises social bonding, interaction, and identity-building.

Lastly, for a business model, emphasising the value of images 'now' rather than 'after a decade' is less risky. Understandably, making business out of something that happens within days is more attractive than investing in something that will happen sometime in the future. In contrast, for Kodak and film technology, there was no 'instant consumption'. Because of the external photo-finishing service, the first time a snapshooter was able to view and share photographs, the images were of the past. The photo-finishing process, which took a few days before the 1-h-photo services, forced the viewing of snapshots always to be about reminiscing – about the past. Polaroid was, of course, the exception to this and anchored much of its marketing message to this fact.[21] Simply put, the memory and reminiscing value of snapshots suited Kodak's business and core technology. Because digital technology shows the images immediately after capture, major businesses in personal imaging, such as Facebook, focus less on the reminiscing and more on immediate social interaction and communication of identity.

It seems that people in the current fermenting form of the Digital Path value snapshots more for their immediate function in social bonding and in demonstrating membership than the function of preserving memories. If we look back at the Portrait Path, when people did not have cameras of their own, we see a reminiscing function but different from that in the Kodak Path. The images of people were predominantly studio portraits, and often the memory function of a portrait was that of a person and a relationship, not a 'Kodak moment' such as a child's first steps or a happy day at the beach. A Portrait Path photograph was given much in the manner of a lock of hair: to reify and strengthen a social bond, but also to make sure that the social bond is remembered.[22] The portraits were not created and given for reminiscing on certain events, holidays, or growing children – the kind of functions marketed by Kodak in the early twentieth century.

Perhaps the memory function on the Digital Path will find a new form, different from the reminiscing and visual history functions supported by Kodak. Perhaps the individuality and intimacy in photographs is valued over the social events typical of the Kodak Path. In other words, perhaps intimate moments such as kisses and cuddling are typical of the Digital Path, rather than the social events typical of the Kodak Path, such as graduation, birth of children, or family vacations. The more intimate moments shared with others seem to celebrate individuality and personality more than the socially acceptable demonstrations of familial life on the Kodak Path.

---

[20]Fletcher 2010.

[21]See, e.g., Buse 2010.

[22]Batchen 2004.

Nevertheless, the type of memories and reminiscing people will be able to do 10 years from now depends greatly on how current photographs are stored, organised, and annotated – on how the digital shoeboxes of photographs will be managed.

7.1.7 Unorganised Images

Another thing that has changed surprisingly little in the past two decades is that people have difficulties finding time to organise their photographs. On the Portrait Path, this was most probably not a problem, because people had very few photographs. It was in the time of the Kodak Path, when people learned to consume inexpensive film, that the problem of too many photographs started to emerge. On the Digital Path, people capture more photographs than ever in history and the problem of organisation is familiar to everyone. Rather surprisingly, the 'information technology revolution' that has taken place in recent decades has not been able to provide a solution for the problem of organising one's photographs.

The film-era cliché that people keep on postponing the organisation of their unsorted collections of photographs (often stashed away in shoeboxes) seems to hold true still. Although people still place a value on having their photographs organised, there seems not to be enough motivation to do extra work for 'preservation for future use'.[23] The result of spending no time on organising is that people have their photographs unorganised, just as in the past,[24] a significant difference being that on the Digital Path there are many more photographs than before.

Paper prints have one advantage over digital photographs that influences their organisation. Paper prints on the Kodak Path were physical objects often shared and displayed in a medium that also served as an archive: the photo album. In the album, the images were organised, annotated, and presented in a manner and format that was resilient to technological changes (i.e., independent of external technologies). This was, of course, only true when someone had made the effort of creating the album in the first place.

Digital photographs are shared and displayed often via commercial Web services that are not primarily designed for archival and long-term storage. Even if they provide archival and storage, commercial services may go bankrupt or change their policies, putting the users' photographs in danger of being lost. Digital photographs stored on personal computers, optical discs, or hard drives are not safe from business and technological changes either: standards change and can become unsupported because sustaining them is no longer commercially attractive or possible. In other words, digital photographs are much more dependent on certain technologies and businesses than paper photographs were on the Kodak Path.

---

[23] See, e.g., Sarvas et al. 2004.
[24] See, e.g., Whittaker et al. 2010.

People archive their digital photographs, for example, by burning images to DVD-ROM. There are strong personal incentives to preserve digital photographs, but the preservation has broader motives also. Looking at people's personal snapshots (and other visual media) as a large body of visual culture, ones sees a societal incentive to keep these visual records accessible and available for decades to come.

7.1.8 The Snapshot Camera and New Domestic Cameras

The principle of a camera has not changed since the introduction of the first photographic cameras in the late 1830s: light passes through a lens and hits a surface where it is recorded. It is the medium for recording the image that has changed, from metal plates and paper to glass plates to celluloid film and more recently to an electronic format decoded into binary numbers. Unlike the recording format, the camera has seen incremental evolution and development, without a radical change in its basic principle.[25] The camera Daguerre used in 1839 is different from a contemporary digital single-lens reflex camera (SLR) in many ways, but both still follow the same principle of capturing light to create an image on a recording medium.

It may sound far-fetched to question the principle of the camera; after all, a device not capturing light through a lens inside a small box would not be a camera. However, not only are there other electromagnetic waves to capture than light (some of which are already widely used outside domestic photography, among them infrared, ultrasound, and x-rays), but there are potential other 'data sources' to capture than light that might serve the same purpose as photographs. Once again, social networking services provide a good example.

Users of social networking services capture and share a variety of information for the same reasons they capture and share photographs: to strengthen and reify social bonds and to demonstrate culture or group membership. People share nonphotographic information such as text, graphics, and sound about their social ties, family relations, meaningful locations, their feelings and preferences, important events, and so on, all of which is the kind of information typically relayed through personal snapshots. From this perspective, could the camera capture something more than just visual data?

There have already been camera phone prototypes that capture, in addition to visual information, contextual information such as location, current calendar status, and Bluetooth identification codes in the vicinity.[26] This information can then be used to infer further information, such as which people were present at the time of

---

[25]This is not to say that within the technologies that make up a camera there have not been radical and disruptive innovations. For example, the use of microprocessors in cameras in the 1970s was a radically new way of automating light measurement. However, it did not radically change the camera.

[26]Raento et al. 2005; Sarvas et al. 2004.

capture.[27] When this kind of context information is aggregated and processed for the snapshooter for specific purposes, then perhaps the visual information of a database of photographs becomes secondary.

There are also other changes that are forcing us to rethink the traditional camera. Camera phones were the first cameras that had an open programming interface. A programmer can write software for the phone that uses the camera as a resource just like any other sensor on the phone. For example, there are mobile phone games that use the camera as a tool in the game (pointing the camera at a specific colour triggers an activity in the game). The Frankencamera[28] is a project that brings the programmability in camera phones to other cameras, mainly high-quality SLRs. In other words, it is an example of how the camera phone has made people rethink what a traditional camera such as an SLR is.

The camera phone and a traditional consumer camera are not that far apart in their uses. Both are carried along and manually operated to capture images (still and video images), and these images are then used more or less in the tradition of the snapshots culture. But these two cameras are not the only classes of cameras in people's homes. Very different types of cameras have already entered the domestic sphere. These cameras were never designed for capturing snapshots: Web cams, surveillance cameras, wearable cameras, and virtual cameras.

Typically Web cams are separate cameras connected via a cable to a computer, though sometimes they are embedded in a laptop computer's screen. The main function for these cameras seems to be in real-time videoconferencing (or chatting).[29] Surveillance cameras have also been 'domesticated' in the sense that they are sold and used as household appliances for monitoring the household, for example, in the fear of burglary, to prevent small children from doing something dangerous, or to monitor a child-minder ('nanny cams').

Wearable cameras have become available for non-professional and domestic uses as well. Wearable cameras may be hidden in other appliances, such as pens, sunglasses, or car keys. But there are also wearable cameras that are fully visible and are used and marketed for very mobile sports such as downhill skiing or surfing. Wearable cameras are also being marketed and studied as 'life logging' devices that automatically capture images of the user's life as the camera is worn as a piece of clothing.[30] As a life-logging camera, the wearable camera suggests that the images are used for reminiscing. It further suggests that our reminiscing on the past is a data query of a database of images rather than viewing ready-made stories such as in traditional photo albums.

The fourth type of domestic camera is perhaps the most radical: capturing images on the computer screen with special 'screenshot' software (often built-in functionality of the operating system). Screenshots become linked to photography

---

[27]Davis et al. 2004.

[28]Adams et al. 2010.

[29]See, e.g., Kirk et al. 2010.

[30]See, e.g., Hodges et al. 2006.

when they are used to capture images from virtual worlds for the purposes for which one would capture photographs from the offline world.[31] For example, players in the virtual world World of Warcraft take so-called 'killshots' after a successful mission. According to Kristine Ask, these 'killshots' are used as proof of the gamers' guild's achievements, and as proof that the gamers were there when the mission was accomplished.[32] It does not seem far-fetched that, as virtual worlds are gaining importance in people's lives, they would start capturing images from these for the same purposes as traditional snapshots.[33]

The traditional domestic camera has not changed radically in the last few decades. The most obvious change has been the integration of a camera into mobile phones, making them the 'other' domestic camera. However, there are already other cameras in the domestic sphere that are more different from the family camera of the Kodak Path than the camera phone is. How these cameras will shape domestic photography, or how domestic photography will shape the uses of these cameras, remains to be seen.

7.1.9 Public and Private Images

The fourth change we draw attention to is the division between personal private photographs and publicly available photographs made for mass appeal. As we have discussed in the previous chapters, this division between private and public photographs has existed ever since the invention of photography. The division existed already before photography in the division between portraits and likenesses of private people, on one hand, and the lithographs and other images sold for the public; photography fell into this division right from the start.

The division does follow common sense. For example, images of family members have relevance to people who have some knowledge of, attachment to, or interest in the people depicted; and often to nobody else. On the other hand, some images simply appeal to many people, meaning that the image has relevance to a large number of people. Between a portrait that is relevant to perhaps one person and a portrait that is interesting for millions are images that can interest any number of people between one and a million.

It is when this simple fact about images is turned into business that a distinct division is created between public and private images. Public images are sold to any potential buyer, and the logic of the marketplace sorts out which images have public appeal and which do not. Private images are the ones that are not sold to the public because either there is no motivation to sell them or they are thought to have no public appeal.

---

[31] Book 2003.

[32] Ask, 2010, personal communication.

[33] See, e.g., Neustaedter and Fedorovskaya 2009.

On the Portrait Path, this division into public and private was supported by the separate business models. A single portrait taken in a studio was sold to an individual customer, and that single sale of a single image had to bring a profit. A photograph with public appeal was copied and sold to potentially tens of thousand of people, and the multiple sales of the multiple copies of the single image had to bring in a profit. As we discussed in Chap. 3, metal plate photography supported the studio portrait model, and the negative/positive process supported mass production and sales.

We also discussed earlier how the almost simultaneous inventions of film photography and halftone printing further separated the businesses and technological infrastructures for public and private photographs. Private photographs were captured with consumer cameras on celluloid film and printed by an external service. Public photographs were captured with similar cameras and on film as well but were printed in newspapers, magazines, and books by means of a different process and different technology. Private photography became the snapshot culture, and public photography became mass media.

On the Digital Path we can still see the division between public and private images, but the grey area between them seems to be growing. This is partly because images captured by private non-professionals have found new ways to broader appeal and reaching of larger audiences[34] but partly also because one business model for profiting from private snapshots is advertising, the same model that is at the core of mass media. Although people's private snapshots often have limited appeal, the cost of printing them has vanished with digital technology and the Internet. For a service providing online advertising space, it makes little difference whether a single image on a Web page is viewed a million times or one million images on individual Web pages are viewed only once each; in both cases, an advertisement can be made visible to a million viewers.

The Internet has also made it easy to make one's photographs visible to a potentially large number of people. Posting an image on a public Web page makes it available to anyone who has access to the Internet, which is roughly two billion people.[35] On the other hand, someone might make a photograph available on the Internet and it would not be surprising if none of the two billion users ever saw it.

To solve that dilemma, the Internet has numerous tools and services to attract attention: photo sharing services with functionality to help viewers find images that match their interests; online forums for showing, discussing, and looking at ordinary people's photographs; tagging and linking tools for making one's photograph more discoverable; convincing a popular Web site that an image has public appeal; and, finally, buying advertisement space on the Internet to attract people to the photograph.

---

[34]The availability of vast collections of non-professional photographs is eroding the demand for professional photography (see, e.g., The New York Times 2010, 29 Mar 2010).

[35]Miniwatts Marketing Group 2010.

There is also a contemporary public interest in images and photographs traditionally considered to be private. Reality shows on television are an example of public interest in images of non-famous people in intimate moments. Therefore, some images that would not necessarily have had public appeal a few decades ago might be interesting to a large audience today. Perhaps it is exactly this voyeurism into strangers' private lives and moments that is also shifting the boundaries of public and private images.

However, the basic fact that some images interest only a handful of people and other images interest millions will not change. There will most probably remain studio photography services for creating high-quality images that are important for a limited audience. There will also most probably be business in creating images for mass appeal. The change that is taking place lies between these two: images that have appeal outside the traditional social circles of family and friends but are not necessarily of interest to 'the wider public'. In addition to the new audiences made possible by the Internet, there are new potential uses for private images as well as publicly available images. Because the technical standards are often the same (e.g., the JPEG format) for the two, a photograph on a news Web page can be used in a photo book made for private family use, and a private snapshot can be made public – for example, through news services that encourage their readers to submit photographs.

7.2 Shaping the Future Digital Path

What will shape the fermenting Digital Path in the next 5–10 years? At the moment, the technologies, businesses, and practices that constitute domestic photography are still changing, and major changes have not really made their final impact. Businesses such as Facebook, Flickr, and YouTube were launched less than a decade ago, in 2004, and digital cameras outsold film cameras for the first time in roughly 2003. It is quite probable that some technology combined with a business model has been launched in the past few years that will shape domestic photography as much as, for example, social networking services have.

Rather than listing our guesses as to which prototypes and new innovations will become dominant and have an impact on people's practices, we try to base our predictions on less technology-centric actors. We draw attention to currently dominant companies and their business models, commercial incentives driving technological development, and regulation and legislation activity, and we also discuss public discourse, standardisation, and economic factors. Our rationale for this is twofold. First of all, from the history of photography it can be seen that there is no technology without a business: every technology that has become widely adopted has been integrated with a business model and a commercial organisation. For this reason, studying technologies without a business perspective seems unfruitful and limited in scope. Second, for practical reasons it is difficult to study or list even a fraction of all prototypes and innovations made in academia and industry that might shape future photography. However, we have included some references to prototypes in the discussion above to shed more light on our argumentation.

In a way, predicting the future is easier than writing about the past: no-one can expect us to predict the future with the same precision we apply when talking about the past. Of course, we hope that at least some of our arguments will prove to be correct, and we do our best in grounding our discussion. In the discussion that follows, we highlight a handful of actors that we expect to have strong agency in shaping the future of domestic photography. At the end of this chapter, we draw together our conclusions on the themes and issues that emerge from our perspective on the future.

7.2.1 Selling Advertisements: Social Networking and Search

Two major trends in consumer information technology overlap significantly with the basic uses and challenges in domestic photography. First, seeking, organising, and analysing information is an answer to the problem of managing, controlling, and effectively using the thousands of personal photographs (and other media) that have been created. Second, online social interaction is centralised with Web services that facilitate socialising with existing and broader social networks. The undisputed champions of these two businesses (in 2010) were Google in the search business and Facebook in the social networking service business. The core business model for both of these companies is selling targeted online advertisement space on the basis of data on the use of their services. In the case of Google, the data pertain to people's search activities (i.e., search queries and selections of answers). For Facebook, the user data consist of demographics, social connections, and preferences. Targeted advertisements are considered better than traditional advertisements for mass audiences. For the advertiser they are more economical in the sense that they focus only on the desired audience. For the consumer they are more relevant, and for the provider of the advertisement space a targeted advertisement can command a higher price than traditional ones.

In the domain of domestic photography, Google provides not only a search service but also a photo organisation program, Picasa, coupled with a photo sharing and publishing Web site, Picasa Web, as well as e-mail and other communication services. The significance of Facebook for domestic photography has been mentioned quite often in the previous chapters: the site hosts around 48 billion images and has over 500 million users globally (more than any other social networking service).

We believe that selling targeted online advertisement space will play a significant role as a business model driving technological and commercial development in domestic photography. As market leaders, both Google and Facebook will therefore be important in shaping the future of domestic photography.

As mentioned above, Google provides more than a search service. In addition to the personal photography technology of Picasa and Picasa Web, Google has services for placing and finding photographs on maps, social networking services, an e-mail service, a video publishing and sharing service, and technology products such as a Web browser and a mobile phone operating system. In other words, Google provides a set of services and products that are combined such that information from one can be transferred to another (e.g., user accounts and photographs). This also means that the company has access to information from various sources, and it can process and quantify this information for the benefit of the user and the company's core business. For example, Google processes e-mail messages both to sell targeted advertisement space and to help the user manage his or her messages. In the case of photography technologies, the information gathered and processed is, for example, location information and face recognition information in photographs. It is not clear how this information is used in targeted advertising, if it is used for that at all. Later in this chapter, we return to potential issues rising from centralising personal information such as face recognition data.

Nevertheless, the core business of Google benefits from centralising personal information and quantifying that information to best suit advertisers.[36] Therefore, the generation of personal information (e.g., location, Web browsing habits, social networks, purchase decisions, and user logs), standardisation of data, and processing of raw data into quantified information are in its interests. From this perspective, devices such as a camera are technologies for generating data (both visual and non-visual) that then can be processed and organised to provide consumers with tools for information management (e.g., to organise unorganised photographs) and to provide advertisers with targeted advertisement space.

The core business model of Facebook too is to sell targeted advertisement space, and most of the demographic information used for targeting advertisements is provided directly by the users of Facebook: gender, age, marital status, home city, religion, political views, and education. But the users also provide information such as employer, social connections, familial relations, and personal likes and interests. The social networking service provides the users of the service with tools for socialising and interaction with other people. On the one hand, the service facilitates people's social interaction, to keep the service interesting and attractive so that people keep using it (i.e., remain an audience for the advertisements). On the other hand, people's interactions keep the demographic and social information up to date and, therefore, enable the service to sell up-to-date information for advertisers. Photographs on Facebook serve both of these purposes: they make the service attractive to other people (mainly the social networks of an individual user), and they can be used to infer information about social networks and connections. However, it is not publicly known whether Facebook is a profitable company or not. Its market value is quite high (estimated at $33 billion[37]), but, because it is a private company, its profit levels are unknown.

---

[36] Other business models and revenue sources exist, but they are secondary to the selling of advertisement space. For example, Picasa Web sells photograph storage space to its users.

[37] See The Guardian 2010d.

Both of these companies benefit from a centralised service, from continuous use, and from collection of user data. Continuous use provides more up-to-date user data, and with a centralised service, the data can be effectively processed to provide information for advertisers' purposes. For domestic photography, this means that there is a commercial incentive for these companies to promote online photo sharing and publishing (rather than sharing personal photographs from one's own computer). The photographs are a source of personal data, such as combinations of location, time, and people that can be processed. Also, photographs are an effective way of 'locking in' a user: a person who has most of his or her personal photographs shared via a service will not move to another service if the photographs and the social networks cannot be easily transferred as well. As we mentioned, tagging of photographs within a service makes them more valuable on both sides, by generating usable information and by further locking in the user.

In addition to the business model discussed here, there is a hybrid model combining the free-of-charge use typical with Facebook and the model in which users are charged for the service. This 'freemium' model provides the service for free for most users and charges a subscription fee to a minority of users, who then get a premium service. Often the free use is covered by advertisements (e.g., in the music service Spotify and the photo publishing service Flickr), and, therefore, this model is related to the fully advertisement-based models.

However, the driving force behind the search business, dominated by Google, and the social networking service business, dominated by Facebook, is selling of online space for targeted advertisements and, thereby, effective coupling of people's social interactions and advertisement business. Making social interaction an activity surrounded by advertisements, or making purchases and consumption a topic of social interaction, is of increasing business interest.[38] These business opportunities seem to be drivers that are pushing domestic photography and social media in the direction of centralised online services that welcome the most possible data and information.

7.2.2   The Home ICT Infrastructure

The second group of commercial actors in domestic photography we identify as the providers of the domestic ICT infrastructure. By infrastructure we mean the network of devices, hardware, software, operating systems, protocols, cables, routers, screens and displays, game consoles, television sets, computers, services, and so on that together enable the use of information and communication technologies in the domestic sphere.[39]

---

[38] The Economist 2010a.

[39] In our use of the term, we include Web services and mobile phone technologies as components of the domestic ICT infrastructure although they physically exist outside the home or are not used within the physical home.

As we have discussed from the standpoint of domestic photography, this infrastructure is heterogeneous and fragmented: there is no single business providing the whole infrastructure, and no two home infrastructures are the same. Therefore, the set-up, maintenance, and configuration work for the home infrastructure becomes an issue. For the designers of technology, the challenge is that any new piece of technology has to operate in an infrastructure the configuration of which cannot be known beforehand.[40]

For the people living in the home, the challenge involves having to configure and maintain the infrastructure, and this 'infrawork' requires skills and knowledge.[41] Typical examples of 'infrawork' are setting up a wireless home network; configuring the transfer of digital photographs from one device to another (e.g., for viewing, online sharing, or printing); and updating to the latest versions of software, drivers, or firmware.

For businesses that sell the components of home infrastructures, this is a mixed blessing. On the one hand, it is challenging to design a compatible and easily configurable product for the heterogeneous infrastructures that people use. On the other hand, it means that people need to buy new versions of the same technology in order to keep the infrastructure working effectively and up to date. For example, buying a new digital camera often means that the size of the photograph files grows. The larger image files put pressure on the computational performance of the personal computer, the storage capacity of the home infrastructure, and the network bandwidth as well. If the home infrastructure is not updated, the newest products and services cannot be used as advertised and suggested by the technology providers. The purchase of a new, high-resolution digital camera can lead to buying a new computer and a faster broadband connection.

In this light, the growth of 'megapixels' in consumer cameras benefits, among others, Internet connection providers (through demand for faster networks), hard disk manufacturers and Web storage services (through demand for more storage space), television and computer screen manufacturers (via demand for higher-resolution displays), and printer manufacturers and printing services (through the demand for higher-resolution prints and printed products). In this kind of perpetual change – in which more computational power, more storage space, more network bandwidth, and better screen resolution are typical of domestic ICT and are often taken for granted – 'more is more' is often cited as the central mantra.[42] The components of the domestic ICT infrastructure have practically become consumables with a life cycle of just a few years.

Homogenising the domestic ICT infrastructure has benefits both for the technology providers and also for the people in their homes. For the technology provider, the benefits are in selling a variety of infrastructure components rather than one. The benefit for the home user would be that potentially the components from a single

---

[40]Edwards and Grinter 2001 call this "impromptu interoperability".

[41]Grinter et al. 2005 discuss the work required to make a home network function.

[42]Frohlich and Fennell 2007.

provider work together better than do components from separate providers. In other words, there are benefits and business potential in providing a variety of compatible technologies for the home or, at least, in providing infrastructure technologies that diminish the compatibility and 'infrawork' issues discussed above.

For example, Apple Inc. is a product and service provider that sells, among other things, desktop computers, laptops, operating systems, displays, camera phones, network routers, online storage space, e-mail services, television receivers, network servers, photo management and editing software, online music and video purchasing services, mp3 players, and a tablet computer. Often, Apple technologies work better together than the many non-Apple technologies do, and sometimes use of an Apple technology is the only possible option (e.g., applications for Apple phones can only be acquired through a service owned by Apple). Technology providers that provide several components in the domestic ICT infrastructure have, of course, a lot of influence on how the infrastructures will change in the future (e.g., by choosing what standards not to support[43]) and, therefore, a lot of influence in shaping domestic photography. However, linking technologies together is not without legal implications, an issue we return to in our discussion of law and regulation.

An alternative, and much advertised, business strategy for providing most of the domestic infrastructure components is to shift most of the components outside the physical home. Rather than software, hard disks, and other technologies being 'local' in the home, some of these components can be provided as a Web service. For example, the storage, organisation, editing, and archival of personal photographs can be done on remote servers and the user has only to access the data through a terminal. This is the promise of the 'cloud services': In a cloud service, the user does not need to install specific software (e.g., a photo editing program) on a computer. He or she instead runs the software through a standard Web browser. In addition to having no installation tasks, the end user does not need to maintain and install any updates either. Also, the data will be stored on a remote hard disk 'in the cloud', and there is no need for extensive storage in the home. Another benefit of the cloud is that it can be accessed outside the home infrastructure as long as there is a network connection.

As an example, it is already possible to transfer photographs from a digital camera or a camera phone directly to a Web service, edit them through a Web browser, and share them with other people either by using e-mail or by printing paper copies of them – all this can be done without the images being stored on a personal hard drive, without an editing program on a computer, and without a printer in the home.

Current Web services can be seen as 'clouds' in the way in which they provide functionality. For example, the above-mentioned Picasa Web provides photo editing in its Web service for photographs stored remotely, and the Facebook service requires only a Web browser to be used. Therefore, the centralisation of people's personal data discussed above is also a key characteristic of 'cloud' services. Transferring part of the home infrastructure into a single Web service also transfers

---

43 The Guardian 2010e.

personal data (e.g., usage data, as well as personal files and information) to the control of a single commercial organisation.

In summary, the future of domestic photography technology cannot be separated from the home ICT infrastructure and discussions of the future of the businesses providing domestic ICTs. We are already witnessing a heterogeneous and fragmented infrastructure that requires skills and money to use and maintain. In response to the fragmentation and heterogeneity, some technology providers promise fuller interoperability between their proprietary components and other providers promote the outsourcing of parts of the infrastructure altogether (i.e., 'the cloud'). These providers of infrastructure components will shape domestic photography through the business models and technological couplings they promote.

7.2.3   Selling Capture: Cameras Vs. Camera Phones

We have already discussed, in previous chapters, how several of the camera manufacturers on the Kodak Path survived the disruption caused by digital technology. In particular, Japanese camera manufacturers, such as Canon, Nikon, Olympus, and Pentax, were significant businesses on the Kodak Path and still are in the current state of the Digital Path. Our historical overview in Chap. 5 also showed that camera phones have become the most popular camera in the household – at least in ownership, not necessarily in use. However, there is competition between traditional camera manufacturers and camera phone manufacturers as to how domestic photography will be shaped. Will people have a camera dedicated only to photography, will they have a camera integrated into their phone that serves all photographic purposes; or will they have both?

Both standalone camera manufacturers and camera phone manufacturers benefit from the continuous 'more is more' culture discussed above. People are buying new cameras (and phones) more often than they ever were on the Kodak Path. However, there are a few technical characteristics that distinguish cameras from camera phones. First, the consumer camera is a dedicated device with no uses other than capturing still (and moving) images. The camera phone, on the other hand, is a multi-purpose device, and capturing images is only one of its several functions. Second, because the camera phone is a general-purpose device, it cannot be optimised as a camera. In other words, the other uses (e.g., telephony, Web browsing, text messaging, and listening to music) shape the device as much as the requirements for photography do. This means that the central processing unit (CPU) of the camera phone, the operating system of the camera phone, and the size and shape of the camera phone have to take into account uses other than photography. This means, for example, that a dedicated camera can always process images more quickly than a camera phone, which means that it can process more 'megapixels' (i.e., capture images with higher resolution) more quickly than a camera phone, and a dedicated camera need not necessarily fit into a pocket or a handbag as a phone is required to do.

However, the multi-purpose quality of the camera phone enables flexibility in the uses of the camera and the photographs. The general-purpose operating system of a camera phone makes it possible to run a variety of programs on the phone, such as for editing, sharing, or transferring the images. The inherent network connection on the phone makes it possible for those programs to use network resources and connect the functionality to Web services. Also, the multiple uses of the device make it possible to utilise a variety of data in the photography-related uses (e.g., location data and social data from a calendar or the address book).

These technical differences between cameras and camera phones can be supported by different practices and values in domestic photography. A photographic practice in which the technical quality of the image (i.e., high resolution and sharpness) and user control over the capture (i.e., focus, focal length, exposure, white balance, etc.) are very important supports the use of dedicated cameras. Digital single-lens reflex (SLR) cameras with interchangeable lenses are the kind of camera that supports this type of photography. Also, computation-heavy functions (in addition to processing of high-resolution images) are better supported by a dedicated camera with a dedicated CPU than a camera phone with a multi-purpose CPU. For example, face recognition, smile recognition, and blink recognition require processing power, so current pocket cameras have these features and promote them as an important part of domestic photography.

On the other hand, the multi-purpose camera phone supports a practice in which the technical quality of the image is not of primary importance. The camera phone is better in supporting domestic photography where instant sharing of images (over the Internet) and the social interaction surrounding the images is important. The camera phone also supports photographic practices wherein information about time, location, and people is important, and the possibility to edit photographs right after capture.

The competition has already shaped both cameras. In the past few years, camera phones have been made and marketed with high-quality lenses and high-resolution CCDs. Dedicated cameras have been made smaller, and some even have a network connection function. However, network connectivity and open programming interfaces have not yet become standard features of dedicated cameras.

There is a clear difference between camera phone and camera manufacturers in the kind of photography capture devices they are making, and this difference reflects the industry structures. Camera phones are manufactured by mobile phone manufacturers, for whom connectivity and communication are important values and core competencies. By contrast, SLR cameras and smaller 'point-and-shoot' cameras are manufactured by companies that have been in the photography business since the Kodak Path. For them the core competencies and values are high-quality photographs and imaging (i.e., what SLRs typically represent). If these two approaches to photography are to merge in cameras that offer the best of both worlds, there would need to be merging in the industries as well: the telecommunications and camera industries. At the moment, they are clearly separate, and this separation will shape domestic photography through the technologies these businesses make available and through the marketing of these technologies.

Perhaps an indication of this separation is the statistics on camera use provided by the photo publishing service Flickr. The five most popular cameras used to capture the photographs in the service were, apart from a camera phone in first place, SLRs.[44] The 'point-and-shoot' cameras that can be said to stand between the two other camera types had not made it into the top five.

7.2.4   Regulating Photography: Data Protection and IPRs

From the history of domestic photography we can see that intellectual property rights (IPRs), mainly patents, have had a major impact on which technologies have become dominant (e.g., daguerreotypes in the 1840s) or have simply disappeared (e.g., Kodak instant cameras and film in 1982). However, in this section we do not focus on existing and future patents. Studying existing patents and predicting their future importance is beyond the scope of this book. Instead, we draw attention to other legal issues that we see as important for shaping the future of domestic photography: copyright laws, data protection laws, privacy regulation, anti-trust regulation, and also the issues of global versus national legislation. As the metadata and usage data for people's domestic photographs gain importance in Internet services, these legal issues become more central in shaping the business, technology, and practice of domestic photography.

The division on the Kodak Path between private snapshots and public mass media was not problematic from the perspective of copyright laws. The private photographs almost never became public, and within the private circles where snapshots were distributed there were no issues about who owned the rights to an image. To put it simply, the creation and distribution of snapshots did not interfere with the business of mass media, so it made little sense to enforce copyright laws with respect to snapshooters who happened to capture, for example, an image of a company logo or an artist's painting.

With the current Digital Path, the distribution of non-professional snapshots is radically different. A private person can capture an image and distribute the image on the Internet with potentially very large audiences. Much in consequence of copyright issues in the music and moving image industries, media companies are cautious about any potential copyright conflicts, and their attitude is by default protective.

The new types of self-made images and the uses for them push traditional copyright practices to their limits. For example, a screenshot capture taken from a computer game, such as a 'killshot' mentioned earlier, has dual ownership: by the person who captured the image and the company owning the game in which the image was taken. To publish a 'killshot' on a personal Web site, it is not enough to

---

[44] See http://www.flickr.com/cameras/ (accessed on 14 Sept 2010).

get the permission of the capturer; one also must ask the game company.[45] However, the example shows that the Internet as a public distribution channel has brought copyright regulation into the sphere of domestic photography.

As a reaction to how people use and reuse publicly available images on the Internet, a new copyright licensing scheme has been created. Creative Commons licences (or 'CC licences') provide a way to facilitate the legal use of publicly available content on the Internet.[46] The owner of a copyright can decide to retain some rights to the content and give away other rights under legally solid CC licences. In other words, the CC licensing model makes it simple for people to reuse images and other content without the risk of copyright infringement. It also makes it simple for copyright holders to retain some rights and still make the digital content publicly available. The ways in which copyrights are enforced, and the way in which these laws are shaped to better fit people's practices, will have an influence on how the boundaries of domestic photography will be drawn. The world in which domestic photography did not overlap publicly available visual media is gone, and new legal tools such as CC licensing are enabling domestic photography to expand from the closed private sphere that traditionally housed it.

In a world where the social and demographic information linked to personal photographs has greater monetary value than the visual content does, data protection has implications for the business, the technology, and people's practices. Therefore, another field of regulation that has seen much change in the past few decades is data protection.[47] As personal photographs and the metadata connected with them are being used for business purposes, the question of what can be collected and by whom becomes important. Commercial organisations that have a major role in domestic photography are collecting personal information as part of their processes. For example, as we mentioned above, the social networking service Facebook collects people's personal information (age, gender, religion, friends, family, etc.) and Google's photo sharing service Picasa Web stores face recognition information from the users' photographs. How data protection laws are shaped in the future will have an influence on how the companies leveraging personal data operate. A liberal interpretation of data protection and privacy would benefit global Internet firms, who could worry less about legal issues. A more protective approach would make companies take greater account of the privacy of their users' data and the uses thereof.[48]

Another legal issue we see affecting domestic photography is privacy regulations affecting where people can take photographs and what can be captured. Already the possibility of taking candid photographs with camera phones and other small cameras has forced some operators of swimming pools and locker rooms to

---

[45] Which Blizzard Entertainment grants by default if it is not for professional purposes and a single copy of the image is involved.

[46] Creative Commons 2010.

[47] See, e.g., European Union 2010.

[48] See, e.g., The Economist 2010b.

regulate camera use and enforce those rules. For example, in July 2010, the City of Helsinki forbade the use of cameras in its outdoor swimming pools, to control photography of children.[49] Family memories of summer days on the beach or at the public swimming hall might have to be accompanied with fewer photographs than before.

Also, anti-trust legislation and regulations on commercial competition can have an impact on the domestic ICT infrastructure and how a single technology provider can couple different technologies. For example, in the last decade, Microsoft has been prohibited from coupling its operating system with its Web browser. Another example is how in Finland, before April 2006, it was prohibited to sell mobile phones and network carrier contracts together. This in practice stopped network carriers from subsidising the costs of an expensive mobile phone, because they could not make long-term contracts with the customer. Once the restriction was removed and this coupling allowed, sales of smartphones increased significantly.

As becomes clear from the examples above, there is a conflict between national legislation and global Internet business and use. On the one hand, heterogeneous legislation adds complexity to Internet use, as the most appropriate legal regime becomes unclear. On the other hand, differences in legal regimes make it possible for organisations to circumvent national legislation. As an example, take BitTorrent index Web sites. The Pirate Bay found a safe harbour in Sweden, where interpretations of copyright infringement were more liberal than in other countries. For domestic photography, the various legal regimes in different countries mean that data protection, IPR enforcement, and privacy regulation in one country does not necessarily force an Internet business or other organisation to change its policy and technology.[50]

Changes in legislation reflect changes in societies, including the interests of business organisations and the attitudes and values of citizens. In the next section, we briefly discuss potential changes in people's attitudes toward personal privacy and their trust in commercial organisations.

7.2.5 Public Concerns About Privacy and Trust

In January 2010, Mark Zuckerberg, the founder and CEO of Facebook, stated: "People have really gotten comfortable not only sharing more information and different kinds, but more openly and with more people. That social norm is just something that has evolved over time." This statement was issued a month after a modification in the social networking service that moved the service's privacy settings for its 350 million users toward more open information.[51] After much public criticism in the media concerning Facebook's privacy policy and the

---

[49] Helsingin Sanomat 2010.
[50] See, e.g., The Guardian 2010f.
[51] Sanghvi 2009.

complexity of managing one's privacy settings in the service, the company replaced the privacy settings in the user interface with a simpler set.[52] In the announcement about the new settings, Zuckerberg wrote: "The number one thing we've heard is that there just needs to be a simpler way to control your information."[53]

Another public comment on people's privacy was made by Google founder and CEO Eric Schmidt in August 2010. He said that he believed that in the future young people will be automatically entitled to change their name in order to disown unwanted information about their past stored on social media Web sites.[54] The statement was made at a time when Google was being investigated by authorities for accidentally gathering personal data by cars mapping for Google's StreetView service, and 6 months after a privacy flaw was detected in Google's Buzz social interaction service.[55]

Both of these comments underscore how commercial information and communication technologies are shaping norms, attitudes, and practices related to privacy. The attention that these two statements have received also demonstrates how very influential global Internet companies, such as Facebook and Google, are in shaping the norm for privacy: statements about the future of privacy made by the leaders of these two companies cannot be ignored, nor can changes in the services they provide. However, the public criticism levelled at Facebook's privacy changes is an example showing that these services are influenced by public opinions and how privacy is shaped in an interaction among technology providers, public debate, and regulation. Boyd and Hargittai found that most of their sample population of Facebook users changed their privacy settings between 2009 and 2010, the time when the service's privacy policy was changed and there was public discussion about the changes.[56] There was a clear reaction from the users of the service to the changes.

Nevertheless, it is clear that people's attitudes toward the privacy of personal data have shifted. Social networking services and other Web services let people make available information such as their name, photograph, address, previous schools and employees, and so on. The motivation for doing so is for people to find each other on the Internet and to keep in touch with those people. However, the ownership of the information and the rights of the service provider to use the data for its own purposes are less celebrated and often are hidden in the legal language of an end-user licence agreement. From the service's perspective, there is a trade-off in which the users share their personal data with the service in return for the benefits the service provides (i.e., facilitating the connecting of people and social interaction among them). In summary, the service provider uses the personal data to target advertisements and personalise the service, and the user uses the personal

---

[52] Kirkpatrick 2010; The Guardian 2010c; The Guardian 2010b; Zuckerberg 2010a.

[53] Zuckerberg 2010a.

[54] See The Wall Street Journal 2010.

[55] See, e.g., Silicon Alley Insider 2010; The Guardian 2010a; TechCrunch 2010.

[56] Boyd and Hargittai 2010.

data to find and interact with other people (e.g., by uploading photographs), and also to personalise the service to work better for him or her.

To share information with a commercial service requires trust in that service to keep the information secure and to store that information for future use. The public debates on online privacy can be seen also in discussions about whether a commercial organisation can be trusted with personal data. As our examples in Chap. 5 showed, photo sharing Web services can go bankrupt or may change their policies such that whatever the user agreed to when starting to use the service does not necessarily hold true after a while. From the standpoint of domestic photography, trusting in commercial services is important in two respects. One must trust in the service to keep personal data secure (i.e., take good care of private photographs and the information associated with them) and, second, trust that the service simply is going to exist in the future.

The trust in services existing in the future (i.e., being available and accessible in the years to come) is not as frequently discussed as privacy concerns, although the existence of these services is critical for the longevity of personal photographs (and other media). Will the 48 billion photographs on Facebook be accessible in 20 years? Perhaps people's attitudes toward photographs as keepsakes and memorabilia are changing such that photographs are presumed to have a short life span, a few years or less. If people value their photographs as personal histories that should be retained for future generations, then trusting commercial services with the archival of photographs has its risks. However, secure and long-term archival can also be seen as a business opportunity for service providers: once people trust their personal media to a service, they have strong incentives to keep the service running and making sure the archives will remain accessible even though standards and formats might change. We return to the issue of long-term storage and endurance of the infrastructure in our concluding section.

7.2.6 Standardisation: Making It All Work Together

Standardisation work is often considered mundane and to have less appeal than designing 'cool' and 'revolutionary' applications or gadgets. Standards are also often seen as belonging to the internal mechanics of ICTs and not the concern of user interface, usability, and human–computer interaction designers – standards are something that happens 'behind the scenes'. However, standards are probably more influential in shaping technology, business, and practices than any single user interface or application. A standard means that there is consensus on how specific technology should be implemented. A standard can be a *de jure* standard, which means that it was specified by a standardisation body. There are also *de facto* standards, wherein a technology has become so dominant that it is in practice standardised.

Standards are created to enable more seamless and complete interoperability: if there is a common standard addressing how to connect two pieces of technology together (e.g., a digital camera and a printer), then it benefits both the users of the technology and the makers of the technology. The user of the camera and the printer can use any combination of the two if both adhere to the same standard (such as the CIPA PictBridge standard). The maker of a technology, such as a printer, needs only to adhere to the standard and, ideally, all cameras that support the same standard can use that printer.

Standards can be proprietary or open. A proprietary standard includes intellectual property rights that the owner wants to keep full control of and often not disclose at all. A company in a monopolistic situation can promote its proprietary standard and force competitors to license the required technology, as was discussed with reference to the Kodak 126 cartridge in Chap. 4. An open standard can include IPRs, but often the standardisation process has made sure that the owner is automatically willing to license the rights on reasonable and non-discriminatory terms. A standard can be open and free, meaning that there are no known intellectual property rights involved in the use of the standard.

As we have discussed above, domestic photography is integrated into a domestic ICT infrastructure that is fragmented and heterogeneous. The future of the domestic ICT infrastructure depends a great deal on how the interconnections between the various components are standardised: the cables, the protocols, the drivers, the formats, and also the operating systems and middleware. Also, the long-term functionality of digital images depends on standardisation. At the moment, the dominant standard for digital photographs is the JPEG image format, which was first used in 1992.[57] However, other standards are in use, especially so-called RAW image standards that are often camera-manufacturer-specific. Nevertheless, the JPEG standard is so dominant that it stands a good chance of being accessible and usable in the future.

This is not the case with video standards and even less with metadata standards for images and other personal media. Neither videos nor metadata have such a dominant standard as JPEG. Personal video clips can be stored in a variety of file formats and compressions: AVI, QuickTime .mov, MPEG (versions 1, 2, and 4), and formats designed for DVDs, to name a few. For image metadata, two standards are widely used. The EXIF standard, from JEITA and CIPA,[58] stores technical information about the captured photograph, such as the time and date of capture, location, aperture, exposure, camera make and model, and colour space. The other popular standard is the IPTC Photo Metadata Standard, by the International Press Telecommunications Council, which is supported by other standards and applications. It enables, among other things, the listing of keywords attached to the image.

However, there is currently no popular and widely used metadata standard that is designed to support the practices of domestic photography. Both of the metadata standards mentioned above have been designed for the purposes of a specific industry. Also, there is no standard way of storing one's personal data so as to ensure portability from one social networking service to another, or to allow storage locally on

---

[57] International Telecommunication Union ITU 1992.
[58] CIPA 2010.

an individual's computer. One reason for the lack of such a standard is that the value of personal data has become so great that companies with access are not willing to standardise and share the data.

The future of domestic photography does not rely solely on the standardisation of image formats and metadata. Because photography is integrated into the broader infrastructure, standardisation efforts for transfer protocols, middleware, operating systems, etc. will influence the ways in which the domestic ICT infrastructure changes – and domestic photography with it. What standards will be open, proprietary, and dominant, and the purposes for which those standards will be designed, have major agency in the future of the technology, business, and practice.

7.2.7   New Photographers

Above we have focused on how commercial organisations and their business models, regulation and legislation, and public discourse can shape future domestic photography. Here we share how we believe new groups of photographers will shape domestic photography through the ways in which they practice photography. We have briefly discussed how the 'family' in domestic photography has changed; here we draw attention to three large populations of photographers: children and teenagers, older adults, and non-Western cultures.

As we mentioned earlier, the children on the Digital Path are in a different situation than those of the same age from the Kodak Path were when it comes to photography. Through camera phones, teenagers and younger children have a camera of their own that is not shared with any other member of the family. Also, because the mobile phone is often taken almost everywhere (the parents often insist on the phone being within a hand's reach all the time), the camera is available in situations where a 'camera-only' device would not necessarily be. In addition to the camera, children have access to the Internet via their mobile phones and computers. Using social networking sites, instant messaging, picture messaging, and e-mail, children can share and discuss photographs with little intervention from their parents. The kinds of photographs teenagers take and teens' photography practices have been studied[59] and found of great interest for both academics and commercial research and development. Children are also being photographed in new environments, such as kindergartens, and getting used to capturing and being captured in photos in environments outside the home.[60] How will these generations shape the practices of domestic photography as they grow older? Will they, as we have suggested, have less interest in photographs as memories and value the social interaction and identity-building functions more?

---

[59] See, e.g., Schiano et al. 2002; Van Dijck 2008.
[60] Lehmuskallio 2010; Näsänen et al. 2009.

Teenagers are not the only generation in an interesting socio-technical situation. The so-called baby boomer generations (born between 1945 and 1955) in the Western world will make up a significant part of the population in European countries and Japan.[61] This generation will be retiring from the workforce within the next decade and will have both a longer life expectancy and more wealth than previous retirees. The ways in which this generation takes photographs differ from the practices of contemporary children and teenagers. The baby boomer generation learned photography on the Kodak Path but have often also learned basic ICT skills. Also, older adults seem to have a more cautious attitude toward online social interaction than teenagers and young adults do,[62] although they seem to be a growing demographic in such services.[63] Nevertheless, the older adults' generation with their free time, wealth, and perhaps emphasis on photographs as memorabilia and visual history are in a position to shape domestic photography as much as children and teenagers do.

The third large population of photographers we draw attention to are people in the so-called emerging economies, mainly Brazil, China, India, Korea, Mexico, and Russia.[64] These six countries make up 44% of the world's population[65] and account for roughly one third of the world's economic growth,[66] and, because of their huge population and potential for growth, they are seen as a future lucrative market.

Photography on the Kodak Path was an industry dominated by companies from Europe, Japan, and the United States, and the practices of the Kodak Culture discussed by Chalfen[67] were very much born of Western culture. In this book, our perspective too has been mainly an Anglo-American one and predominantly Western. However, as mentioned, the emerging economies are growing, and as the purchasing power of those economies grows, they start acquiring domestic ICT equipment such as digital cameras and camera phones.

The business opportunities in the emerging markets will bring the ICT infrastructure required for domestic photography within the reach of these populations. How will the new markets shape domestic photography business and technologies? Or perhaps the technologies sold to the new markets will shape the photography practices of people in the developing world to resemble more the practices in the developed countries. In other words, perhaps the uptake of ICTs in developing economies will further homogenise the global domestic photography culture. For example, already more than 500 million people are using Facebook, which must have a homogenising effect on the online social interaction practices of those 500 million people.

---

[61]Eurostat 2008; National Institute of Population and Social Security Research 2006.

[62]Lehtinen et al. 2009.

[63]Riddle 2010.

[64]See, e.g., MSCI (2010) for a listing.

[65]U.S. Census Bureau 2010.

[66]EconomyWatch.com 2010.

[67]Chalfen 1987.

7.3   Looking Forward

Photography used to be an industry of its own, a set of specific practices carried out with photography technology. Since its digitisation, domestic photography has become increasingly integrated into information and communication technologies, business, and practices. It is no longer obvious where the boundaries of the photography industry are. People's needs for social bonding, demonstrating identity and membership, and recording personal histories are practised with a variety of networked digital media (e.g., text, video, audio, graphics, and computer-generated images). The technologies for photography are no longer restricted to the camera and its images. Equally important are Web services, e-mail, instant messaging, multimedia messages, and the infrastructure that enables these.

In this sense, the practice of domestic photography today has become a practice of *social media generation and exchange*. In social media, the social interaction is emphasised, the potential for societal impact is celebrated, the message is not limited to one medium, the Internet is taken for granted, and the commercial organisations profiting from social media are stretching the boundaries of traditional industries. In other words, the technology is no longer photography-centric. It is now ICT-centric with an emphasis on immediate social interaction and personal representation over the recording of memories for future reminiscing. The core business has also changed from selling consumables to selling advertisement space and perpetually changing technology.

What does this change mean for the non-professional snapshooter? How does the change from film-based photography to the information and communications technology of social media affect domestic photography as a practice and as a form of visual culture? What kinds of design alternatives are there for shaping the future of domestic photography?

7.3.1   Complexity and Expressiveness

Looking at the gradual shift from the Kodak Path to the beginning of the Digital Path, we highlight two major changes in the technology and how it is intertwined with the world we live in.

First, from the perspective of the home photographer, the Kodak infrastructure was very simple but also very restrictive. The process of creating photographs required very little skill ('You press the button, we do the rest'), and, especially in the later half of the twentieth century, it was not expensive. Simple point-and-shoot cameras were accessible to all social classes in the West, and a 24-exposure roll of film was priced quite reasonably. However, the simplicity was achieved by automating most of the process: focusing, exposure and aperture metering, developing the film, and printing the film. There was hardly a chance to edit the image between the time of capture and getting the prints from the photo-finishing service. A person who wanted to be more expressive with his or her photography had to take the development and printing process into his or her own hands, which is something that many people did, becoming labelled as 'hobbyists' or 'serious amateur' photographers. Taking this step revealed the complexity of the process, and skills, time, and effort were required.

The transformation of domestic photography into an ICT activity has increased the potential for expression in the editing of snapshots, but it has also turned ordinary image capture and sharing into a more complex process. To put it simply, digital domestic photography is more complex than domestic photography on the Kodak Path. The infrastructure for digital photography permits a variety of ways to practice photography (not only editing), and there is no escape from this heterogeneity and complexity. Individually, a person can do domestic photography very simply: push the button and take the memory card to a photo-finishing service for printing. However, even the simplest of practices such as this cannot ignore *other people's practices* that include various ways of sharing images over networks, editing with professional-grade software tools, creating beautiful photo books, and so on. Receiving and sharing photographs is elemental in our social relationships, and people are drawn into revising their practices in line with each other to maintain those relationships. Even the most conservative and 'Luddite' domestic photographer has to face the complexity of the Digital Path or otherwise risk becoming anti-social and excluded from social networks.

7.3.2 Increased Dependence on Infrastructure

The second major change from the Kodak Path we note is the *dependence* of domestic photography on the ICT infrastructure. On the Kodak Path, the domestic photographer depended on camera manufacturers to make new cameras, and on repair shops to repair broken ones. Also, the photographer depended on film manufacturers to make film and photo-finishing services to make prints of exposed film. If any of these businesses were to stop providing the service or the technology, the photographer would be without a functioning infrastructure. This happened, for example, in 1982 when Kodak was forced to stop manufacturing its instant photography cameras and film, and it happened again in 1988 when Kodak stopped its support for Disc film. The people who had invested in either Kodak instant cameras or Disc cameras were disappointed and had to buy new equipment if they wished to continue snapshooting. However, they still had the prints they had developed from the instant and Disc film; the photographic prints themselves were not dependent on the continuation of the film or the cameras. The prints were paper, and no device is required to look at paper prints – the prints were autonomous technology, with little dependence on the underlying infrastructure.

The shift to an ICT infrastructure has made domestic photography less autonomous and more dependent on other technologies. Digital photography depends on camera manufacturers and photo-finishing service, as photography has for 170 years, but in recent decades the dependence has expanded to cover the images as well. Digital photographs cannot be viewed without a screen, a computer, and a computer program that understands the format of the digital images. If the photographs reside in a Web service, viewing them requires a Web connection and for the service to be accessible. As we mentioned in Chap. 5, the online photo sharing service Ringo serves as an example of how a service was terminated and personal content lost forever.[68]

Domestic photography as a set of practices and a form of culture has become dependent on technology and service providers to function, more dependent than in the era of film photography. For good or ill, domestic photography is increasingly reliant on commercial services that host the images and the interaction around them, and on technology providers that create technologies and standards. Perhaps from this perspective the heterogeneity and fragmentation of the industry is beneficial: we can distribute the dependence over several technology and service providers rather than putting all our eggs in the same basket.

7.3.3 Room for Innovation: Infrastructural Simplicity and Endurance

The complexity of the domestic photography infrastructure and people's increased dependence on that infrastructure can be taken as design challenges for future technology's development. To address the complexity of the heterogeneous networks of devices, we pose the question of how to build simplicity and usability into an infrastructure rather than single applications or individual user interfaces. To address the increasing dependence on ICT infrastructures for domestic photography, we ask how to build enduring technology that will enable people to access their photographs and other media decades from now.

The requirement for more simplicity is one of accessibility. As discussed above, the use of domestic photography technology requires special skills and knowledge of the use of the ICT infrastructure. Not only special skills are required; using the infrastructure requires financial investments in devices, services, and their maintenance. The current complexity in domestic photography runs the risk of excluding people from domestic photography on the basis of income and education.

The building of simpler infrastructures requires interaction designers and usability experts to look under the hood, so to speak. For an infrastructure to be simple, it has to be understood, and this requires breaking down the walls between user interface technology and infrastructure technology. These two fields of technology are seldom designed, studied, and discussed by the same people, at the same conferences, in the same journals, or in the same projects. There is a natural

---

[68] The photographs in the service were available for download for a while. The comments and the videos uploaded to the service could not be downloaded.

presumption that people working with applications and user interfaces, both of which work on top of an infrastructure, need not concern themselves with the internal structures and workings of that infrastructure. There is a division between 'above the hood' and 'under the hood' technology. For this reason, applying best practices and well-known principles of usability and building simple technology into the infrastructure are problematic. For example, running user tests on an infrastructure cannot rely on simulations and mock-ups in the same way a usability test of a user interface can.

Perhaps the main challenge in designing simple infrastructures is that there is no central owner of an infrastructure.[69] An infrastructure as a network of technologies, organisations, people, legal contracts, and interconnections is fragmented and heterogeneous. Making such a network simple requires a different approach to design, in which standardisation is critical. As we discussed earlier, the common strategy for achieving infrastructural simplicity is either to lessen the heterogeneity or to standardise the interconnections. With the first option, an organisation, such as a company, aims to make parts of the infrastructure proprietary and control the heterogeneity by providing a set of products and services that inter-operate together better than technologies from other providers. With the second option, the goal is to pursue open and standardised interconnections that enable variety and choice in the components of the infrastructure. Whether simplicity can be achieved through a closed proprietary system or an open network of components is something for designers, policymakers, consumers, and businesspeople to think about. We see room for innovation, potential business, and future research in making infrastructures simpler and more usable.

The challenge is to build enduring technology at a time when technology seems to be in a state of continuous change. As part of this, we see demand for a service or a product that ensures the long-term archival of personal photographs and other media. We believe that people will continue reflecting on their personal and family histories, and photographs and other media will play an important role. We also believe that photographs, video clips, blog posts, status updates, and e-mail messages are an important source for understanding societies' and people's everyday life from a perspective broader than that of an individual. In other words, photographs and other self-made media have a cultural value in addition to individual personal value.

An enduring technical solution would also require an organisation that lasts a long time and whose goal is long-term archival and accessibility. Such organisations are typically museums or public archives, but also more commercially minded organisations have the potential to persist for decades, especially if that is in the interest of their clients and customers. That organisation would be trusted with people's personal media and with keeping them accessible even if standards for file formats, image compression, and metadata change (i.e., curation work). Long-term archival of millions of digital images and other media, and the curation of the images, creates significant costs that require a business model to cover them as well as innovative technology to make the service accessible and easy to use.

---

[69] Norman 2009; Star 1999.

We also emphasise standardisation of technologies in domestic photography for ensuring archival for decades to come – especially open standards. Openness in standards such as image formats, transfer protocols, and metadata ontologies would enable free competition among providers of archival services, and also allow people to archive their images in several places, to reduce the risk of dependence on a single provider. Perhaps an open-source technology with a business model to cover the costs would be a solution.

In the following chapter, we finish the book by discussing future research in domestic photography, and especially, the lessons we have learned for each of the three main academic fields we have applied in our study: human–computer interaction, visual studies and photography, and science and technology studies.

References

Adams A, Talvala E-V, Park SH, Jacobs DE, Ajdin B, Gelfand N, Dolson J, Vaquero D, Baek J, Tico M, Lensch HPA, Matusik W, Pulli K, Horowitz M, and Levoy M (2010) The Frankencamera: an experimental platform for computational photography. In: Proceedings of the ACM SIGGRAPH 2010, Los Angeles, 2010. ACM, New York, pp 1–12

Anderson P, Tushman M (1990) Technological discontinuities and dominant designs: a cyclical model of technological change. Adm Sci Q 35(4):604–633

Batchen G (2004) Forget me not: photography and remembrance. Van Gogh Museum; Princeton Architectural Press, Amsterdam

Book B (2003) Traveling through cyberspace: tourism and photography in virtual worlds. In: Proceedings of the tourism & photography: still visions – changing lives, Sheffield, 2 May 2003, pp 1–24

Boyd D, Hargittai E (2010) Facebook privacy settings: who cares? First Monday 15(8)

Buse P (2010) Polaroid into digital: technology, cultural form, and the social practices of snapshot photography. Continuum 24(2):215–230

Chalfen R (1987) Snapshot versions of life. Bowling Green State University Popular Press, Bowling Green

CIPA (2010) What is exif? CIPA. http://www.cipa.jp/exifprint/contents_e/01exif1_e.html. Accessed 2 Sept 2010

CNET News (2007) Cameras: shipments rising, but prices falling. 19 Sept 2007

Creative Commons (2010) Creative commons. http://creativecommons.org/. Accessed 2 Sept 2010

Davis M, King S, Good N, Sarvas R (2004) From context to content: leveraging context to infer media metadata. In: Proceedings of the 12th annual ACM international conference on multimedia, New York, 1 Oct 2004

Durrant A (2010) Family portrayals: design to support photographic representations of intergenerational relationships in family homes. Doctoral dissertation, Department of Psychology, University of Surrey, Guildford

Durrant A, Frohlich D, Sellen A, Lyons E (2009) Home curation versus teenage photography: photo displays in the family home. Int J Hum Comput Stud 67(12):1005–1023

EconomyWatch.com (2010) World economy, global economy, international economics. EconomyWatch.com. http://www.economywatch.com/world_economy/. Accessed 9 Jan 2010

Edwards WK, Grinter RE (2001) At home with ubiquitous computing: seven challenges. In: Proceedings of the UbiComp 2001, Atlanta, 15 Aug 2001, pp 256–271

European Union (2010) Data protection. European Union. http://ec.europa.eu/justice/policies/privacy/index_en.htm. Accessed 16 Sept 2010

Eurostat (2008) Ageing characterizes the demographic perspectives of the European societies, statistic in focus 72/2008. Office for Official Publications of the European Communities, Luxembourg

Fletcher D (2010) How Facebook is redefining privacy. Time Magazine
Frohlich D, Fennell J (2007) Sound, paper and memorabilia: resources for a simpler digital pho-
  tography. Pers Ubiquit Comput 11(2):107–116
Giddens A (1998) The third way: the renewal of social democracy. Polity Press, Cambridge
Giddens A (2000) The third way and its critics. Polity, Cambridge
Grinter RE, Edwards WK, Newman M, Duchenaut N (2005) The work to make a home network.
  In: Proceedings of the Ninth European conference on computer-supported cooperative work
  (ECSCW 2005), Paris, 18–22 Sept 2005, pp 469–488
Harrison B (2002) Photographic visions and narrative inquiry. Narrat Inq 12(1):87–111
Helsingin Sanomat (2010) Kuvaamista maauimaloissa halutaan rajoittaa pedofiilien pelossa. 12
  July 2010
Hodges S, Williams L, Berry E, Izadi S, Srinivasan J, Butler A, Smyth G, Kapur N, Wood K (2006)
  SenseCam: a retrospective memory aid. In: Proceedings of the eighth international conference
  of ubiquitous computing (UbiComp 2006), Orange County, 27 July 2006, pp 177–193
Hsu J (2009) The worldwide mobile phone camera module market and Taiwan's industry, 2009
  and beyond. Market Intelligence & Consulting Institute (MIC), Taipei
International Telecommunication Union ITU (1992) T.81: information technology – digital com-
  pression and coding of continuous-tone still images – requirements and guidelines. ITU,
  Geneva
Kirk DS, Sellen A, Cao X (2010) Home video communication: mediating 'closeness'. In:
  Proceedings of the 2010 ACM conference on computer supported cooperative work, Savannah,
  2010. ACM, New York, pp 135–144
Kirkpatrick M (2010) The day has come: Facebook pushes people to go public. ReadWriteWeb.
  http://www.readwriteweb.com/archives/facebook_pushes_people_to_go_public.php Accessed
  1 Sept 2010
Lehmuskallio A (2010) Non-professional camera pictures in a 'Cam Era' – empirical studies in
  non-professional uses of user-created pictorial content. Unpublished Work
Lehtinen V, Näsänen J, Sarvas R (2009) "A little bit foolish and light-headed" – Older adults'
  understandings of social networking sites. In: Proceedings of the 23rd BCS conference on
  Human Computer Interaction, British Computer Society, Cambridge, 2009, pp 45–54
Miniwatts Marketing Group (2010) World internet usage and population statistics. Miniwatts
  Marketing Group. http://www.internetworldstats.com/stats.htm. Accessed 6 Aug 2010
MSCI (2010) MSCI international equity indices. http://www.mscibarra.com/products/indices/
  international_equity_indices/. Accessed 2 Sept 2010
Näsänen J, Oulasvirta A, Lehmuskallio A (2009) Mobile media in the social fabric of a kindergar-
  ten. In: Proceedings of the 27th international conference on human factors in computing
  systems CHI'09, Boston, 2009. ACM, New York, pp 2167–2176
National Institute of Population and Social Security Research (2006) Population statistics of
  Japan. National Institute of Population and Social Security Research, Tokyo
Neustaedter C, Fedorovskaya E (2009) Capturing and sharing memories in a virtual world. In:
  Proceedings of the 27th international conference on human factors in computing systems,
  Boston, 2009. ACM, New york, pp 1161–1170
Norman D (2009) Designing the infrastructure. Interactions 16(4):66–69
PMA (2009a) U.S. households make photo books for family keepsakes. PMA. http://pmafore-
  sight.com/?p=40. Accessed 2 Sept 2010
PMA (2009b) Printing behavior of U.S. consumers. PMA. http://pmaforesight.com/?p=92.
  Accessed 2 Sept 2010
PMA (2009c) Percentage of U.S. households receiving digital images from family and friends
  down from previous years. PMA. http://pmaforesight.com/?p=123. Accessed 2 Sept 2010
Raento M, Oulasvirta A, Petit R, Toivonen H (2005) ContextPhone: a prototyping platform for
  context-aware mobile applications. IEEE Pervasive Comput 4(2):51–59
Riddle W (2010) Social networking experiences a great migration of maturity in Switched. http://
  www.switched.com/2010/08/28/social-networking-experiences-a-great-migration-of-maturity/.
  Accessed 2 Sept 2010

Rose G (2003) Family photographs and domestic spacings: a case study. Trans Inst Br Geogr 28(1):5–18

Sanghvi R (2009) New tools to control your eExperience. The Facebook Blog. http://blog. facebook.com/blog.php?post=196629387130. Accessed 1 Sept 2010

Sarvas R, Herrarte E, Wilhelm A, Davis M (2004) Metadata creation system for mobile images. In: Proceedings of the 2nd international conference on mobile systems, applications, and services, Boston, 2004. ACM, New York, pp 36–48

Sarvas R, Oulasvirta A, Jacucci G (2005) Building social discourse around mobile photos: a systemic perspective. In: Proceedings of the 7th international conference on human computer interaction with mobile devices and services, MobileHCI '05, Salzburg, 1 Sept 2005. ACM, New York

Schiano D, Chen CP, Isaacs E (2002) How teens take, view, share, and store photos. In: Proceedings of the computer supported cooperative work (CSCW 2002), New Orleans, 2002

Shove E, Watson M, Hand M, Ingram J (2007) The design of everyday life. Berg, New York

Silicon Alley Insider (2010) WARNING: Google Buzz has a huge privacy flaw. http://www. businessinsider.com/warning-google-buzz-has-a-huge-privacy-flaw-2010-2#. Accessed 19 Mar 2010

Star SL (1999) The ethnography of infrastructure. Am Behav Sci 43(3):377–391

TechCrunch (2010) Watch out who you reply to on Google Buzz, you might be exposing their email address. http://techcrunch.com/2010/02/11/reply-google-buzz-exposing-email/. Accessed 19 Mar 2010

The Economist (2010a) Selling becomes sociable. 9 Sept 2010

The Economist (2010b) The clash of data civilisations. 17 June 2010

The Guardian (2010a) Google Wi-Fi data capture cleared by information commissioner. 29 July 2010

The Guardian (2010b) Privacy no longer a social norm, says Facebook founder. 11 Jan 2010

The Guardian (2010c) Facebook reveals new privacy controls following intense criticism from users. 26 May 2010

The Guardian (2010d) Shareholder trading values Facebook at more than $33bn. 25 Aug 2010

The Guardian (2010e) Apple's iPad war on Adobe and Flash. 18 Apr 2010

The Guardian (2010f) Internet pirates find 'bulletproof' havens for illegal file sharing. 5 Jan 2010

The New York Times (2010) For photographers, the image of a shrinking path. 29 Mar 2010

The Wall Street Journal (2010) Google and the search for the future. 14 Aug 2010

United Nations (2000) Charting the progress of populations. United Nations Population Division, New York

US Census Bureau (2010) U.S. and world population clocks. U.S. Census Bureau. http://www. census.gov/main/www/popclock.html. Accessed 16 Sept 2010

Van Dijck J (2008) Digital photography: communication, identity, memory. Vis Commun 7(1):57–76

Van House N (2007) Flickr and public image-sharing: distant closeness and photo exhibition. In: Extended abstracts on human factors in computing systems (CHI '07), San Jose

Whittaker S, Bergman O, Clough P (2010) Easy on that trigger dad: a study of long term family photo retrieval. Pers Ubiquit Comput 14(1):31–43

Zuckerberg M (2010) Making control simple. In: The Facebook Blog. http://blog.facebook.com/ blog.php?post=391922327130. Accessed 1 Sept 2010

Chapter 8
Future Research

Our background, from which we approached this book, is in human–computer interaction (HCI). This field seeks to build technological prototypes that either facilitate understanding of people's behaviour with new technologies or feed ideas in to the design of innovative products and services. Most often, the method in HCI and related fields of research is to build a prototype, empirically study its use, and report the results of the study in the form of implications for design. A piece of technology without a user study is considered half-done, and a study of people using technology is also unfinished unless there is a discussion of how to apply the knowledge created, in building new technology.

In our desire to write a book about domestic photography from the perspective of system and application design, we ran into a problem with the method described above. We wanted to discuss the past, present, and future of domestic photography, but the related literature in HCI was somewhat problematic for our goal. There were few studies on the uptake of commercial technologies. No-one seemed to be interested in studying, for example, the use of existing document-scanners for photographs at the beginning of the digital photography era. Instead, the majority of studies concerned lab prototypes rather than off-the-shelf technology. These are useful for reasoning about hypothetical future technologies but not for understanding how actual technologies are changing social practices in the real world. Fortunately, there were a substantial set of residual user studies in HCI that examined the very early uptake of *new* digital photography products, or the small-scale use of prototypes that *eventually* had an impact on the mass market.

In contrast, we did find studies and writings on past and present photographic behaviours in visual media studies, including work on photography and visual culture. These articles and books have proved to be elemental for us in understanding domestic photography. Newspaper articles, second-hand cameras, marketing reports, and informal conversations complemented this understanding. To make sense of this disparate information, we needed a theoretical framework in which we could synthesise the design-oriented HCI literature with visual media studies and also our streams of non-academic sources. How could we intuitively blend our technological understanding with critical and empirical data about domestic photography? Science and technology studies provided one answer.

R. Sarvas and D.M. Frohlich, *From Snapshots to Social Media - The Changing Picture of Domestic Photography*, Computer Supported Cooperative Work, DOI 10.1007/978-0-85729-247-6_8, © Springer-Verlag London Limited 2011

The field of science and technology studies (STS) looks at technology as something to study rather than something to improve by designing and building. Unlike the goal of engineering and design sciences, that of STS is not to produce inventions, better technology, and an understanding of the use of specific implementations: STS looks at technology as an integral part of our society, how values and heterogeneous actors shape technology, and how technology shapes those actors and values. These studies take into account interactions of practice, technology, and business factors that we felt were critical for understanding the evolution of domestic photography technology and its effects on everyday life. Hence, in Chap. 2, we used the concept of technological paths and the theory of dominant designs in describing the changes and stabilisations in domestic photography as a socio-technical system.

In this final chapter, we reflect on what we see as the main lessons learnt for each of the three fields of academic literature we brought together in this way. We go on to argue that in such a broad area as photography, academic boundaries and barriers are artificial and can often hinder the exchange of information and the development of knowledge. As Bijker et al. write at the beginning of their book: "System builders are no respecters of knowledge categories or professional boundaries. In his notebooks Thomas Edison so thoroughly mixed matters commonly labelled economic, technical, and scientific that his thoughts composed a seamless web."[1] In our conclusions, we therefore recommend the interdisciplinary study of domestic photography and describe some of its current research challenges.

8.1 Lessons for Human–Computer Interaction

Typically, the research of new technologies in human–computer interaction turns a blind eye to the commercial actors shaping technology. Technology design in these fields seldom makes explicit the commercial actors shaping the requirements for the prototype: industry structures, business models associated with existing technologies, and commercial organisations that fund the research. Also, the design process does not pay much attention to the processes of further innovation and commercialisation required to take a prototype out of the academic world and shape it into something for mass adoption, and often this is not seen as within the scope of HCI research. However, as the history of domestic photography shows, no technology gets widely adopted without strong and obvious backing by companies, sustainable business models, and individual customers' purchasing decisions.

The goal of research is to create knowledge that has an impact, and we argue that, to have an impact, the design of technology prototypes should acknowledge the inherently commercial nature of technology. Information and communication

---

[1]Bijker et al. 1987, p. 9.

technologies are intertwined through complex infrastructure such that it is almost impossible to build information and communication technology that is not dependent on commercial actors: broadband providers, device manufacturers, business models, pricing policies, companies' product portfolios, and so on. This means that no design can start with a 'clean slate'. For example, the design and implementation of a photo organisation application for a mobile phone has to take into account what operating system it will support, and that decision limits what kind of application distribution and sales model is possible, and which organisations can benefit from that model.

Studying and designing for the commercial as well as the social context of technology use will require two new forms of HCI study. First, it requires the incorporation of business analysis and research into the HCI field so that business factors can be taken into account much earlier in the design process. Business researchers should be brought into research and development (R&D) teams themselves rather than consulted from within marketing departments, so that novel business models can be co-designed with novel technology in the light of user and producer understandings. Second, the framing of user research should be expanded to include studies of the uptake of new and existing technologies over much longer periods of time, and it should be expanded to cover a wider network of actors and influences that shape the uptake process. Current studies stop too soon in the life cycle of a product, which continues to be shaped for many years beyond early lab and field prototypes or design exhibitions.

These changes would begin to address what Don Norman has recently referred to as the Research–Practice gap.[2] By this he means the ineffectiveness of research insights for informing design and leading to successful innovations. Although he puts this down to a difference in the aims and culture of science and business practitioners, we believe it is largely due to an ignorance of or indifference to commercial factors in HCI. This could be put right by studying the operation of such factors and taking them into account more explicitly within interactive system design.

This solution would also address a second criticism Norman makes of HCI: that it has only incremental impact on product development.[3] His observation that needs often follow, rather than lead, new technologies acknowledges the social shaping of technology so prevalent in the history of photography we have reviewed. By studying this process more carefully, and designing for it to happen, HCI might have a bigger impact on products and ultimately on society. We are less keen, however, on Norman's preference for a technology-driven approach in which "inventors will invent" and "the needs will slowly follow".[4] In our opinion, Norman overlooks the influences that shape the inventors. Inventors are members of their society and society shapes them to create products and services that seem rational and inventive at the time. Many inventors work for a company whose values will shape the ideas of the inventor.

---

[2] Norman 2010.

[3] *Ibid.*, p. 39.

[4] *Ibid.*, p. 42.

Neither are inventors immune to existing technologies, public discourse, traditions, personal histories, laws and regulations, and economic situations in the world touching them.

In general, this perspective suggests that HCI should take on more of a computer-supported co-operative work (CSCW) mindset, in viewing human actors and digital products as elements in a socio-technical system or network. We hope that this book provides an example of how socio-technological systems are shaped over time. We especially hope that our history of domestic photography and our view of the future draws attention to actors and influences often overlooked in HCI and even CSCW. These include commercial organisations and business models, industry structures, law and regulation, the legacy of old and existing interconnected technologies, economic changes, and cultural differences. We see understanding these actors and stakeholders as an important factor for designing components for the current and future ICT infrastructure.

8.2 Lessons for Visual Media Studies

Visual media studies often look at photography in the context of societal phenomena – for example, urbanisation and the rise of the middle class in the nineteenth century, the sensitisation of society to media, or changes in the family in the industrialised world. Such studies are also valuable for highlighting differences in image and media *content* across various contexts of use. In our experience, studies of this sort are not, however, widely adopted in the research and design of interactive systems. We believe that the broader perspective on technology that we argue for would make it easier to connect the discourses in visual media studies with those in HCI and technology design. Such discourses should seek to position their conclusions as relevant to new technology development and might even explore their implications for design.

We also see visual media studies as themselves benefiting from a deeper understanding of technologies and other non-human actors shaping the productions and consumption of images. Our discussion of the shift from a film-based infrastructure to an ICT infrastructure has pointed out that changes in the mediating technologies have a profound effect on the practice and content of domestic photography. As Lehmuskallio and Sarvas discuss, the change in infrastructure has highlighted the role of hybrid networks in connecting photography to related technologies, the 'infrawork' required to maintain those networks, and the business models and monetary transactions driving the commercial incentives behind the infrastructure.[5] To put it simply, we see the benefit for visual media studies in collaboration with HCI practitioners in opening the 'black box' of infrastructure and making the connections between its various components more transparent.

---

[5]Lehmuskallio and Sarvas 2010.

8.3 Lessons for Science and Technology Studies

We see photography as an exceptionally rich domain of study for science and technology studies. Photography has a long history of change of technology, it is a widespread practice, and it is in the middle of another major transition. Perhaps most importantly, photography has been studied from a variety of academic perspectives ever since photographic cameras were invented. Few systems have had the privilege of being studied in the arts and humanities, engineering, design, the social sciences, and business studies. The ongoing transition and the rich academic activity focusing on it make photography a fruitful area of research into innovation and socio-technical systems in the midst of an era of ferment.

We hope our study and the discussion earlier in this chapter have also shown that there is a pragmatic connection between the *study* of technology and the *development* of technology. The broader perspective familiar in science and technology studies can be used to better identify stakeholders, agencies, and values in technology design, especially for understanding the infrastructure in which a new design is intended to operate.

The literature on technology management has a pragmatic dimension to the perspective it takes on systems. It looks at the evolution of technology and industries in transition through the lens of innovation activity. This approach can be seen as integral to science and technology studies, as Munir and Jones suggest.[6] However, the technology management literature has a clear business-orientation, and could benefit from a more in-depth understanding of people's practices and the way these change over time.

8.4 Conclusions

Most of the research lessons we recommend for the individual disciplines mentioned above involve greater acknowledgement of each other's contribution to understanding photography. Applying these lessons across the board could therefore result in a more fully integrated and interdisciplinary study of domestic photography and its associated technology. This would involve more than we have been able to do in this book by reviewing work carried out in three separate fields. It would mean practitioners in those fields talking to one another and eventually planning new kinds of studies, studies that bring the best of their theories, methods, and analyses together.

Such studies would be more longitudinal than is common in HCI or the visual media field. They would incorporate the empirical data collection of HCI and STS studies but also the critical content analysis of media studies. Their findings would be used to speculate about novel design and business possibilities as well as to

---

[6]Munir and Jones 2004.

understand real-world interactions of business, technology, and practice. A role might be found for *intervention* in STS and media studies through the use of design probes and market tests. Finally, and perhaps most importantly, interdisciplinary studies might examine technology–business–practice interactions at a variety of levels.

For example, numerous studies of technology examine the design and adoption of photography technology at a *micro* level: designing the features of a product, user trials with prototypes, etc. There are also studies of technology approached from a *macro* level, such as this book and other writings on systems and industries.[7] What we see as missing is a *meso* level: looking at a single service or product from a broader perspective than typical design research does but at the same time having a closer focus than studies on organisations or industries.[8] A meso perspective could pay more attention to the network of actors shaping technology, business, and practice in the context of a product or a service – from a historical perspective and from a contemporaneous perspective. We see such studies as being extremely informative, illuminating how inventions turn into innovations (successful or not); what constitutes technology and how it might vary between times and locations; and how technology, business, and practices, in addition to other actors, shape the technology. For example, the concept of domestic photography could be studied over a long period of time from the standpoint of a service, an organisation behind the service, and the people involved with these.

For now, we must be content with the conclusion of our current analysis that domestic photography has moved from an activity carried out with a dedicated set of photographic tools in its own industry to one involving a set of multi-purpose tools embedded in the broader ICT infrastructure. Snapshots have evolved into social media and are just as likely to circulate between the screens of Internet appliances as they are to be passed from hand to hand as a printed photograph. Indeed, it is hard to know today what counts as a photograph and where to draw the boundaries around the activity of domestic photography. Is photography still *domestic* when it involves sharing images outside the family or beyond the confines of a domestic space? Is the activity still *photography* when it involves posting a self-portrait on a social networking site and adding textual details to a public profile? Right now, the meanings and definitions of both words in the term 'domestic photography' are somewhat outdated in an age of heterogeneous ICT infrastructures and social media.

In the future, new understandings will be needed that take into account some of the trends we pointed to in the previous chapter. As people accumulate collections of tens of thousands of photographs with metadata about time, location, people, and personal keywords, the database of metadata becomes as important as the images themselves. It is the metadata that will allow consumers to find images again and

---

[7]For example, in this book we have often referenced the work of Reese Jenkins (1975) and also a few histories of photography written from the perspective of an individual, such as Edwin Land (Wensberg 1987), or an organisation, such as Kodak (Collins 1990).

[8]Hyysalo discusses the longitudinal analyses of the biography of technologies (Hyysalo 2010).

reflect on important people, places, and events in their lives. For advertising purposes, which are becoming more important to the imaging industry, the visual content of personal photographs is already secondary to the metadata addressing who, what, where, and when. The growing importance of metadata is changing people's relationship to photographs. No longer are photographs predominantly visual objects for communication, identity-building, and memory. The digital photograph is also a container of information that can be linked to other information in a heterogeneous infrastructure. In general, the increasing importance of non-visual data in photographs is a result of the shift toward an ICT-based infrastructure, and we see it as a potentially fundamental change in people's relationship to photographs and photography. To study and shape this change, we believe, it will be necessary to adopt the kind of interdisciplinary approach we have followed in this book and recommend above. The history, formats, contents, meanings, values, and costs of future photography must be studied together if we are to understand its new role in our lives.

References

Bijker WE, Hughes TP, Pinch TJ (1987) The Social construction of technological systems: new directions in the sociology and history of technology. MIT Press, Cambridge

Collins D (1990) The story of Kodak. H.N. Abrams, New York

Hyysalo S (2010) Health technology development and use: from practice-bound imagination to evolving impacts. Routledge, London

Jenkins R (1975) Images and enterprise: technology and the American photographic industry, 1839–1925. Johns Hopkins University Press, Baltimore

Lehmuskallio A, Sarvas R (2010) The agency of ICT in shaping non-professional photo use. In: Proceedings of the Nordic Network for Visual Studies in Social Science Workshop: from Family Album to Social Media – traditions and Change, Stockholm, 2010

Munir KA, Jones M (2004) Discontinuity and after: the social dynamics of technology evolution and dominance. Organ Stud 25(4):561–581

Norman D (2010) The way I see it: technology first, needs last: the research–product gulf. Interactions 17(2):38–42

Wensberg PC (1987) Land's Polaroid: a company and the man who invented it. Houghton Mifflin, Boston

List of Figures

R. Sarvas and D.M. Frohlich, *From Snapshots to Social Media - The Changing Picture*   187
of Domestic Photography, Computer Supported Cooperative Work,
DOI 10.1007/978-0-85729-247-6, © Springer-Verlag London Limited 2011

Bibliography

Aaland M, Burger R (1992) Digital photography. Random House, New York

Adams A, Talvala E-V, Park SH, Jacobs DE, Ajdin B, Gelfand N, Dolson J, Vaquero D, Baek J, Tico M, Lensch HPA, Matusik W, Pulli K, Horowitz M, and Levoy M (2010) The Frankencamera: an experimental platform for computational photography. In: Proceedings of the ACM SIGGRAPH 2010, Los Angeles, 2010. ACM, New York, pp 1–12

Ahern S, Eckles D, Good NS, King S, Naaman M, Nair R (2007) Over-exposed?: Privacy patterns and considerations in online and mobile photo sharing. In: Proceedings of the SIGCHI conference on human factors in computing systems, San Jose, 2007. ACM, New York, pp 357–366

Allison D (1989) Photography and the mass market. In: Ford C (ed.) The Kodak Museum: the story of popular photography. Century, London, pp 42–59

Ames M, Naaman M (2007) Why we tag: motivations for annotation in mobile and online media. In: Proceedings of the SIGCHI conference on human factors in computing systems, San Jose, 2007. ACM, New York, pp 971–980

Ames M, Eckles D, Naaman M, Spasojevic M, Van House N (2010) Requirements for mobile photoware. Pers Ubiquit Comput 14(2):95–109

Anderson R (1994) Representation and requirements: the value of ethnography in system design. Hum Comput Interact 9(2):151–182

Anderson P, Tushman M (1990) Technological discontinuities and dominant designs: a cyclical model of technological change. Adm Sci Q 35(4):604–633

Apted T, Kay J, Quigley A (2006) Tabletop sharing of digital photographs for the elderly. In: Proceedings of the SIGCHI conference on human factors in computing systems, Montreal, 2006. ACM, New York, pp 781–790

Arthur WB (1994) Increasing returns and path dependence in the economy. University of Michigan Press, Ann Arbor

Auer M (1975) The illustrated history of the camera from 1839 to the present. New York Graphic Society, Boston

Balabanović M, Chu L, Wolff G (2000) Storytelling with digital photographs. In: Proceedings of the SIGCHI conference on human factors in computing systems (CHI '00), The Hague, 1 Apr 2000. ACM, New York, pp 564–571

Barthes R (2000) Camera Lucida: reflections on photography. Vintage Books, London

Batchen G (1997) Burning with desire: the conception of photography. MIT Press, Cambridge

Batchen G (2004) Forget me not: photography and remembrance. Van Gogh Museum; Princeton Architectural Press, Amsterdam

Batchen G (2009) Dreams of ordinary life: Cartes-de-visite and the Bourgeois imagination. In: Long JJ, Noble A, Welch E (eds) Photography: theoretical snapshots. Routledge, London, pp 80–97

Benson R (2008) The printed picture. Museum of Modern Art, New York

Bentley F, Metcalf C, Harboe G (2006) Personal vs. commercial content: the similarities between consumer use of photos and music. In: Proceedings of the SIGCHI conference on human factors in computing systems, Montreal, 2006. ACM, New York, pp 667–676

Besmer A, Lipford H (2009) Tagged photos: concerns, perceptions, and protections. In: Proceedings of the 27th international conference on human factors in computing systems, Boston, 2009. ACM, New York, pp 4585–4590

Bijker WE (1995) Of bicycles, bakelites, and bulbs: toward a theory of sociotechnical change. MIT Press, Cambridge

Bijker WE, Law J (1992) Shaping technology/building society: studies in sociotechnical change. MIT Press, Cambridge

Bijker WE, Hughes TP, Pinch TJ (1987) The Social construction of technological systems: new directions in the sociology and history of technology. MIT Press, Cambridge

Book B (2003) Traveling through cyberspace: tourism and photography in virtual worlds. In: Proceedings of the tourism & photography: still visions – changing lives, Sheffield, 2 May 2003, pp 1–24

Bourdieu P (1990) Photography: a middle-brow art. Polity Press, Cambridge

Boyd D, Ellison N (2008) Social network sites: definition, history, and scholarship. J Comput Mediated Commun 13(1):210–230

Boyd D, Hargittai E (2010) Facebook privacy settings: who cares? First Monday 15(8)

Buse P (2007) Photography degree zero: cultural history of the Polaroid image. New Form 62(Autumn):29–44

Buse P (2010) Polaroid into digital: technology, cultural form, and the social practices of snapshot photography. Continuum 24(2):215–230

Canon Inc (2010) Canon camera museum. Canon Inc. http://www.canon.com/camera-museum/camera/film/data/1976-1985/1979_af35m.html?lang=eu&categ=srs&page=ab&p=1. Accessed 6 Sept 2010

Chalfen R (1987) Snapshot versions of life. Bowling Green State University Popular Press, Bowling Green

Chambers D (2003) Family as place: family photograph albums and the domestication of public and private space. In: Schwartz JM, Ryan JM (eds) Picturing place: photography and the geographical imagination. I.B. Tauris, London

Christensen CM (1997) The innovator's dilemma: when new technologies cause great firms to fail. Harvard Business School Press, Boston

CIPA (2010) What is exif? CIPA. http://www.cipa.jp/exifprint/contents_e/01exif1_e.html. Accessed 2 Sept 2010

CNET News (2002) Toshiba crops digital camera price. 1 Mar 2002

CNET News (2007) Cameras: shipments rising, but prices falling. 19 Sept 2007

Coe B (1988) Kodak cameras: the first hundred years. Hove Foto, Hove

Coe B (1989) The Rollfilm revolution. In: Ford C (ed) The Kodak Museum: the story of popular photography. Century, London, pp 60–89

Coe B, Gates P (1977) The snapshot photograph: the rise of popular photography, 1888–1939. Ash & Grant, London

Collins D (1990) The story of Kodak. H.N. Abrams, New York

Crabtree A, Rodden T, Mariani J (2004) Collaborating around collections: informing the continued development of photoware. In: Proceedings of the 2004 ACM conference on computer supported cooperative work, Chicago, 2004. ACM, New York, pp 396–405

Crawley G (1989) Colour comes to all. In: Ford C (ed) The Kodak Museum: the story of popular photography. Century, London, pp 128–153

Creative Commons (2010) Creative commons. http://creativecommons.org/. Accessed 2 Sept 2010

Czech KP (1996) Snapshot: America discovers the camera. Lerner, Minneapolis

Data Center Knowledge (2009) Facebook now has 30,000 servers. Data Center Knowledge. http://www.datacenterknowledge.com/archives/2009/10/13/facebook-now-has-30000-servers/. Accessed 19 Mar 2010

Datamonitor (2009) Global Photographic Products – Industry Profile. Datamonitor, New York

Davis M, King S, Good N, Sarvas R (2004) From context to content: leveraging context to infer media metadata. In: Proceedings of the 12th annual ACM international conference on multimedia, New York, 1 Oct 2004

Davis M, House N, Towle J, King S, Ahern S, Burgener C, Perkel D, Finn M, Viswanathan V, Rothenberg M (2005) MMM2: Mobile media metadata for media sharing. In: Proceedings of the CHI '05 extended abstracts on human factors in computing systems, Portland, 1 Apr 2005. ACM, New York

Digital Imaging Plus (1994) Apple quicktake 100. Mar 1994

Drazin A, Frohlich D (2007) Good intentions: remembering through framing photographs in english homes. Ethnos 72(1):51–76

Drucker S, Wong C, Roseway A, Glenner S, Mar S (2004) MediaBrowser: reclaiming the shoebox. In: Proceedings of the working conference on advanced visual interfaces (AVI '04), Gallipoli

Durrant A (2010) Family portrayals: design to support photographic representations of intergenerational relationships in family homes. Doctoral dissertation, Department of Psychology, University of Surrey, Guildford

Durrant A, Taylor AS, Taylor S, Molloy M, Sellen A, Frohlich D, Gosset P, Swan L (2008) Speculative devices for photo display. In: Proceedings of the CHI '08 extended abstracts on human factors in computing systems, Florence, 2008. ACM, New York, pp 2297–2302

Durrant A, Frohlich D, Sellen A, Lyons E (2009a) Home curation versus teenage photography: photo displays in the family home. Int J Hum Comput Stud 67(12):1005–1023

Durrant A, Taylor A, Frohlich D, Sellen A, Uzzell D (2009b) Photo displays and intergenerational relationships in the family home. In: Proceedings of the 23rd BCS conference on human computer interaction, Cambridge, 2009. British Computer Society

Eastman G (1888) Camera. #388850, United States Patent Office

EconomyWatch.com (2010) World economy, global economy, international economics. EconomyWatch.com. http://www.economywatch.com/world_economy/. Accessed 9 Jan 2010

Edwards WK, Grinter RE (2001) At home with ubiquitous computing: seven challenges. In: Proceedings of the UbiComp 2001, Atlanta, 15 Aug 2001, pp 256–271

Edwards D, Middleton D (1986) Joint remembering: constructing an account of shared experience through conversational discourse. Discourse Process 9(4):423–459

European Union (2010) Data protection. European Union. http://ec.europa.eu/justice/policies/privacy/index_en.htm. Accessed 16 Sept 2010

Eurostat (2008) Ageing characterizes the demographic perspectives of the European societies, statistic in focus 72/2008. Office for Official Publications of the European Communities, Luxembourg

Finnerty TC (2000) Kodak vs. Fuji: the battle for global market share. Unpublished work

Ford C (1989) The Kodak Museum: the story of popular photography. Century, London, 184

Freund G (1982) Photography & society. David R Godine, Boston

Frohlich DM (2004) Audiophotography: bringing photos to life with sounds. Kluwer, Dordrecht/London

Frohlich D, Daly-Jones O (1995) Voicefax: a shared workspace for voicemail partners. In: Proceedings of the Conference companion on Human factors in computing systems, Denver, 1995. ACM, New York, pp 308–309

Frohlich D, Fennell J (2007) Sound, paper and memorabilia: resources for a simpler digital photography. Pers Ubiquit Comput 11(2):107–116

Frohlich D, Kuchinsky A, Pering C, Don A, Ariss S (2002) Requirements for photoware. In: Proceedings of the 2002 ACM conference on computer supported cooperative work (CSCW '02), New Orleans

Frohlich DM, Wall S, Kiddle G (2011) Re-discovery of forgotten images in family photo collections. Submission to HCI journal special issue on Designing for Personal Memories

Giddens A (1998) The third way: the renewal of social democracy. Polity Press, Cambridge

Giddens A (2000) The third way and its critics. Polity, Cambridge

Goldberg V (1991) The power of photography: how photographs changed our lives, 1st. Abbeville, New York

Grinter RE, Edwards WK, Newman M, Duchenaut N (2005) The work to make a home network. In: Proceedings of the Ninth European conference on computer-supported cooperative work (ECSCW 2005), Paris, 18–22 Sept 2005, pp 469–488

Gustavson T (2009) Camera: a history of photography from daguerreotype to digital. Sterling Pub, New York

Harmant P (1977) Anno Lucis 1839: 1st Part. Camera 5

Harrison B (2002) Photographic visions and narrative inquiry. Narrat Inq 12(1):87–111

Helsingin Sanomat (2010) Kuvaamista maauimaloissa halutaan rajoittaa pedofiilien pelossa. 12 July 2010

Hernandez V (2008) Ringo photo sharing Website bows out of cyber space by end of June. All Headline News. http://www.allheadlinenews.com/articles/7011151890. Accessed 19 Mar 2010

Hilliges O, Kirk DS (2009) Getting sidetracked: display design and occasioning photo-talk with the photohelix. In: Proceedings of the 27th international conference on human factors in computing systems, Boston, 2009. ACM, New York, pp 1733–1736

Hodges S, Williams L, Berry E, Izadi S, Srinivasan J, Butler A, Smyth G, Kapur N, Wood K (2006) SenseCam: a retrospective memory aid. In: Proceedings of the eighth international conference of ubiquitous computing (UbiComp 2006), Orange County, 27 July 2006, pp 177–193

Hofmeester K (1999) Introduction. Interactions 6(6):8–10

Holland P (2009) 'Sweet is to scan...': personal photographs and popular photography. In: Wells L (ed) Photography: a critical introduction. Routledge, London, pp 113–158

Hsu J (2009) The worldwide mobile phone camera module market and Taiwan's industry, 2009 and beyond. Market Intelligence & Consulting Institute (MIC), Taipei

Hughes TP (1989) The evolution of large technological systems. In: Bijker WE, Hughes TP, Pinch TJ (eds) The social construction of technological systems. MIT Press, Cambridge, pp 51–82

Humphries M (2004) MMS not popular in EU. Geek.com. http://www.geek.com/articles/mobile/mms-not-popular-in-eu-20040513/. Accessed 19 Mar 2010

Hyysalo S (2010) Health technology development and use: from practice-bound imagination to evolving impacts. Routledge, London

International Telecommunication Union ITU (1992) T.81: information technology – digital compression and coding of continuous-tone still images – requirements and guidelines. ITU, Geneva

Isaacs E, Whittaker S, Frohlich D, O'Conaill B (1997) Informal communications re-examined: new functions for video in supporting opportunistic encounters. In: Finn K, Sellen A, Wilbur S (eds) Video-mediated communication. Lawrence Erlbaum, Mahwah

Isaacs E, Walendowski A, Ranganathan D (2002a) Mobile instant messaging through Hubbub. Commun ACM 45(9):68–72

Isaacs E, Walendowski A, Whittaker S, Schiano DJ, Kamm C (2002) The character, functions, and styles of instant messaging in the workplace. In: Proceedings of the 2002 ACM conference on computer supported cooperative work, New Orleans, 2002. ACM, New York, pp 11–20

IT Facts (2005) Film sales drop by 20% every year. IT Facts. http://www.itfacts.biz/film-sales-drop-by-20-every-year/4889. Accessed 6 Sept 2010

Jenkins R (1975) Images and enterprise: technology and the American photographic industry, 1839–1925. Johns Hopkins University Press, Baltimore

Johansen R (1988) Groupware: computer support for business teams. The Free Press, New York

Johnson WS, Rice M, Williams C (2005) The George Eastman House collection, a history of photography, from 1839 to present. Taschen, Hong Kong

Joinson AN (2008) Looking at, looking up or keeping up with people?: motives and use of Facebook. In: Proceedings of the twenty-sixth annual SIGCHI conference on human factors in computing systems, Florence, 2008. ACM, New York, pp 1027–1036

Kao DM (1999) Innovation/imagination: 50 years of Polaroid photography. H. N. Abrams, New York/London, p 120

Kenyon D (1992) Inside amateur photography. Batsford, London

Kim J, Zimmerman J (2006) Cherish: smart digital photo frames for sharing social narratives at home. In: Proceedings of the CHI '06 extended abstracts on human factors in computing systems, Montreal, 2006. ACM, New York, pp 953–958

Kindberg T, Spasojevic M, Fleck R, Sellen A (2005) I saw this and thought of you: some social uses of camera phones. In: Proceedings of the CHI '05 extended abstracts on human factors in computing systems, Portland, 1 Apr 2005

King G (1984) Say 'cheese'!: the snapshot as art and social history. Collins, London

Kirk D, Sellen A, Rother C, Wood K (2006) Understanding photowork. In: Proceedings of the SIGCHI conference on human factors in computing systems CHI '06, Montreal, 1 Apr 2006. ACM, New York, pp 761–770

Kirk D, Sellen A, Harper R, Wood K (2007) Understanding videowork. In: Proceedings of the SIGCHI conference on human factors in computing systems CHI '07, San Jose, 1 Apr 2007. ACM, New York, pp 61–70

Kirk DS, Izadi S, Sellen A, Taylor S, Banks R, Hilliges O (2010) Opening up the family archive. In: Proceedings of the 2010 ACM conference on computer supported cooperative work, Savannah, 2010. ACM, New York, pp 261–270

Kirk DS, Sellen A, Cao X (2010) Home video communication: mediating 'closeness'. In: Proceedings of the 2010 ACM conference on computer supported cooperative work, Savannah, 2010. ACM, New York, pp 135–144

Kirkpatrick M (2010) The day has come: Facebook pushes people to go public. ReadWriteWeb. http://www.readwriteweb.com/archives/facebook_pushes_people_to_go_public.php Accessed 1 Sept 2010

Kodak Imaging Network Inc (2009) Terms of service at Kodak gallery. Kodak Imaging Network Inc. http://www.kodakgallery.com/gallery/footerLinksContent.jsp?pageID=600010. Accessed 29 Apr 2010

Koskinen I (2005) Sound in Mobile Multimedia: a mobile design challenge. In: Proceedings of the designing pleasurable products and interfaces 2005 (DPPI 2005), Eindhoven, 2005

Koskinen IK (2007) Mobile multimedia in action. Transaction, New Brunswick

Koskinen I, Kurvinen E, Lehtonen T-K (2002) Mobile image. Edita, Helsinki

Kuchinsky A, Pering C, Creech M, Freeze D, Serra B, Gwizdka J (1999) FotoFile: a consumer multimedia organization and retrieval system. In: Proceedings of the SIGCHI conference on human factors in computing systems: the CHI is the limit CHI '99, Pittsburgh, 1 May 1999. ACM, New York

Kuhn TS (1962) The structure of scientific revolutions. University of Chicago Press, Chicago

Kun LMA, Marsden G (2007) Co-Present photo sharing on mobile devices. In: Proceedings of the 9th international conference on human computer interaction with mobile devices and services, Singapore, 2007. ACM, New York, pp 277–284

Larish J (2008) Silver to silicon: a journalist looks back at the changes that have brought us to the era of digital photos. CreateSpace, Seattle

Latour B (1987) Science in action. Harvard University Press, Cambridge

Lehmuskallio A (2010) Non-professional camera pictures in a 'Cam Era' – empirical studies in non-professional uses of user-created pictorial content. Unpublished work

Lehmuskallio A, Sarvas R (2008) Snapshot video: everyday photographers taking short video-clips. In: Proceedings of the 5th Nordic conference on human–computer interaction: building bridges, Lund, 1 Oct 2008. ACM, New York, pp 257–265

Lehmuskallio A, Sarvas R (2010) The agency of ICT in shaping non-professional photo use. In: Proceedings of the Nordic Network for Visual Studies in Social Science Workshop: from Family Album to Social Media – traditions and change, Stockholm, 2010

Lehtinen V, Näsänen J, Sarvas R (2009) "A little bit foolish and light-headed" – Older adults' understandings of social networking sites. In: Proceedings of the 23rd BCS conference on human computer interaction. British Computer Society, Cambridge, 2009, pp 45–54

Leong TW, Vetere F, Howard, S (2005) The serendipity shuffle. In: Proceedings of the 17th Australia conference on computer-human interaction: citizens online: considerations for today and the future, Canberra, 2005. Computer-Human Interaction Special Interest Group (CHISIG) of Australia, pp 1–4

Leong T, Howard S, Vetere F (2008) Choice: abdicating or exercising? In: Proceedings of the twenty-sixth annual SIGCHI conference on human factors in computing systems CHI '08, Florence, 2008. ACM, New York, pp 715–724

Lewis G (1991) The history of the Japanese camera. The international museum of photography at George Eastman House. Rochester, New York

Life Magazine (1972) A genius and his magic camera. 27 Oct 1972

Lindley S, Monk A (2006) Designing appropriate affordances for electronic photo sharing media. In: Proceedings of the CHI '06 extended abstracts on human factors in computing systems, 1 Apr 2006, Montreal. ACM, New York

Lindley S, Monk A (2008) Social enjoyment with electronic photo displays: awareness and control. Int J Hum Comput Stud 66(8):587–604

Lindley SE, Durrant A, Kirk D, Taylor AS (2009) Editorial: collocated social practices surrounding photos. Int J Hum Comput Stud 67(12):995–1004

Lister M (1995) The photographic image in digital culture. Routledge, London

MacKenzie DA, Wajcman J (1999) Introductory essay: the social shaping of technology. In: MacKenzie DA, Wajcman J (eds) The social shaping of technology. Open University Press, Buckingham/Philadelphia, pp 3–27

Mäkelä A, Giller V, Tscheligi M, Sefelin R (2000) Joking, storytelling, artsharing, expressing affection: a field trial of how children and their social network communicate with digital images in leisure time. In: The SIGCHI conference on human factors in computing systems CHI '00, The Hague. ACM, New York, pp 548–555

Manovich L (2002) The language of new media. MIT Press, Cambridge, 1st MIT Press pbk

Michaud F (2010) Monthly Prices in Angoulême, 1819–1880. International Institute of Social History.http://www.iisg.nl/hpw/angouleme.php. Accessed 7 Sep 2010

Miller A, Edwards W (2007) Give and Take: a study of consumer photo-sharing culture and practice. In: Proceedings of the SIGCHI conference on human factors in computing systems CHI '07, San Jose, 1 Apr 2007. ACM, New York, pp 347–356

Mills TJ, Pye D, Sinclair D, Wood KR (2000) Managing photos with AT&T shoebox (demonstration session). In: Proceedings of the 23rd annual international ACM SIGIR conference on research and development in information retrieval, Athens, 2000. ACM, New York, p 390

Miniwatts Marketing Group (2010) World internet usage and population statistics. Miniwatts Marketing Group. http://www.internetworldstats.com/stats.htm. Accessed 6 Aug 2010

MSCI (2010) MSCI international equity indices. http://www.mscibarra.com/products/indices/international_equity_indices/. Accessed 2 Sept 2010

Munir KA (2005) The birth of the 'Kodak Moment': institutional entrepreneurship and the adoption of new technologies. Organ Stud 26(11):1665–1687

Munir KA, Jones M (2004) Discontinuity and after: the social dynamics of technology evolution and dominance. Organ Stud 25(4):561–581

Munir KA, Phillips N (2002) The concept of industry and the case of radical technological change. J High Tech Manag Res 13:279–297

Musello C (1979) Family photography. In: Wagner J (ed) Images of information: still photography in the social sciences. Sage, Beverly Hills, pp 101–118

Näsänen J, Oulasvirta A, Lehmuskallio A (2009) Mobile media in the social fabric of a kindergarten. In: Proceedings of the 27th international conference on human factors in computing systems CHI'09, Boston, 2009. ACM, New York, pp 2167–2176

National Institute of Population and Social Security Research (2006) Population statistics of Japan. National Institute of Population and Social Security Research, Tokyo

Nerwin H (1964) Roll Film Magazine. #3138081, US Patent Office

Neustaedter C, Fedorovskaya E (2009a) Capturing and sharing memories in a virtual world. In: Proceedings of the 27th international conference on human factors in computing systems, Boston, 2009. ACM, New York, pp 1161–1170

Neustaedter C, Fedorovskaya E (2009b) Understanding and improving flow in digital photo ecosystems. In: Proceedings of the graphics interface 2009, Kelowna, 2009b. ACM, New York

PR Newswire (1995) Fargo introduces FotoFUN!: Digital color photo printer comparable to a photo lab. 8 Aug 1995

Norman D (2009) Designing the infrastructure. Interactions 16(4):66–69

Norman D (2010) The way I see it: technology first, needs last: the research–product gulf. Interactions 17(2):38–42

O'Conaill B, Geelhoed E, Toft P (1994) Deskslate: a shared workspace for telephone partners. In: Proceedings of the conference companion on human factors in computing systems, Boston, 1994. ACM, New York, pp 303–304

O'Hara K, Perry M, Churchill E (2004) Public and situated displays: social and Interactional aspects of shared display technologies (Cooperative Work, 2). Kluwer Academic Publishers, Norwell

Okabe D, Ito M (2003) Camera phones changing the definition of picture-worthy. Jpn Media Rev

Olshaker M (1978) The instant image: Edwin Land and the Polaroid experience. Stein and Day, New York

Peres MR (2007) Focal encyclopedia of photography: digital imaging, theory and applications, history, and science, 4th edn. Focal, Amsterdam/London

PMA (2009a) U.S. households make photo books for family keepsakes. PMA. http://pmaforesight. com/?p=40. Accessed 2 Sept 2010

PMA (2009b) Printing behavior of U.S. consumers. PMA. http://pmaforesight.com/?p=92. Accessed 2 Sept 2010

PMA (2009c) Percentage of U.S. households receiving digital images from family and friends down from previous years. PMA. http://pmaforesight.com/?p=123. Accessed 2 Sept 2010

Raento M, Oulasvirta A, Petit R, Toivonen H (2005) ContextPhone: a prototyping platform for context-aware mobile applications. IEEE Pervasive Comput 4(2):51–59

Riddle W (2010) Social networking experiences a great migration of maturity in Switched. http://www.switched.com/2010/08/28/social-networking-experiences-a-great-migration-of-maturity/ Accessed 2 Sept 2010

Rodden K, Wood K (2003) How Do people manage their digital photographs? In: Proceedings of the SIGCHI conference on human factors in computing systems CHI '03, Fort Lauderdale, 2003. ACM, New York, pp 409–416

Rogers Y, Lindley S (2004) Collaborating around vertical and horizontal large interactive displays: which way is best? Interact Comput 16(6):1133–1152

Rose G (2003) Family photographs and domestic spacings: a case study. Trans Inst Br Geogr 28(1):5–18

Rosenblum N (2007) A world history of photography, 4th edn. Abbeville, New York

Sanghvi R (2009) New tools to control your eExperience. The Facebook Blog. http://blog.facebook.com/blog.php?post=196629387130. Accessed 1 Sept 2010

Sarvas R, Herrarte E, Wilhelm A, Davis M (2004a) Metadata creation system for mobile images. In: Proceedings of the 2nd international conference on mobile systems, applications, and services, Boston, 2004. ACM, New York, pp 36–48

Sarvas R, Viikari M, Pesonen J, Nevanlinna H (2004b) MobShare: controlled and immediate sharing of mobile images. In: Proceedings of the 12th annual ACM international conference on multimedia, New York, 2004. ACM, New York, pp 724–731

Sarvas R, Oulasvirta A, Jacucci G (2005) Building social discourse around mobile photos: a systemic perspective. In: Proceedings of the 7th international conference on human computer interaction with mobile devices and services, MobileHCI '05, Salzburg, 1 Sept 2005. ACM, New York

Schiano D, Chen CP, Isaacs E (2002) How teens take, view, share, and store photos. In: Proceedings of the computer supported cooperative work (CSCW 2002), New Orleans, 2002

Shove E, Watson M, Hand M, Ingram J (2007) The design of everyday life. Berg, New York

Silicon Alley Insider (2010) WARNING: Google Buzz has a huge privacy flaw. http://www.businessinsider.com/warning-google-buzz-has-a-huge-privacy-flaw-2010-2#. Accessed 19 Mar 2010

Slater D (1995) Domestic photography and digital culture. In: Lister M (ed) The photographic image in digital culture. Routledge, London, pp 129–146

Staal G (1999) Strategic outlook: from ears to eyes. Interactions 6(6):64–67

Star SL (1999) The ethnography of infrastructure. Am Behav Sci 43(3):377–391

Stelmaszewska H, Fields B, Blandford A (2008) The roles of time, place, value and relationships in collocated photo sharing with camera phones. In: Proceedings of the 22nd British HCI group annual conference on HCI 2008: people and computers XXII: culture, creativity, interaction – vol 1, Liverpool, 2008, pp 141–150

Strategy Analytics (2005) Camera phone sales surge to 257 million units worldwide in 2004. Strategy Analytics. http://www.strategyanalytics.com/default.aspx?mod=PressReleaseViewer& a0=2354. Accessed 19 Mar 2010

Swan L, Taylor A (2008) Photo displays in the home. In: Proceedings of the 7th ACM conference on designing interactive systems (DIS '08), Cape Town

Swasy A (1997) Changing focus: Kodak and the battle to save a great American company. Times Business, New York

Tang JC, Isaacs EA, Rua M (1994) Supporting distributed groups with a montage of lightweight interactions. In: Proceedings of the 1994 ACM conference on computer supported cooperative work, Chapel Hill, 1994. ACM, New York, pp 23–34

Taylor A, Swan L, Durrant A (2007) Designing family photo displays. In: Proceedings of the 10th European conference on computer-supported cooperative work (ECSCW 2007), Limerick, 2007. Springer, pp 79–98

TechCrunch (2009) Who has the most photos of them all? Hint: it is not Facebook. TechCrunch. http://techcrunch.com/2009/04/07/who-has-the-most-photos-of-them-all-hint-it-is-not-facebook/. Accessed 19 Mar 2010

TechCrunch (2010) Watch out who you reply to on Google Buzz, you might be exposing their email address. http://techcrunch.com/2010/02/11/reply-google-buzz-exposing-email/. Accessed 19 Mar 2010

The Economist (2010a) Selling becomes sociable. 9 Sept 2010

The Economist (2010b) The clash of data civilisations. 17 June 2010

The Guardian (2010a) Google Wi-Fi data capture cleared by information commissioner. 29 July 2010

The Guardian (2010b) Privacy no longer a social norm, says Facebook founder. 11 Jan 2010

The Guardian (2010c) Facebook reveals new privacy controls following intense criticism from users. 26 May 2010

The Guardian (2010d) Shareholder trading values Facebook at more than $33bn. 25 Aug 2010

The Guardian (2010e) Apple's iPad war on Adobe and Flash. 18 Apr 2010

The Guardian (2010f) Internet pirates find 'bulletproof' havens for illegal file sharing. 5 Jan 2010

The New York Times (1991) Kodak settles with Polaroid. 16 June 1991

The New York Times (2010) For photographers, the image of a shrinking path. 29 Mar 2010

The Wall Street Journal (2010) Google and the search for the future. 14 Aug 2010

Time Magazine (2010) How Facebook is Redefining Privacy. 31 May 2010

Trotman N (2002) The life of the party – the Polaroid SX-70 Land camera and instant film photography. Afterimage 29(6):10

United Nations (2000) Charting the progress of populations. United Nations Population Division, New York

US Census Bureau (2001) Home computers and Internet use in the United States. Aug 2000

US Census Bureau (2010) U.S. and world population clocks. U.S. Census Bureau. http://www.census.gov/main/www/popclock.html. Accessed 16 Sept 2010

Utterback JM (1994) Mastering the dynamics of innovation: how companies can seize opportunities in the face of technological change. Harvard Business School Press, Boston

Van Dijck J (2008) Digital photography: communication, identity, memory. Vis Commun 7(1):57–76

Van House N (2007) Flickr and public image-sharing: distant closeness and photo exhibition. In: Extended abstracts on human factors in computing systems (CHI '07), San Jose

Van House N (2009) Collocated photo sharing, story-telling, and the performance of self. J Hum Comput Stud 67(12):1073–1086

Van House N, Ames M (2010) The social life of camera phones. Unpublished work

Van House N, Davis M, Ames M, Finn M, Viswanathan V (2005) The uses of personal networked digital imaging: an empirical study of cameraphone photos and sharing. In: CHI '05 extended abstracts on Human factors in computing systems (CHI '05), Portland

Wade J (1979) A short history of the camera. Fountain Press, Watford/New York

Wang H (2007) Digital Photo Frames: Picture a Good Year. Parks Associates, Dallas

Wang H (2009) Digital Photo Frames: Annual Global Market Analysis and Forecasts. Parks Associates, Dallas

Wensberg PC (1987) Land's Polaroid: a company and the man who invented it. Houghton Mifflin, Boston

West NM (2000) Kodak and the lens of nostalgia. University Press of Virginia, Charlottesville

Whittaker S, Swanson J, Kucan J, Sidner C (1997) TeleNotes: managing lightweight interactions in the desktop. ACM T Comput Hum Interact 4(2):137–168

Whittaker S, Bergman O, Clough P (2010) Easy on that trigger dad: a study of long term family photo retrieval. Pers Ubiquit Comput 14(1):31–43

Wichard R, Wichard C (1999) Victorian cartes-de-visite. Shire, Princes Risborough

Zuckerberg M (2010a) Making control simple. In: The Facebook Blog. http://blog.facebook.com/blog.php?post=391922327130. Accessed 1 Sept 2010

Zuckerberg M (2010b) 500 million stories. The Facebook Blog. http://blog.facebook.com/blog.php?post=409753352130 Accessed 6 Aug 2010

Zuromskis C (2009) On snapshot photography: rethinking photographic power in public and private spheres. In: Long JJ, Noble A, Welch E (eds) Photography: theoretical snapshots. Routledge, London, pp 49–62

Index